Development Strategies as Ideology

Development Strategies as Ideology

Puerto Rico's Export-Led Industrialization Experience

Emilio Pantojas-García

Lynne Rienner Publishers · Boulder & London

Editorial de la Universidad de Puerto Rico · Río Piedras

AIV 2972 - 0/2

Published in the United States of America in 1990 by
Lynne Rienner Publishers, Inc.
1800 30th Street, Boulder, Colorado 80301

and by
Editorial de la Universidad de Puerto Rico
Apartado 23322
Estación de la Universidad
Río Piedras, Puerto Rico 00931-3322

Published in the United Kingdom by
Lynne Rienner Publishers, Inc.
3 Henrietta Street, Covent Garden, London WC2E 8LU

Library of Congress Cataloging-in-Publication Data
Pantojas-García, Emilio.
 Development strategies as ideology : Puerto Rico's export-led
industrialization experience / by Emilio Pantojas-García.
 Includes bibliographical references.
 ISBN 1-55587-198-4
 1. Puerto Rico—Economic policy. 2. Exports—Puerto Rico.
3. Foreign trade promotion—Puerto Rico. I. Title
HC154.5.P36 1990
338.97291—dc20   90-33397
                                                        CIP

British Cataloguing in Publication Data
A Cataloguing in Publication record for this book
is available from the British Library.

ISBN: 1-55587-198-4 (Rienner)
ISBN: 0-8477-0175-1 (EDUPR)

Printed and bound in the United States of America

The paper used in this publication meets the requirements
of the American National Standard for Permanence of
Paper for Printed Library Materials Z39.48-1984.

To the memory of my father, Emilio Pantojas-Soto

To my mother, Libertad García-López

To my wife, Luz del Alba Acevedo

Contents

List of Tables and Figures

Tables

Figures

List of Abbreviations

AFE	Administración de Fomento Económico de Puerto Rico (Puerto Rico Economic Development Administration)
CBI	Caribbean Basin Initiative
CI/EP	Capital Importation/Export Processing
CFPR	Compañía de Fomento de Puerto Rico (Puerto Rico Development Company)
CGT	Confederación General de Trabajadores (General Confederation of Labor)
CORCO	Commonwealth Oil Refinery Corporation
CPI	Congreso Pro Independencia (Pro-Independence Congress)
ECLA	United Nations Economic Commission on Latin America
EP	Export Promotion
FLT	Federación Libre de Trabajadores (Free Federation of Labor)
Fomento	Administración de Fomento Económico (Puerto Rico Economic Development Administration)
GAO	Government Accounting Office
GDP	Gross Domestic Product
GNP	Gross National Product
IRC	United States Internal Revenue Code
IRS	United States Internal Revenue Service
ISAs	Ideological State Apparatuses
ISI	Import Substitution Industrialization
MPI	Movimiento Pro Independencia (Pro-Independence Movement)
PAC	Partido Acción Cristiana (Christian Action Party)
PCP	Partido Comunista Puertorriqueño (Puerto Rican Communist Party)
PER	Partido Estadista Republicano (Statehood Republican Party)
PIP	Partido Independentista Puertorriqueño (Puerto Rican Independence Party)
PL	Partido Liberal (Liberal Party)
PN	Partido Nacionalista (Nationalist Party)
PNP	Partido Nuevo Progresista (New Progressive Party)

PP	Partido del Pueblo (People's Party)
PPD	Partido Popular Democrático (Popular Democratic Party)
PR	Partido Republicano (Republican Party)
PRDC	Puerto Rico Development Company
PREDA	Puerto Rico Economic Development Administration
PRERA	Puerto Rico Emergency Relief Administration
PRP	Partido de Renovación Puertorriqueña (Puerto Rican Renovation Party)
PRRA	Puerto Rico Reconstruction Administration
PRUSA	Puerto Rico U.S.A. Foundation
PSP	Partido Socialista Puertorriqueño (Puerto Rican Socialist Party)
PS	Partido Socialista (Socialist Party)
PUP	Partido Unión Puertorriqueña (Puerto Rican Union Party)
TNCs	Transnational Corporations

Acknowledgments

Every product of human activity is ultimately the result of a collective process, during which one learns and receives support from many people and in many ways. In the long process of gestation of this book, many have provided support, encouragement, and valuable insights and ideas. I cannot mention here all who have helped along the way, but I would like to recognize publicly those who helped me directly.

First, I must thank Carmen Diana Deere, James Dietz, Consuelo López Springfield, and Helen Safa, who read the whole manuscript and made important suggestions. From my days at the University of Liverpool, I am deeply indebted to Colin Henfrey, my thesis advisor, whose ideas are embedded throughout the text, although in ways that he would not always agree with. Also from those days I must thank Benny Pollack, Hernán Rosenkranz, Joseph Femia, Walter Little, and Antonio Herrera, all of whom played a key role in the formation of some of my ideas. My intellectual curiosity was forever stimulated by some of my teachers and friends at the University of Puerto Rico, and in this regard I especially thank Gamaliel Ortíz, Pablo García Rodríguez, Barry Levine, Irene Rivera, and Benjamín Rivera (my *compadre*). I was given much valuable help by Isabel López, the librarian of the Puerto Rico Economic Development Administration, and her assistant, Nimia Tosca; Cynthia Rodríguez of the computer center at the University of Illinois at Chicago (UIC); and Elizabeth Román, a former UIC student. Others that offered help and encouragement were my friends John Valadez and Jim English, formerly of UIC, Carmen Gautier Mayoral of the University of Puerto Rico, and Richard Barrett of UIC. The head of the Latin American Studies Program at UIC, Otto Pikaza, and the dean of the College of Liberal Arts and Sciences, Jay Levine, generously provided much needed time and resources to complete this project.

I must also thank the older members of my family and my wife's family for sharing with me their views and feelings on the golden age of developmentalism, the Muñoz era. Much of my understanding of that period comes from my long talks with my uncles, aunts, and in-laws about the "old days." Finally, I must thank the most important person in this process, Luz del Alba Acevedo, my wife and colleague. She shared with me her research and insights. She patiently read, listened, and criticized all my ideas. Throughout this process she has been all, teacher, critic, and companion.

I have tried to the best of my abilities and within the normal editorial constraints to give credit throughout the text and in the bibliography to all those who have contributed to the ideas in this book. I apologize if I have omitted any due credit. In a gestation process that takes over a decade, one sometimes forgets where some things came from.

Emilio Pantojas-García

Development Strategies as Ideology

Introduction

Operation Bootstrap, also known as the "Puerto Rican model" of industrialization, is the oldest version of what today is called an "export promotion" development model. With few exceptions, the academic literature presents development strategies as theoretical models of opposing rationalities among which a varied assortment of policymakers (technocrats, militaries, autocrats) have to choose in order to determine the socioeconomic course of a country.

The systematic arrangement and classification of economic policies into development models can be a useful tool for understanding some of the underlying assumptions, objectives, and structural constraints of the development policy of a country. But to confuse a model with reality is to leave out the social or real-world basis of development options and to underestimate the role of political conflict in the adoption of particular policies to the detriment of others.

In the real world, development strategies are a product of what Albert O. Hirschman calls "hidden rationalities"—that is, ideology, not the results of a selection from a menu of options prepared by academics or experts from international organizations.[1] The decisions that lead to the adoption of a particular development strategy are a function of political struggles and, more importantly, which social groups or classes emerge victorious and assume political control. It is the interests of the power bloc in a society that, within particular structural constraints, determine the adoption of a development strategy and shape its implementation, not the rational maximization schemes of government bureaucrats looking after the well-being of society.

Political realities notwithstanding, over the past two decades the academic debate on economic development strategies has centered on two models: import-substitution industrialization (ISI) and export promotion (EP). ISI first gained prominence during the 1950s, and its main proponents were members of the United Nations Economic Commission on Latin America (ECLA).[2] The debates on the ECLA-inspired ISI model, in turn,

1

gave birth to "dependency theory" and the Latin American regional integration schemes so popular in the 1960s. Dependency theory advocated development strategies based on a new international economic order and the satisfaction of basic needs. The proponents of ISI and dependency shared at least one basic assumption originating in ECLA's structuralist economics: that there is an unequal distribution of the benefits from global exchange.[3] They reject the neoclassical assumption that international trade and the division of labor result in benefits to all involved. Hence, in order to achieve economic development, a country must pursue policies that will counterbalance the negative effects of unequal exchange in the international economy.

On the other side of the ledger, the EP model, which started to gain ascendancy in the 1970s, became the model of choice among mainstream economists and policymakers. Grounded in neoclassical economics, it assumes that all countries do benefit from international exchange and specialization. Inequalities are not a function of unequal exchange but of market conditions (supply and demand variations) or initial resource endowment of countries, which will be leveled by trade. Based on this assumption, this "neoliberal" economics predicates free trade and international specialization in the production of commodities and manufactures for the global economy, i.e., the open-economy approach. The bastion of this new orthodoxy is another international organization, the World Bank.[4]

The open-economy approach of neoliberal economics is not new; its roots are found in nineteenth-century Ricardian free-trade doctrine. What is new is that it predicates export diversification or substitution. Rather than the traditional division of labor between producers of manufactures and producers of primary commodities, the "new orthodoxy" argues that international exchange will produce development if the countries involved adopt adequate policies for promoting exports of those goods for which they have a comparative advantage in the international economy. This does not limit production to primary goods. On the contrary, the idea is to compete in other areas, such as labor-intensive manufacturing, high-tech consumer goods, and agroindustrial products.[5]

The current debate on development strategies between ISI and EP proponents in academia and in international organizations misses two key points. First, the real-world debate on development options does not revolve around the superiority of ISI versus EP strategies. Even those who reject the new orthodoxy agree that no country can achieve significant economic growth by withdrawing from the international economy. The real issue is the conditions under which the countries in the periphery of the world capitalist economy should organize their production and exchange relations vis-à-vis the developed or core capitalist countries.

Second, they do not identify the main beneficiaries of any development strategy chosen; who stands to gain the most from the partnerships formed in the relations of international exchange. This issue is often ignored in the debate, and most mainstream economists assume that the decisions on economic strategy are taken by technocrats above particular class interests.[6] In order to understand why one development strategy is preferred over another one must go beyond pure economics into the realm of political sociology. Economists usually avoid these kinds of political questions. Nevertheless they are the crux of any debate on development strategies.

This book focuses on how development strategies, as ideological constructs, articulate or express class interests. This work disputes the technocratic notion that development strategies are a set of neutral policies promoted by the state (usually conceived of also as a neutral agent) for the benefit of all of society, or a series of technical and scientific principles (rational models) that serve to guide the process of economic development of a country. Development strategies are examined here as part of the political projects of class coalitions.

A development strategy is an ideological representation of a particular mode of capital accumulation;[7] that is, it presents a given mode of organizing the production and distribution of the social surplus in a manner that is congruent with the interests of a coalition of classes and class fractions that promote the strategy and presents the interests of that sociopolitical coalition as the basis for the "rational" or "technical" decisions of the state and leading economic groups (class fractions) for the benefit of a country. A development strategy is thus part of a larger political project of classes that aspire to organize the productive and reproductive processes in a society according to their own interests.[8] If a political project is the articulation of the interests and aspirations of class coalitions for political and economic power, then in order to achieve power a class coalition must incorporate and reconcile in its political project often contradictory interests. The class coalition that succeeds in presenting its political project as representative of the interests of the majority of society is the one most likely to succeed in its bid for power. In Gramsci's terms it would be able to establish political hegemony. Put another way, the strategic objectives of economic development and the means by which to achieve them, when articulated as a development strategy, may appear as in the general, classless interests of all of society, but they are a function of the interests, expressed or implicit, of groups that are in power or aspire to achieve it. Development strategies are therefore a key terrain of ideological class conflict.

The concept of political project can be defined as a set of social, economic, and political measures promoted by a class or class coalition that articulates the interests, preferences, values, and aspirations of such a class or coalition for the organization and distribution of political power and the production and distribution of the social surplus vis-à-vis other classes or groups in society. These interests and preferences are expressed concretely through political parties and other sociopolitical groups in society. However, a political project is not the same as a party platform or the political program of an organization. A political project is often articulated in a contradictory and fragmented manner in party platforms and political programs because it is the sum of social propositions and policies developed and promoted by groups bidding for political power in the process of political conflict. That is, a political project is the expression of the interests of class coalitions in their praxis rather than in official party documents and sociopolitical institutions. To talk about political projects is to talk about the unity of thought and action in the Gramscian sense. What groups say about development is as important as what they actually do about it.

The implementation of a particular development strategy, within certain structural constraints, is a function of the interests of whatever group or class coalition holds political and economic power, not of abstract rational choices of individual or social actors. Yet the presentation of a particular model of accumulation as a "development strategy" beneficial to all of society is crucial in providing political support and legitimacy for that particular model vis-à-vis competing ones. Therefore, development strategies constitute the ideological terrain where the "superiority" of the economic component of competing political projects is determined. It is the thesis of this study that development strategies are the ideological representation of class interests as "rational economic models" or "neutral" sets of development policies and programs of the state.

Starting from this view of development strategies as ideologies, this study sets out to uncover the social basis of export-led industrialization in Puerto Rico using an interpretive method grounded in class analysis and historical sociology.[9] It applies theoretical concepts from various disciplines (sociology, economics, and political science) to explain the sociopolitical dynamics of the capital-importation/export-processing development strategy in Puerto Rico. Indeed, the study of Puerto Rico is crucial for any study of the sociology of export-led industrialization since it was the first country in the capitalist periphery to adopt this kind of development strategy. In the 1960s, similar U.S.-promoted EP strategies, adopted in Taiwan and across the Mexican border, followed the lead of Puerto Rico's experience.[10] What is known today varyingly as export processing, out sourcing, or *maquiladoras*, characterizing industries in peripheral countries, was first developed in the late 1940s and early 1950s in Puerto Rico.[11]

Certainly, conditions in Puerto Rico were propitious for this kind of development. Unlike other peripheral countries, the island is a U.S. "possession" (the North American government term for colony), which means the absence of tariff restrictions in trade with the United States and no foreign exchange problems (the U.S. dollar has been the currency of Puerto Rico since 1901). With markets and trade infrastructure already in existence by the 1940s, over 80 percent of Puerto Rico's external trade was with the

United States. This, coupled with the differential applicability of U.S. tax and wage laws, placed the island's economy in the unique position of having free access to the metropolitan market while being a peripheral economy—the best of both worlds for those fractions of U.S. capital looking to expand internationally after World War II. The open colonial economy thus presented the ideal structural condition for this kind of economic strategy. Reality, as usual, predated theory.[12]

In studying Puerto Rico's EP strategy, it is not necessary to analyze the shifts in structural variables, such as foreign exchange and tariffs. The key condition of the EP model, as presented by Jagdish Bhagwati, that the effective exchange rate of exports has to be equal to or greater than that of imports in order not to discriminate against exports, is always met in the colonial context of Puerto Rico.[13] With this as a constant, it is easier to analyze the political sociology of export-led industrialization and the ways in which this strategy constitutes the ideological terrain where political hegemony is built and disputed.

Two other factors make Puerto Rico an important case in the analysis of the sociology of EP strategies. First, the fact that this strategy has been in place there longer than anywhere else in the Third World permits a clear assessment of the long-term impact of this strategy on the social structure and the dynamics of politicoideological conflict and accommodation within which it evolves. Second, since Puerto Rico also serves as a "model" for current U.S. policy in the Caribbean and Central America (e.g., the Caribbean Basin Initiative), this study hopes to contribute to the demystification of the image of "technical soundness" with which this policy and its implicit EP strategy are being presented, providing keys for understanding the class basis, political character, and long-term implications of adopting EP strategies in neighboring countries.

Notes

1. Hirschman, "A Dissenter's Confession," pp. 91–94.
2. Rodríguez, *La teoría*, Chap. 3.
3. There is more than one view of dependency, yet all *dependentistas* share certain basic assumptions, such as the core/periphery dichotomy and some version of unequal exchange. See Henfrey, "Dependency, Modes of Production."
4. Lewis, "Development Promotion," p. 9.
5. The new orthodoxy is grounded in some of the postulates of neoclassical economics, but it rejects some of the premises of the old neoclassical theory. See Myint, "The Neoclassical Resurgence."
6. This technocratic view of development strategies is taken, for example, by the various contributors to the volume edited by Lewis and Kallab, *Development Strategies*; and in Balassa et al., *Development Strategies in Semi-Industrial Economies*.
7. The first to advance this view of development strategies was Ricardo

Kesselman, *Estrategias de desarrollo*, pp. 11, 15. The difference between his view and the one developed here is discussed in Chap. 1.

8. Limoeiro Cardoso, *La ideología dominante*, pp. 11–13.

9. Skocpol, "Emerging Agendas," pp. 368–374.

10. Teodoro Moscoso, creator of the Puerto Rico Economic Development Administration (Fomento) and the architect of export-led industrialization in Puerto Rico, told me in a conversation on 21 April 1988 that during a visit to Taiwan the son of Chiang Kai-shek showed him the Chinese translation of the book *Fomento: The Economic Development of Puerto Rico* by William H. Stead. He mentioned this as evidence that Puerto Rico's Operation Bootstrap had influenced the thinking of the Taiwanese government. Whether it influenced the Taiwanese or the U.S. Agency for International Development advisers who were behind Taiwan's strategy, the Puerto Rican experience became a "model" for peripheral capitalist growth in the 1960s. AID's influence on Taiwan's economic reforms in that period is discussed in Gold, *State and Society*, Chap. 6.

11. James L. Dietz argues that Operation Bootstrap turned Puerto Rico into an export processing zone long before this became conceptualized as part of the incentive package of industrial development strategies. "Maquiladoras in the Caribbean," p. 2.

12. Moscoso argued that the industrialization program in Puerto Rico was developed intuitively and theory came afterwards. He also mentioned that Sir Arthur Lewis used data from Fomento to develop his theory on industrial development in surplus labor economies. These and other exchanges then led to the conceptualization of what began as a strategy dictated by immediate needs and constraints. Both Lewis and Moscoso assumed capitalism to be the only way of achieving development. Conversation of 21 April 1988.

13. Bhagwati, "Rethinking Trade Strategies."

1

Development Strategies as Ideology

The view that a development strategy is a technical construct that guides the process of economic growth and "progress," devoid of any consideration of conflicting interests and political conflict, has been termed *desarrollismo*, or developmentalism, by Latin American social scientists. Initially, *desarrollismo* was used to refer specifically to the state-based, nationalist-oriented development policies of populist political projects. But with the collapse of populist regimes and the emergence of "bureaucratic authoritarian" developmentalist regimes, the concept was used to define generically the technocratic view of development.[1]

In his study of Argentina after the 1966 coup d'état, Ricardo Kesselman was the first to argue that "development strategies are ideological projects of economic direction sustained by different classes or class fractions, and, as such, they are structured upon a sizeable technical scaffolding in which the state frequently appears as an instrument of a determined economic policy to be put into practice."[2] For him the articulation of development strategies was a function of the civil society rather than the state. He held that the dominant classes were united in relation to a development strategy as an ideological project, rather than in relation to the state. The state was seen as an instrument to implement the class interests articulated in economic policies. While this work agrees with Kesselman's view of development strategies as ideology, our view coincides with that of Limoeiro Cardoso, whose study of the populist policies of the Kubitschek government in Brazil defines developmentalism as an ideology articulated by the state that expresses a particular class project as a societal or generalized political project.[3]

Defining the state as the articulating point of developmentalism implies a view of the peripheral state as a key arena of class conflict. The economic policies of peripheral countries are viewed here as a means of mediating the conflicting interest of the dominant classes, the intermediary sectors that run the state apparatus, the metropolitan or imperialist bourgeoisie of advanced capitalist countries, and, in some cases, the working classes. The question is

7

how is this mediation achieved, and how are the interests of the dominant classes articulated and presented by the state as being in the interests of society in general? As Kesselman points out, a development strategy is a series of strategic principles that articulate the economic project of a class or a class coalition. Yet it is the state that offers development strategies as rational policies beneficial to all of society. State bureaucracies, which appear to be devoid of class links, are better able to present development strategies as "neutral" and technically sound socioeconomic policies. In this sense, from a class perspective, a successful development strategy is one that achieves not only economic growth but sociopolitical stability and consensus on the basic economic direction of a country; that is, one that generalizes the interests of the ruling coalition, ensuring the preservation and reproduction of the strategic interests of the power bloc, while allowing for accommodation with the subordinate classes through mediation and compromise in nonstrategic interests.

The concept of class interests can be troublesome and elusive to a social scientist. Since the concept of class is itself a theoretical construct, identifying class interests means infering or imputing preferences to groups identified as classes. These inferences are based on the observed behavior of groups as well as on statements and documents of institutions representing them. In this work, class interests are divided into immediate interests and strategic interests.[4] The first refer to the desire of every class to get a larger share of the social surplus product, to gain access to positions of political power, and to maintain its social well-being. In other words, immediate interests deal with the question of how to distribute the economic and political benefits and privileges within the existing order. On the other hand, strategic interests refer to the necessary conditions for the maintenance and reproduction of the existing order. For example, bourgeois dominance requires the existence of private property and wage labor. If these two elements were abolished, capitalism, the bourgeois social order, would collapse and the material basis of bourgeois dominance would disappear, just as the dominance of the aristocracy disappeared with the abolition of feudal forms of property and servile labor.

This distinction between the two types of interests is important in understanding the terms and implications of class struggle because it distinguishes different types of political and economic change. For example, within this definition a process of politicoeconomic reform refers to allowing or inducing changes that affect immediate interests, leaving intact strategic ones. Thus, in times of crisis, the state may promote reform programs in which the dominant classes are compelled to accept a certain degree of redistribution of the social surplus product and even of political power in order to preserve the strategic basis for their dominance. The power bloc yields on their immediate interests to preserve the substance of their dominance. Conversely, a revolutionary process refers to changes that affect strategic interests, transforming radically the political and economic base of society. If this is correct, then the nature of any political project and its concomitant development strategy (whether it is conservative, reformist, or revolutionary) can only be measured in terms of its impact on the social structure as a whole.

The implementation of any political project, then, is a function of the capacity of the class or class coalition that promotes a particular project to achieve political power (i.e., control over the state). If the development strategy is a crucial ideological component of a political project and the state is the structure that makes possible its implementation, then it can be said that development strategies constitute the key ideological terrain of the state in peripheral capitalist countries. It is on this terrain that class contradictions are condensed and mediated, class alliances are forged within the power bloc, and certain accommodations are worked out between the power bloc and the subordinated classes.[5] Development strategies, the formulation of economic policy, provide the ideological unity (a conflictive or dialectical unity) of peripheral states.

Ideology, State, and Class

The fact that the social sciences lack a unified paradigm makes it necessary to define the use of the key theoretical concepts in this research. When social scientists discuss ideology, state, and class they may be expressing quite different concepts. A class, for example, may be defined in terms of its relation to the means of production (social relations of production) or in terms of market relations (income), which have very different analytical implications. Hence, researchers are always compelled to specify the theoretical coordinates within which their work moves.

Ideology as Lived Relations

The view that ideology is "lived relations," rather than ideas or ideal forms of consciousness (i.e., doctrines, creeds), is grounded in the Marxist tradition within the social sciences. It was Marx who first advanced the view that human beings in their most important activity, the social production of their material life conditions, produce not only commodities but also a series of real and symbolic relationships among themselves and between them and nature. Hence, the productive process is the basis of all ideology, and understanding it is only possible through an understanding of the contradictions of material life.[6]

This view of ideology has been characterized often as deterministic, where economics explains the rest of society. But arguing that the organization of a society is conditioned by the mode of production of its material life conditions does not necessarily mean that it is determined by economic production alone. On the contrary, it can be said that this is a holistic view in which ideology and politics are seen as integral parts of the process of production. The process of production then is not a mechanical economic process of commodity production but a social process in which ideas, values, and institutions are produced as well. In this view, material reality cannot be reduced to tangible things (e.g., commodities). Material reality refers to the real products of society, tangible or not, such as institutions, traditions, and knowledge, which are necessary for the process of social reproduction. Politics and ideology shape the production process as much as structural economic constraints shape politics and ideology.

If ideology is not a set of floating ideas, but rather a set of ideas and representations grounded and expressed in social relations, then it can be understood as the terrain where class relations are reproduced and legitimized in society; where people become aware of and represent social conflicts and strive to resolve them. In short, ideology is a world view, the basis on which the world is perceived and acted upon. Ideology is not merely an abstract idea. It is rather a concrete understanding of the world expressed in an objectively identifiable, if contradictory, ideological practice enmeshed in social relations.[7]

One of the foremost contemporary proponents of the view of ideology as lived relations was the French philosopher Louis Althusser. For Althusser, "ideology represents the imaginary relationship of individuals to their real conditions of existence."[8] In the structuralist view of Althusser, "ideology has very little to do with 'consciousness.' "[9] Ideology is an objective element, a level of the structure or, better yet, "structures" imposed upon the vast majority of people. The main function of ideology, for structuralists, is the concealment of real relations and their distortion through their representation in an imaginary form. This process of concealment is achieved through the articulation and reproduction of ideology in ideological state apparatuses (ISAs). It is through specific, concrete practices in ISAs (e.g., churches, schools, political parties, trade unions) that individuals participate in ideology and "accept" and reproduce the existing social relations of production. The "acceptance" of the dominant ideology is not an act of consciousness but a function of objective social relationships in which individuals are voluntarily or involuntarily involved through their participation in ISAs.[10]

In short, Althusser and the structuralist school conceive of ideology as an objective level of society in which the social conditions necessary for the reproduction of the existing relations of production can be secured. This is done through the ISAs, which guarantee the reproduction and distorted representation, at an ideal level, of the lived relations of individuals. It is through the "imaginary" representation of lived relations in ISAs that individuals "accept," in practice, the validity and universality of the dominant ideology. Thus, ideology is produced "automatically" (structurally reproduced) by society in the process of production. Althusser argues that "human societies secrete ideology as the very element and atmosphere indispensable to their historical respiration and life," and all classes are inscribed in the dominant ideology and are converted into its bearers.[11] Social classes are not the dynamic element of ideological practice but its victims, the "bearers" of the ideological structure. In this sense, society becomes a self-reproductive totality to which individuals or classes are subjected. Ideology guarantees the subjugation of individuals or classes to existing social relations and the reproduction (in a quasi-mechanical manner) of such relations. Thus society, and not classes, are the real subjects of history for Althusser and the structuralists.

This view reifies society and loses sight of the dynamics of social relations. The structuralists ignore the fact that ideology may serve to preserve a class order but dialectically it may serve to articulate political projects for change. If ideology is the terrain where people become aware of their social situation and strive to change it, then social change implies, necessarily, class struggle at the level of ideology. This means that any class that aspires to achieve power needs to establish its ideology as dominant and replace or redefine the ideology of the class that ruled before. If this is correct, then the function of ideology is not merely distortion and preservation, as Althusser argues. It is also, dialectically, understanding and making possible political change. The abolition of ideology as a distortive, conservative force is not the precondition for revolution, as Althusser believes. No class, including a revolutionary class, is above ideology. In fact, a class that leads a revolution or any process of change becomes a leading social force in the process of ideological struggle by opposing an alternative ideology.

Ideology is not necessarily distortive and conservative in a universal sense. It is not a mere instrument of reproduction but a terrain of class struggle that makes possible the reproduction of an historically determined social order and, at the same time, dialectically makes possible social change. ISAs do exist but they are not monolithic structures, nor can all ideological activity be reduced to them.

Another precursor of the view of ideology as lived relations was Antonio Gramsci. In his now famous *Prison Notebooks*, Gramsci defines ideology as "a conception of the world that is implicitly manifest in art, in law, in economic activity and in all manifestations of individual and collective life."[12] This conception permeates all aspects of human social activity, unifying and "cementing" society and providing a unitary significance, a raison d'être for human social activity, praxis.

However, this sense of unity provided by ideology does not mean the absence of class conflict. On the contrary, it is in the process of class struggle that the ruling classes impose their ideological dominance, their intellectual and moral leadership. Gramsci makes a distinction between the capacity of a class to dominate and its capacity to lead. The capacity to dominate comes from the exercise of coercive force, but the capacity to lead comes from the exercise of ideological (moral and intellectual) leadership. For a ruling class to be truly dominant, it must be able to control the means of violence as well as the means of persuasion in society. This capacity to lead, to use persuasion over force, in the exercise of political power is what Gramsci calls hegemony.[13]

In this sense, the social order imposed by the ruling classes rests upon a relatively precarious balance between coercion and persuasion, between repression and ideology. The imposition of the interests of the ruling classes upon the rest of society is not exclusively the result of a unilateral act of violence; it is also the result of an ideological process through which the dominated classes accept and internalize the interests of the ruling classes as part of their everyday life.

The acceptance of the ideology of the ruling classes does not mean total submission to it nor is it an act of the will of the subordinate classes. Rather, it is the product of a process of praxis where the subordinate classes are inscribed in the categories and the conception of the world of the ruling classes. They are "immersed" in ideology. Also, if the dominant ideology is the ideology of the ruling classes, then humans live and understand their relation according to the categories of the ruling classes. However, if the dominant ideology is imposed through class struggle, through a process of coercion and persuasion, this means that the subordinate classes, while living within the categories of the ruling class, are developing at the same time their own ideology, an ideology that expresses the tensions and contradictions of the very process of class conflict through which the dominant ideology is imposed.

In Gramsci's view, the ruling class, in the process of establishing its hegemony, creates a vast and complex structure that guarantees its dominance even in times of crisis, particularly economic crisis. This structure is civil society, composed of those "private" institutions that secure the leading capacity of the ruling class through the institutionalization and diffusion throughout society of its view of the world, its ideology.[14] Civil society for Gramsci is the principal domain of ideological praxis. Its function is fundamentally to organize the ideological praxis of the ruling classes and establish its hegemony (i.e., the establishment of rule by consent).

The fact that civil society becomes a primary terrain of ideological praxis does not imply that ideology is constrained to the practices of civil institutions. But it is the complexity of the institutions of civil society that allows for the condensation of ideological contradictions. The huge apparatus of civil society creates a complex mesh of social relations that obscure class contradictions. This is not the result of a willful act of the ruling classes but the result of the fragmentary nature of quotidian praxis in a complex social structure. Class contradictions may be obscured for both the subordinate and the dominant classes.

In viewing ideology as a level of praxis, Gramsci argues that ideologies are not necessarily logically consistent but are in fact contradictory. In Gramsci's view, people have two theoretical consciousnesses or one contradictory consciousness. People have a consciousness (a view of the world, an ideology) that is implicit in their activity and unites them with their peers (e.g., other workers). People also have a "superficially explicit or verbal" consciousness that they inherit from the past and absorb uncritically. The first form of consciousness emerges from the social relations established in the productive process and is shared by those who occupy the same social and economic position in this process. The latter is the link of the subordinated classes with the dominant ideology, the element that provides social unity, and the medium through which ideological dominance is articulated. These two consciousnesses express the contradiction between the "acceptance" of the ideology of the ruling classes in the verbal or explicit consciousness and its implicit rejection, albeit in a fragmented manner, in the practical or implicit consciousness (i.e., in the consciousness expressed in lived relations). The solution to this contradiction can only be provided in the process of political and ideological struggle.[15] The contradictory nature of ideology is thus a function of class struggle (i.e., of the imposition of the hegemony of a class). It is in the politicoideological terrain that classes can identify and express with some coherence their position in society, their particular interests, and their antagonisms with other classes.

It is worth noting here that the contradiction between verbal or explicit consciousness and practical or implicit consciousness is not posed as a contradiction between the false and the authentic. Rather, it is posed as the expression of the contradiction of a process of domination (i.e., of the establishment of the hegemony of a ruling class). The subordinate classes, by "accepting" in their verbal consciousness the views of the hegemonic class, are not merely being deceived; actually, they are being "immersed" in the categories of the ruling class by a complex process of coercion and persuasion. And the solution to this contradiction is not found in the scientific pursuit of "truth" but rather in politicoideological class struggle, in the "struggle of political hegemonies."

In sum, for Gramsci, ideology is a view of the world that is explicitly or implicitly present in all aspects of human social activity. The particular content of ideology has a class character that, through the process of ideological class struggle, extends beyond the boundaries of a single class. Ideology is thus a concrete form of social knowledge. It is not a formal system of ideas and concepts unified by a particular logic but rather the knowledge of everyday life, the "philosophy" on which concrete human activity is based, a level of praxis.

Throughout this work ideology will be understood then in the Gramscian sense as a set of explicit and implicit, and often contradictory, values, ideals, preferences, interests, etc., grounded in social relations in a class-divided society. Ideology is thus seen as a view of the world expressed in lived relations (praxis), in the process of class conflict. The notion that ideology is merely a false or distorted view of the world is rejected.

Hence, arguing that development strategies are ideology does not mean that they are simple misrepresentations of the "truth" about development. There is no such thing as "true" or "good" development. There are alternative development strategies representing particular views—interests and preferences—about the production and distribution of the social surplus product. Alternative development strategies are not divided between technically sound ones and ideological ones. They are divided by class interests. So the opposition of one development strategy to another is not the opposition between science and ideology but between alternative sets of policies that reflect competing class-based political projects.

Viewing development strategies as the key ideological terrain of the state does not mean that the state is seen as the only arena of conflict but as the principal one. Moreover, this argument is applicable to peripheral states with interventionist developmental policies and is not meant to be taken as an axiom about the relations among state, ideology, and development strategies. The relation between state and ideology cannot be explained by a fixed formula, be it Althusser's ISAs or the Gramscian antinomy of political society/civil society. The indiscriminate application of either of these formulas to all capitalist states may obscure differences between core and peripheral states as well as among different forms of the ideological function of the state in different societies. What determines the concrete form in which the state and ideology relate is the level of class struggle in a given society at a particular point in history—that is, the concrete needs of the process of social reproduction within the context of the specific antagonisms and conflicts generated by particular social relations of production.

The Capitalist State

The predominant views on the state up to the early sixties saw it either as a reflection of society or an instrument of the ruling classes. The first view was associated with pluralist theories that argued that the state was a reflection of competing forces in society with equal chances to influence the state through elections and pressure mechanisms. The latter view was associated with the Marxist theory of the state as a class dictatorship, where an economically dominant class used the state to become the politically ruling force. These liberal and instrumentalist views were profoundly challenged by the end of the 1960s.

In his book, *The State in Capitalist Societies*, Ralph Miliband thoroughly refuted pluralist claims about the state being a mirror of society or a neutral mediator of the interests of equally competing social forces. For his part, Nicos Poulantzas did the same to Marxist instrumentalism in *Political Power and Social Classes*. He levied a crushing critique against the notion of the state as an instrument of the economically dominant class, arguing that the state was a relatively autonomous entity that acted to reproduce capitalist relations through a complex mechanism of conflict and mediation.

Both these critiques influenced substantially future views on the state. Notions of the state as an instrument or as a neutral reflection of social forces were rejected as naive. Concepts such as relative autonomy, class conflict, and mediation became commonplace in any discussion of the state. The debate started by Miliband and Poulantzas spawned alternative views of looking at the state and led to the rediscovery and reformulation of Gramsci's concept of bourgeois power (hegemony) and the relation between the state and civil society.[16]

For Gramsci, political dominance or hegemony was achieved through a combination of coercion and persuasion (repression and consent). Coercion was the function of the political society, the state, and persuasion was the function of the civil society, ideological institutions. Although the relation between these two levels of society was seen as complementary, and class hegemony was a function of class dominance at the two levels simultaneously, there was the risk of mechanically reproducing a dichotomy that would leave out ideology as a key function of the modern capitalist state.

The post-Miliband and Poulantzas scholarship on the state sees it as a nonneutral mediator that condenses contradictions and forges a political equilibrium in a dialectical or conflictive manner. The state establishes class hegemony through conflict and accommodation. The function of the capitalist state is then seen, in general terms, as the reproduction of the political conditions necessary for the dominance of a ruling coalition at the least possible social, economic, and political cost. The state guarantees the organization and functioning of the social structure according to the needs of the dominant mode of capital accumulation. It not only represses but also organizes and maintains the functioning of the social structure within the limits of bourgeois social order, setting the rules and the limits of the conflict.

The state function can thus be said to be twofold. On the one hand, the state maintains class rule and, on the other, it fosters the support and/or acceptance (in a conflictive manner) of other classes and class fractions of the dominance of the ruling coalition, thus securing its hegemony. This double function of the capitalist state is fulfilled through three mechanisms: (a) the repressive apparatus, which is the ultimate guarantee of all political domination; (b) the direct intervention of the state in ideological institutions (schools, regulation of the media), thus participating in the forging of social consensus; and (c) direct and indirect state intervention in the economy through fiscal policy and the policies of the productive sector in the hands of the state (public utilities, state-owned industries), which gives the state a great degree of influence over the process of accumulation. The last two mechanisms are distinctive of the modern capitalist state, and they have become a most important element in establishing and maintaining bourgeois hegemony during the period that followed World War II. Indeed it could be said that the direct intervention of the capitalist state at the ideological level goes hand in hand with its direct intervention in the economy.

In the attempt to overcome the reductionist and instrumentalist view of the state, the notion of a ruling class has been replaced by the concept of "power bloc." Class rule is not the rule of a single class but of a conflictive coalition that "agrees" on strategic interests. They may fight among themselves but will unite against common enemies who threaten their shared strategic interests.[17]

Another important concept emerging from the Miliband/Poulantzas debate is that of relative autonomy.[18] Political power in advanced capitalism is shared by a power bloc; but this type of political arrangement also implies a state apparatus that is relatively autonomous from the interests of any single class. This concept, however, has at least two different connotations. To some, such as Theda Skocpol, it has come to mean the constitution of the state bureaucracy into independent social actors, class-like groups that pursue the interest of the state in opposition to other classes. Although Skocpol argues that state autonomy is not a fixed structural feature of any governmental system, her analysis emphasizes the "independence" of state bureaucracies.[19] To others, such as Nora Hamilton, state autonomy is a function of the level of class conflict. For Hamilton, the ability of state bureaucracies to pursue their own interests lies not in their entrenchment in a strong state but in a combination of conditions dictated by political and economic conflict.[20] It may well be that the difference between Hamilton and Skocpol stems from the fact that one is focusing on a peripheral state while the other is dealing mainly with advanced capitalist states, where the entrenchment of civil servants in state structures has achieved greater stability. Whatever may be the case, it is clear that for modern sociology and neo-Marxist thinkers, the capitalist state is not simply a committee of the ruling class but a complex structure that condenses political conflict through complex ideological, administrative, and repressive mechanisms. The particular manner in which these mechanisms may be combined to mediate conflicts cannot be defined by an abstract formula but by the concrete study of patterns of conflict.

It has been noted by some analysts that in the countries on the periphery of capitalism the state has historically played a larger role in mediating class conflict than in core societies. One key legacy of colonialism has been a strong state. The need to mediate conflicts between local and external forces and the double constraints that this implies have required a strong state around which irreconcilable and often highly conflictive interests are articulated and condensed.[21] Fernando Henrique Cardoso suggests that, in Latin America, it is around the state, not in political parties, that the dominant classes organize and express their interests. The interests of these classes, according to Cardoso, are articulated by bureaucratic cliques that form rings of politicoeconomic power inside the state apparatus.[22] In this same vein, Hamza Alavi argues that the rise to power of bureaucratic-military oligarchies in postcolonial societies reflects a particular accommodation between the relatively weak local propertied classes and the neocolonialist metropolitan bourgeoisie. In Alavi's view, the relative weakness of the local dominant classes in peripheral capitalist societies promotes the development of a relatively autonomous but sizeable and centralized state whose role is the mediation of the competing interests of the local dominant classes and the neocolonialist bourgeoisie.[23]

In a later elaboration on his view, Alavi argued that the peripheral state constitutes an arena of class struggle.[24] This is a more dynamic formulation of the nature of the peripheral state. Alavi's arguments imply that the strong state in the periphery may assume authoritarian or "democratic" forms depending on the level of class conflict. Moreover, he argues that the working classes may indeed influence or have access to the state in the periphery depending on the level of class conflict.

This is a more fruitful point of departure. Peripheral states indeed articulate class alliances between metropolitan and local classes. Yet it would be mistaken to argue that the power relations involved are fixed or predetermined in a formula of asymmetrical relationships. Like most power relations, the power arrangements in peripheral states are constantly changing, and their outcome can only be predicted by analyzing these relations in a historical context. The key elements that condition the nature of power relations in the periphery can be theoretically identified, of course. The mode of insertion of a country into the international division of labor, the position of the country in geopolitical arrangements, the internal structure of production, the internal class structure, and so on are key ingredients in determining the makeup of the state in a peripheral country.[25] What must be borne in mind, however, is that the articulation of these ingredients and their outcome as democratic or authoritarian power arrangements can only be understood in a concrete historical context.

One crucial question remains open: What is the specific character of the ideological function of the peripheral state and how is it articulated? In our view, the peripheral state has—aside from absorbing a part of ideological institutions normally associated with the civil society (e.g., schools) and transforming them into ISAs—created its own particular ideological terrain. This terrain is the area of economic policy, and this has become the dominant ideological terrain in peripheral capitalist societies since the popularization of

Keynesian and structuralist economic theories after World War II. This ideological function, rather than being reduced to a single unit or a specific ISA, is carried out by a set of administrative and political units within the state apparatus in charge of the various aspects of economic policy. In fact, one of the problems with identifying economic policy as the principal terrain of the ideological function of the state is the impossibility of reducing this function to a single unit or institution within the state apparatus. It can be said, as a matter of fact, that the majority of the administrative and political units of the state are involved in this ideological activity.

The peripheral state possesses both political-administrative and productive economic means to intervene in the pattern of economic accumulation. The state has the power to transfer economic surplus from certain sectors of the economy to others through both fiscal mechanisms and its economic power as a producer and consumer of goods and services in the economy. Examples of these are the subsidies for energy consumption granted to corporations in the form of discount rates given by state-owned utilities, guaranteed profits in state contracts with private corporations, state financing of research, and joint ventures in high-capitalization projects that have continued in spite of the emerging dominance of neoliberal laissez-faire policies.

The political class struggle for the control of the state apparatus becomes crucial. The state becomes the "nerve center" of the capitalist society. It is through the state and in the state that contradictions generated at the level of production are condensed and mediated. The state becomes the terrain where alliances are forged and conflicting interests mediated between the different fractions of the dominant classes that form the power bloc and between these fractions and the working classes. Economic policies are at the center of this process of condensation and mediation. Wage settlements worked out by the state, price policies, state investment policy, monetary policy, and all other economic policies represent crucial accommodations in the process of class struggle. The market alone does not set the rules for the distribution of a share of the social surplus product in capitalist society. The state dictates the rules and the limits of the political conflict for the control of the economy, and it becomes the center of the process of class struggle.

If these arguments are correct, the political struggle that takes place in and around the peripheral capitalist state implies a struggle among different fractions of the propertied classes (and in some cases between these and the working classes) to secure a larger share of the social surplus product and to secure the continuity and expansion of the process of capital accumulation. In this sense, the capitalist state can assume a democratic or pluralistic form because the terms of political conflict are set around distributive policies (wages, social services). One may even find working-class parties running the administrative apparatus of the capitalist state (e.g., the Labour parties of British Commonwealth countries), as long as the basis of capitalist accumulation is not questioned and the key conflicts involved are dealt with in terms of different views on how to distribute a share of the social surplus product. But when the basis of capitalist accumulation—the subordination of wage labor to capital and the dominance of private property over the means of production—is called into question by the working classes, the struggle for the control of state power in peripheral capitalist society becomes violent. In such cases, the state may even be taken over by repressive forces to suppress the challenge of the working classes. The political conflict around the peripheral state assumes a pluralistic form, a diversity of political parties and pressure groups, because it expresses a particular accommodation to and condensation of contradictions on the basis of capitalist accumulation.[26] When this basis is challenged, the ruling bloc may resort to violence as the main means to settle the conflict.

The economic policies of the peripheral state are then an expression of class struggle and represent a particular articulation and condensation of conflicting interests necessary for the continued reproduction of capitalist social relations of production. These policies are presented, at a formal level, in economic plans and programs, messages of the heads of states, and other formal presentations of governments and are implemented through legislation, budget policy, incentive programs, subsidies, tax policies, the policies of public corporations, monetary policy, etc. They involve a particular concept of how the economy ought to be organized and function and what economic interests should be favored. In other words, economic policies involve a set of priorities that are a function of class interests. However, it is difficult to lay bare these underlying interests by analyzing economic policies at the formal level (government statements, speeches). Invariably, the heads of state and government agencies in charge of designing economic policies present these policies as good for "the people," in the interest of "the nation," or in other rhetorical clichés that assert the universal goodness of the economic policies of the capitalist state. It is necessary to analyze economic policies in the process of their implementation. It is then that they reveal their class character and their importance as a concrete ideological force in the process of class struggle.

On the Concept of Class

Generally speaking, there are two views of class in the social sciences. One is rooted in the Weberian definition of class as a group that shares similar access to economic means under conditions determined by the market. This market-based definition is the basis of further elaborations of the concept of class as an income category and other classifications based on access to wealth, education, power, and prestige. The other definition is rooted in the Marxist view of class as a group that shares similar relations to the means of production. This "productionist" view is the basis for definitions of class that emphasize occupational and other "structural" (economic) conditions as criteria for defining class. Although the sociological implications of these two definitions are quite different, they both assume that class is a significant concept in explaining social relations. Shared interests, at the level of the market or of production, are in both views a key ingredient of political activity. Power relations have, ultimately, a class dimension.

Marxists have been accused traditionally of reducing the determination of class to economic criteria. According to this view, Marxists would argue that not only is a class determined by its position in the process of production but the politics and ideology of a class are a function of this position.[27] Reductionism, however, is not necessarily a corollary of using class as a key explanatory concept of social relations. Nonetheless, one must be careful to avoid class reductionism in a double sense. First, it must be clear that class is not merely an economic category defined by market or production criteria. Second, one should not reduce all social conflict to class conflict. Class antagonisms may be the underlying basis of social conflict but not all social conflict is expressed as class antagonisms. Human beings do not necessarily perceive their existence as members of a social class. In quotidian praxis people enter into relations that are constituted by nonclass categories. Gender, race, and ethnicity are also key components of political and ideological conflict. It is my view, however, that class determinations underlie all social conflict, although it is not always expressed and cannot be reduced to class conflict.

Throughout this work, the concept of class is used as a theoretical construct that defines the function of a group of people in the social division of labor. Class identities cannot be reduced to places in the productive structure. People are not what they produce but what they do in society, which extends to the political and ideological structures. Structural locations in the productive process are a component of class identities, but the political and the ideological spheres are also key elements of class identities—that is, a class is not simply an economic category but a sociopolitical one. The concept of class does not exist without that of class struggle. Classes are not things or entities. As a theoretical construct, the concept of class represents an organizing principle that enables the researcher to explain the dynamics of society as driven by a particular way of social relations, class conflict.

Assuming a class perspective means that this study focuses its analysis on macroscopic social, economic, and political questions. Since the objective of the study is to analyze the process of formulating social and economic policies of development, the concept of class allows us to understand the economic basis of political conflict and the political basis of economic strategies. This does not negate the autonomy of the political and ideological from the economic. Heuristically, however, the concept of class facilitates uncovering the linkages among the economic, political, and ideological.

Developmentalism as a Dominant Ideology

Developmentalism became the leading ideology in Latin America immediately after World War II. This coincided with the process of redefining the international division of labor and the forms of exploitation of imperialist capitalism in peripheral capitalist countries. In the period between the late nineteenth century and World War I, the dominant form of expropriation of surplus value in the periphery was based on the extraction of absolute surplus value, the appropriation of surplus value based on activities with relatively low or stagnant rates of labor productivity. This implied what some called the "superexploitation" of labor in agrarian or extractive activities in Latin America.[28] The other main form of expropriation that accompanied this superexploitation of labor was the unequal exchange between the core and the periphery. The structure of unequal exchange implied the asymmetrical exchange of quantities of labor or products of labor in the exchange of raw materials and agricultural goods from the periphery for manufactured goods from the core. This stage of "classical" imperialism was characterized by the predominance of the *haciendas*, agricultural and mining enclaves, and commercial activities (large import/export houses) controlled by metropolitan capital and local landed oligarchies in Latin America.

The restructuring of imperialist capitalism initiated after World War I and culminating with World War II resulted in the internationalization of capitalist production. In this stage the dominant form of expropriation of surplus value became based on the extraction of relative surplus value, the exploitation of labor in activities with increasing rates of labor productivity. This meant an increase in direct industrial investment in some peripheral countries and the expansion and control by the imperialist bourgeoisie (the internationalization) of the internal markets of peripheral countries. Surplus value was not only extracted from the workers but part of it was realized in the markets of the peripheral countries as well. This process was accompanied by a deepening in the structure of unequal exchange. Insofar as industrial advance in the periphery did not lead to closing the gap in the rates of productivity between the core and the periphery, the structures of unequal exchange were reinforced. Put another way, as the process of internationalization of capitalist production developed unevenly, not tending to the homogeneous transfer of the factors of production, the basis for unequal exchange—differential levels of capital accumulation, labor productivity, and rates of surplus value expropriation—remained. But the forms and mechanisms of unequal exchange changed from the classical form of exchange of raw materials for manufactured goods to more sophisticated forms. A new international division of labor emerged in which technology and capital are exchanged for cheap labor and access to the markets of peripheral countries. Capital and technology are controled by the metropolitan centers. This has led to the development of a complex international financial structure that contributes to the siphoning off of surplus value from the periphery to the center.[29]

In this sense, the restructuring of imperialist capitalism between the two world wars favored the emergence of the industrial bourgeoisie and the urban middle classes as leading forces in those sectors that supported industrial development in Latin America. The political changes and the articulation of the class alliances needed to make viable the implementation of a political project that favored industrialization were fostered by the formation and emergence into political power of populist movements. These movements represented an alliance among the Latin American industrial bourgeoisie, the urban middle sectors, and the working classes in favor of industrial development. At that time, populist developmentalism was opposed to the agrarian export economic model supported by the Latin American oligarchies and the fractions of metropolitan capital allied to them (merchant and financial capital linked to the production of primary goods); hence, the initial anti-imperialist nationalistic positions of populist movements.[30]

With the coming to power of the populist forces, the contradictions between the strategic interests of the industrial bourgeoisie and the working classes surfaced. The exacerbation of the contradictions within the populist alliance coincided with the redefinition of the international division of labor and the consequent redefinition of the interests of the metropolitan bourgeoisie regarding Latin America. Metropolitan interests were now shifting toward direct investment in manufacturing industries, which meant the convergence between the populist development project of the Latin American bourgeoisie and the interests of the imperialist bourgeoisie in Latin America. This convergence eventually brought about the rapprochement between the Latin American bourgeoisie and the metropolitan bourgeoisie, deepening the crisis of populism.[31] The populist alliance was restructured with metropolitan and local industrial sectors and the urban middle sectors emerging as the leading forces.

It must be added that the Latin American and the metropolitan bourgeoisies each saw their role in the process of industrial development as the dominant one and the role of the other as secondary. Hence, the convergence did not mean an absence of conflict.[32] The Latin American bourgeoisie believed the process of industrialization should be based on import substitution, and the role of foreign capital should be a supportive or secondary one. The imperialist bourgeoisie did not see its role as supportive and, in fact, came to control the strategic areas of industrial production (e.g., capital goods, durable consumer goods).

The ideology of development came to represent, explain, and legitimize the rearticulation of class alliances in favor of the interests of the bourgeoisie. Developmentalism legitimized the new relations of production (the new forms of exploitation and domination of the working classes) implicit in the strategy favored by the industrial bourgeoisie and presented it as the only viable alternative for development.[33] The concept of development was framed in the categories of capitalist development. The proponents of developmentalism presented society as divided between a "dynamic" industrial sector and a "traditional" agricultural sector, not between social classes. The fundamental problems of society, in the view of developmentalist theoreticians, were backwardness, economic stagnation, and poverty, rather than exploitation.[34] Concepts like progress, modernization, and social mobility became part of the developmentalist jargon. However, behind all this terminology was the political project of a class coalition. Populist developmentalism became the political project of the emerging Latin American industrial bourgeoisie at a particular juncture. The first theoretical formulation of developmentalism was found in the theories of development of ECLA in the 1950s. Octavio Rodríguez, a former ECLA economist, argues that the economic theories developed by this organization were the technical representation of the populist political project. In other words, the ISI polices recommended by ECLA in the 1950s articulated a class-based political project and attempted to provide an aura of theoretical legitimacy to it.[35]

However, populist developmentalism is only one of the forms taken by the ideology of development. Later, during the 1960s and 1970s, it was reformulated by the advocates of national capitalist development within dependency, also known as structuralists.[36] Since then, the categories of developmentalism have been articulated by diverse fractions of the Latin American bourgeoisie, often supporting opposing political projects (e.g., liberal democratic, authoritarian bureaucratic, etc.) but maintaining the basic principles of capitalist development.

In this sense, the version of developmentalism favored by metropolitan groups has been articulated by the various modernization theories produced by the social scientists of the core. These theories support the adoption of the politicoideological tenets of capitalism (private property, wage labor, unrestricted international trade). In general, the policies favored by these theories present foreign investment as a necessary element for development. The imperialist bourgeoisie, termed the foreign sector, is presented as a necessary ally, and sometimes benefactor, of development.[37]

With varying nuances, developmentalism became the dominant ideology in Latin America after World War II. The particular twists of emphasis on one or another aspect of developmentalism were a function of particular accommodations and shifts in class alliances. They represented a form of condensation of competing or conflicting interests, hence the necessity to analyze the concrete expression of class interests in developmentalism at the level of praxis, i.e., in the process of implementation of developmentalist political projects.

The Case of Puerto Rico

Contrary to the rest of Latin America, Puerto Rico never became independent from Spain; in 1898, as a result of the Spanish-American War, it became a colony of the United States. This presents certain peculiarities in the analysis of the relationship between the state and the ideology of development in Puerto Rico.

If, as Alavi argues, the renegotiation of the colonial pact that leads to the establishment of a postcolonial state implies the enhancement of the relative autonomy of the peripheral state,[38] the opposite should hold true for societies that remain under colonial rule—that is, the persistence of colonialism should imply a restricted state autonomy, since the metropolis maintains direct control of the colonial state. In a colony the state becomes the most important social structure, as the ruling class is an absent class that needs to control the state directly in order to create the social and political conditions for its economic dominance. The colonial state is a highly centralized apparatus that tends to assume many functions normally associated with the domain of the civil society. It tends to regulate most of the social activity in the colony in its attempt to legitimize the dominance of the absent class and to neutralize the potential forces of opposition within the colony.

However, if this is true of classic colonialism, in modern colonialism— that which survived the postwar decolonization movement—the colonial state becomes the center for the condensation of both the metropolis/ colony contradiction and that internal to the colony, the labor/capital contradiction. The complexities this presents in a postcolonial world make it impossible to argue that the colonial state is simply an instrument of repression for the absent class. The colonial state principally articulates the interests of the absent ruling class, but not exclusively. In a secondary manner, it articulates the interests of the local propertied classes and intermediary groups, condensing the conflicts implied by the metropolis/colony contradiction as well as mediating internal class conflicts in the colony. The specific form that this accommodation may take depends on the particular correlation of forces in the process of class struggle at a particular juncture. That is, it depends on the level at which class contradictions are exacerbated in the colony and between the classes in the colony and the metropolis.

The Great Depression of the 1930s prompted the expansion of the colonial state in Puerto Rico to maintain control over the colony. This expansion, at a time when the metropolis was itself in crisis, implied the incorporation of more and new local elements into the state apparatus. This, in time, expanded the basis of legitimation of colonial domination. However, this does not mean that the local intermediaries were mere puppets used by the metropolis at will. The process of integrating local elements into the colonial state is a dialectical process of accommodation, articulation, and condensation of often competing, and sometimes conflictive, interests between the local and metropolitan groups.

The expansion of the colonial state in the 1930s facilitated a state-based strategy of industrial development that articulated a political project for restructuring colonial domination. Thus the Puerto Rican process of industrialization varies greatly from the rest of Latin America, where the main push for industrialization came from the local bourgeoisie. Furthermore, the crisis of the thirties induced in Latin America an expansion of local industrial production, which tended to strengthen, at least temporarily, the political position of the local bourgeoisie giving it a greater degree of autonomy from the metropolitan centers. In the case of Puerto Rico, the crisis of the 1930s increased dependence on the metropolis and the industrialization strategy was to a large extent promoted by metropolitan groups.[39]

The changes in the structure and functions of the colonial state in Puerto Rico that took place between the 1930s and the 1950s can be explained in terms of the need to restructure imperialist capitalism both in Puerto Rico and the world. The wide range of functions that make the state in Puerto Rico seem neocolonial rather than classical colonial are a function of the need for the reproduction of imperialist capitalism in the postwar era. In order to lay the basis for a new economic model, it was necessary to relegitimize the colonial relation and to expand the structure and functions of the colonial state into the economic and ideological levels of society.[40]

At the economic level, a vast public sector was created that in the 1940s included productive enterprises, public utilities, and social welfare institutions. At the ideological level, many of the existing institutions of the state as well as newly created ones (e.g., the Puerto Rico Planning Board, the Industrial Development Company) became involved in designing the development strategy, making it appear to respond to the "general interests" of society. Developmentalism became the dominant ideology, and the agencies of the state became its principal bearer.

If this is correct then it can be argued that development strategies in Puerto Rico are the ideological representation of the political project of a class coalition that represents the interests of metropolitan and local dominant sectors. Development strategies within the colonial context represent particular modes of accumulation of imperialist capitalism that assume the subordination of wage labor to capital as well as the political subordination of the colony to the United States. Now we turn to the substantiation of this hypothesis.

Notes

1. Vasconi, "Cultura, ideología, dependencia y alienación," p. 133.
2. Kesselman, *Estategias de desarrollo*, p. 11.
3. Limoeiro Cardoso, *La ideología dominante*, pp. 12–14.

4. This distinction is made by Peralta Rámos, *Etapas*, p. 69.

5. Throughout this work the term "condense" means to transform conflicts and contradictions and provide them with a new form.

6. Marx, "Preface," pp. 182–183.

7. This should not be construed as the only possible interpretation of Marx's view of ideology. Using Marx's ideas, Gregory Lukács developed a view of ideology as a form of class consciousness. He defined this as "the appropriate and rational reactions 'imputed' to a particular position in the process of production." For Lukács, however, all class consciousnesses, except that of the proletariat, were false since they expressed fragmentary views of society. Marx's view of ideology also influenced the views of the Frankfurt school, which moved in the direction of sociopsychological analysis. These divergent interpretations are rooted in the ambiguities of Marx himself. Throughout his work, Marx refers to ideology as a reflex of material (economic) relations, as distorted consciousness, and as a form of social consciousness. See Larrain, *The Concept*, Chap. 2; Lukács, *History and Class Consciousness*; and Connerton, *Critical Sociology*, Introduction.

8. Althusser, *Lenin and Philosophy*, pp. 153–155.

9. Althusser, *For Marx*, p. 233.

10. Althusser, *Lenin and Philosophy*, pp. 156–160.

11. Althusser, *For Marx*, p. 232.

12. Gramsci, *Prison Notebooks*, p. 328.

13. Ibid., pp. 57–58 and passim. For a comprehensive discussion of Gramsci's concept of hegemony see Femia, "Hegemony and Consciousness."

14. Gramsci, *Prison Notebooks*, pp. 12–13, 235, and passim; see also Femia, "Hegemony and Consciousness," p. 35.

15. Gramsci, *Prison Notebooks*, p. 333.

16. Stuart Hall points out that "Poulantzas clearly attempted to give Gramsci's concept of 'hegemony' a more theoreticized and systematic formulation," in Hall, "Nicos Poulantzas," p. 62. The debate between Poulantzas and Miliband appeared in issue numbers 51, 59, 82, and 95 of the *New Left Review*.

17. See Poulantzas, *Political Power*, p. 234.

18. Poulantzas, *Political Power*, p. 256.

19. Skocpol, "Bringing the State Back In," p. 4.

20. Hamilton, *Limits of State Autonomy*, Chap. 1.

21. See Evers, *El estado capitalista*; Thomas, *The Rise*.

22. Cardoso, "As contradiçoes."

23. Alavi, "The State in Post-Colonial Societies."

24. Alavi, "State and Class."

25. See Evers, *El estado capitalista*, for the discussion of these criteria.

26. Democracies in Latin America have been described as systems of elite accommodation, where fractions of the power bloc "agree" to take turns in government to ensure political stability and the exclusion of radical popular alternatives. See Peeler, *Latin American Democracies*.

27. Hindess, "The Concept of Class."

28. Marini, *Dialéctica*, pp. 38–49.

29. This is certainly a sketchy characterization of the later stages of imperialism. It is difficult to provide a clear model for the periodization of imperialism without entering into a comparative study of the development of metropolitan centers, the forms of exploitation, and the definition of different fractions of capital dominant in the different stages. This is beyond the scope of this study. For some interesting analyses of this see Mandel, *Late*

Capitalism; Magdoff, *Imperialism*, especially Chap. 3; Beaud, *A History of Capitalism*; Cardoso and Faletto, *Dependencia y desarrollo*.

30. See Ianni, *Formación del estado populista*.

31. Cardoso and Faletto, *Dependencia y desarrollo*, pp. 130–140.

32. The necessity of the Latin American bourgeoisie to establish first an alliance with the working classes against the oligarchy and then with the imperialist bourgeoisie to contain the potential threat to their rule from the working classes can be explained by the relative weakness of the bourgeoisie and, therefore, its incapacity to impose its hegemony over the rest of society. On this question see Ianni, *Formación del estado populista*, Pt. 3.

33. See Limoeiro Cardoso, *La ideología dominante*, Pt. 2, for a detailed analysis of populist developmentalism in Brazil.

34. See Prebisch, "The System."

35. Rodríguez, *La teoría*, pp. 276–298.

36. See, for example, the works of Sunkel and Paz, *El subdesarrollo*; Furtado, *La economía*; and Jaguaribe, "Dependencia."

37. See Alavi, "State and Class," p. 289.

38. Alavi, "The State in Post-Colonial Societies."

39. This argument does not intend to overemphasize the role of the local bourgeoisie in the industrialization process of Latin America. The point is made to stress the different character of the social forces behind the industrialization process in Puerto Rico and Latin America. For example, the state-based development attempted in Chile as a response to the crisis of the mining enclave during the 1930s and 1940s is different from the state-based development attempted in Puerto Rico. In the Chilean case, the classes in control of the state were local classes, while in Puerto Rico the state was run by a local and North American bureaucracy headed by a U.S. governor appointed by the U.S. president. See Cardoso and Faletto, *Dependencia y desarrollo*, pp. 91–94; and Furtado, *La economía*, Chap. 11.

40. Mattos Cintrón has termed this the "hypertrophy of the colonial state" in *La política y lo político*, p. 131.

2

Populist Reformism and the Origins of Developmentalism

Immediately after the U.S. invasion in 1898, the colonial state apparatus in Puerto Rico was swiftly taken over by U.S. colonial administrators. The share of power attained by the Puerto Rican *hacendados* in the Autonomic Charter of 1897 was quickly wiped out and local groups were only allowed subordinate participation in the executive and the legislative branches of government. The new metropolis set up a military government that ruled the island by decree until 1900. With the Foraker Act in 1900, the military government was replaced with a civil colonial government run by North American officials designated by the president of the United States. The Foraker Act established a highly centralized colonial government wherein representatives of Puerto Rican political forces had limited participation and the U.S. governor, Congress, and the president had the power to veto any laws that the colonial legislature recommended.[1]

The policies of the new metropolis transformed Puerto Rico from a coffee export economy, based on the *hacienda* (estate) as the basic productive unit, into a sugar export economy, with plantations and sugar *centrales* (mills) becoming the center of the productive process. The local dominant class, the Puerto Rican *hacendados*, were displaced from their prominent socioeconomic position and gradually replaced by local sugar barons, who became allied with the powerful North American sugar corporations.[2]

Under the sway of North American capitalism, U.S. sugar corporations came to control the island's main industry. By 1929, the total land dedicated to sugarcane production was 251,000 acres, one-third of all the land cultivated. Four U.S. sugar corporations controlled (owned or rented) 68 percent of this land. These same four corporations owned eleven of the forty-two *centrales* that operated in the country and were responsible for producing

Parts of this chapter appeared in the *Journal of Latin American Studies* 21 (October 1989).

50 percent of the country's sugar.[3] In addition to controlling the most important sector of production, the interests of these corporations extended to investments in railways, utilities, and other public services. The dividends paid by these corporations were very high as were the rates of capitalization. It was estimated that by 1930 the assets of these four corporations represented 10 percent of the total wealth of the country and 40 percent of the agricultural wealth.[4]

Even though sugar was the center of the agroexport accumulation model, North American capital did not limit itself to this area. U.S. companies also controlled tobacco manufacturing, which since 1911 had become the second most important export, accounting for 17 percent of total exports. One-third of the banking resources of the island were controlled by the National City Bank of New York and the American Colonial Bank. U.S. capital also invested in fruit production, where it controlled 64 percent of the land dedicated to this activity. Finally, four North American shipping companies controlled all freight movement between Puerto Rico and the United States.[5]

Clearly, after the invasion of 1898, U.S. capital achieved a hegemonic control over the productive process in Puerto Rico. The first three decades of North American domination shaped Puerto Rico's development as a monoproductive, agricultural export-oriented economy. The bulk of the capital investment in Puerto Rico and the fundamental decisions affecting its economy originated outside of Puerto Rico, and the capital generated there was accumulated outside also. The dominant sector of the Puerto Rican economy was articulated as a function of the North American economy and of U.S. capital in such a way as to form an integral part of them, and it responded, in the main, to the interests of this external sector. Thus, paradoxically, although Puerto Rico had an agrarian economy it imported the majority of the foodstuffs it consumed.[6]

In many respects the sugar economy of Puerto Rico in this period fits the definition that Fernando Henrique Cardoso and Enzo Faletto give of an enclave economy: production was a direct extension of the core economy; investment decisions and the benefits generated by capital merely passed through the local economy in a circulatory flow that ended up increasing the mass of capital in the United States; there were very few linkages between the export sector and the subsistance and local agricultural sectors, although there were connections with the local society through the power system; and the links of the local economy to the world market were established in the sphere of the core markets.[7]

Political conflict took the form of a triangle: the coffee *hacendados* led the opposition to the colonial government, the local sugar growers and urban middle classes formed the local base of support for the colonial government, and the working classes tried to establish an autonomous political base. The three main political groups during the first two decades of the century were the Partido Unión Puertorriqueña (PUP), dominated by the coffee growers; the Partido Republicano (PR), dominated by the sugar growers; and the Federación Libre de Trabajadores (FLT), which gave birth to the Partido Socialista (PS) in 1915.[8] As these groups had no access to executive power, they competed to influence colonial officials and strove to pressure the United States to alter the colonial relation—the PR and the FLT/PS favored statehood; the PUP favored self-rule, autonomy, or independence.

By the 1920s a colonial power bloc had been clearly established and consolidated beyond partisan divisions. The imperialist bourgeoisie had incorporated and co-opted elements from diverse political sectors and social classes within its power sphere. A good inventory of these sectors is provided by North American colonial governor Rexford G. Tugwell:

> Half a dozen of these enterprises controlled by New York and Boston banks among them owned or leased about half the Island's really productive land—and the mills which processed its crop. . . . They pay large fees to many technicians and professional people, they leased much land besides what they owned, and so controlled its owners; they bought the large farmers' cane and so determined the policies of the farmers' associations (here again was my old friend the Farm Bureau, acting as a stooge for the absentee corporations); they supported research at the university and furnished the only extensive market for its graduates and so had the expected influence on university policy. . . . These would include those middle class people who were not employed by the corporations, merchants and other businessmen, professional people and so on, but more importantly the Puerto Ricans who themselves owned or operated sugar properties.[9]

The consolidation of colonial power is further illustrated by the political realignment that occurred during this period. In 1924, the PUP and the PR entered into an electoral alliance known as the Alianza Puertorriqueña (Puerto Rican Alliance). The Alianza won the elections of 1924 and 1928, governing the country from 1925 until 1932. It was formed to advance the demands for self-rule by Puerto Ricans; the key issue was the right of Puerto Ricans to elect the colonial governor. In entering the Alianza, the PUP dropped all demands for independence. For its part, in 1924 the PS entered into an alliance with a splinter faction of the PR, which opposed the alliance with the PUP, known as the Coalición (Coalition); it favored statehood.[10] This alliance of former enemies to demand political reforms within the colonial framework or alternatively annexation to the metropolis clearly points to the success of the imperialist bourgeoisie in consolidating its power in the colony.

The 1930s: The Political and Economic
Crisis of the Sugar Economy

The Great Depression had a devastating impact on Puerto Rico. The price of sugar went from 5.24 cents per pound in 1923 to 2 cents per pound in 1929 and to .93 cents per pound in 1932.[11] However, the sugar companies succeeded in maintaining large profits during the first half of the 1930s by increasing production, lowering wages, and taking advantage of extraordinary protectionist measures in the United States. The U.S. boycott of the international agreement to limit sugar production, known as the Chadbourne Plan, and the enactment of the Smoot-Hawley tariff, which increased the duty on foreign sugar entering the United States in 1930, virtually closed the U.S. market to foreign producers and provided a temporary cushion to U.S. companies in Puerto Rico.[12] These companies also instituted drastic cuts in the salaries of workers. For fiscal year 1928/29, the average salary of a laborer in the sugar fields was 95.75 cents per day; for 1933/34 the average was only 62.25 cents per day, a reduction of 35 percent. In 1928/29, laborers in mills earned an average of $1.37 per day, but by 1933/34 their salary was reduced to $1.20 per day, a drop of slightly more than 12 percent.[13] These factors enabled U.S sugar corporations to pay dividends of up to 30 percent per share to their stockholders in the midst of the depression.[14]

But behind this short-term bonanza enjoyed by the companies and their local allies, troubles were brewing. It was estimated that one hundred and fifty thousand heads of families were unemployed, which affected nearly half of the population of the country. The prices of most basic foodstuffs, which were imported, increased significantly, partly because of the continued deterioration in the terms of trade after the latter half of the 1920s. Between 1932 and 1933 the price of kidney beans and flour increased 75 percent; rice, 70 percent; cod fish, 47 percent; ham, 25 percent; and lard, 24 percent. Overall, the cost of living increased by about one-third in that period.[15]

Although the deterioration in the living standards of a large majority of the population provided the social basis for political unrest, it was the approval of the Jones-Costigan Act of 1934 that dealt the coup de grace to the sugar economy. This act undermined the very basis upon which the dominance of the sugar sector rested by imposing a quota on sugar exports to the United States. The quota forced a reduction in production of one hundred seventy thousand tons of sugar, valued at approximately $8.5 million. This sudden reduction had negative effects not only for the fifteen thousand workers who lost their jobs (added to the one hundred fifty thousand already unemployed) but also for the small and medium growers for whom the mills refused to grind sugarcane and to whom banks denied financing.[16] As a result of the quota, small and medium *colonos* (sugar growers) faced the possibility of losing their crops and their land.

The negative effects of the quota were not limited to the subordinate classes. The large U.S. sugar corporations and the local sugar bourgeoisie faced serious financial problems as well. North American banking institutions denied them credit because of the uncertainties created by the quota. Corporate representatives began to talk about the dangerous conditions for the business sector on the island.[17]

The Political Dimension of the Crisis

The collapse of the economic base of the island was accompanied by a questioning of the colonial regime and the breakdown of political order. A fraction of the petty bourgeoisie began to articulate a militant proindependence political project. This sector blamed U.S. corporate interests for the extremely poor social and economic conditions of the island. They denounced the colonial exploitation that U.S. corporate interests had imposed on Puerto Rico and called for a nationalist revolution that would put an end to North American domination on the island. The political expression of this sector was the Partido Nacionalista (PN).

During the 1930s, the PN led many protests against the colonial government and U.S. interests, including a series of strikes and boycotts against U.S. corporations not involved in sugar production. The most visible of these were the service station and garage owners' strike against oil corporations, protesting the high cost of imported gasoline; the food distributors' boycott against U.S. flour exporters for the high cost and poor quality of imported flour; and the boycott on mortgage collections by small farmers against the Federal Land Bank of Baltimore. Other protests included the 1931 and 1933 university students' strikes and the 1934 general sugar-workers' strike.[18] Although the main political base of the PN was clearly petty bourgeois, the PN was attracting the attention of other social sectors most affected by the crisis, the rural proletariat and the unemployed.

The rural proletariat had traditionally been represented by the FLT, the local affiliate of the American Federation of Labor, and by the PS. Late in 1933, the FLT had signed a contract with the sugar corporations that was rejected and denounced as treason by the workers. They went on strike against the will of the FLT leadership. This rejection was more than a mere disagreement between the leaders and the rank and file of the FLT. Having repudiated the FLT leadership, the workers called upon the president of the PN, Pedro Albizu Campos, to represent them in the bargaining process with the sugar corporations. The strike had now become a symbol of the rejection of the politics of collaboration with the colonial regime in which the PS had engaged through the Coalición, which was in power at the time. With the deepening of the crisis, workers' demands turned from simple wage-oriented issues to calling into question the arrangements that the leadership of the PS had with the PR. The sugar-workers' strike thus highlighted the political crisis facing the colonial regime during this period. If the PS, which was in power, could not control the workers, who could? The strike began to break the almost monolithic control of the FLT on the organized proletariat, a process that culminated in the creation of a new nationwide trade union council, the Confederación General de Trabajadores (CGT).[19]

The 1934 strike represented the juncture at which two potentially revolutionary forces established a significant political collaboration. The convergence of the interests of a fraction of organized labor and the nationalist petty bourgeoisie had the potential of becoming a strong anti-imperialist alliance. The most threatening move, in the eyes of the dominant classes, was that the workers had called on the leader of the PN to lead the strike. The strike took place in a period of increasing social unrest. Between 1931 and 1936 there were a total of 207 strikes, of which ninty-one were between July 1933 and June 1934.[20] The PN was the only party then calling for the immediate liquidation of colonialism, thus questioning the very basis of North American domination in Puerto Rico. The workers, under the moderate leadership of the pro-American FLT, were a manageable force, hence the U.S. corporations and the colonial authorities wanted to put an end quickly to any collaboration between the Nationalists and the workers to prevent the formation of an organization that would bring these sectors together in a durable alliance. The possibility of such an anti-imperialist alliance, as had happened in Cuba and other Caribbean countries in the 1930s, explains why the corporations sent the chief of police, Colonel Elisha Francis Riggs, to negotiate with Albizu and granted all the demands sought by the workers.[21]

Indeed, the collaboration between Nationalists and the dissidents of the FLT did not materialize into a long-term political alliance that could capitalize on the economic crisis. Georg Fromm has noted perceptively that the political and ideological views of the FLT dissidents were different from those of the PN. The PN wanted to establish a republic dominated by the traditional petty bourgeoisie and other small proprietors (e.g., small farmers); the workers, accustomed to the socialist rhetoric of the PS leadership, looked at this with distrust.[22]

In addition to the ideological differences that prevented the emergence of an anti-imperialist popular movement, the colonial regime took action to suppress the nationalist threat. The government implemented a policy that combined the "iron fist" with the "velvet glove."

At the political level, the appointment of General Blanton Winship as governor in 1934, and the earlier appointment of Colonel Riggs as the chief of police, set the stage for things to come. Immediately after the 1934 sugar-workers' strike, the government unleashed a campaign of political repression directed against the PN, starting with the Río Piedras Massacre in 1935 and culminating in the Ponce Massacre in 1937. During this period, PN leaders were imprisoned and any individuals or groups who opposed colonial rule on the island were harassed and persecuted.[23] The sugar economy may have been doomed to failure because of the economic crisis and the restructuring of the international sugar market, but this did not mean that the sugar interests in Puerto Rico were about to relinquish their privileges without a fight. In any case, the sugar corporations represented but one fraction of the imperialist bourgeoisie. The strategic interests of the North American state were also a key factor in determining the political future of the colony.

Repression, however, was only one way of preventing the emergence of a nationalist-led, radical, anti-imperialist popular movement. There was a need to address the socioeconomic conditions that were the breeding ground for a possible popular uprising. To deal with this side of the problem the metropolitan state intervened directly by creating welfare programs that ran parallel to the existing administrative apparatus of the colonial state. The most important programs were the Puerto Rico Emergency Relief Administration (PRERA) and the Puerto Rico Reconstruction Administration (PRRA). The significance of these programs went beyond their immediate effect in terms of aid to the population. In the long run, they would constitute the basis for the mobilization of the political forces that could provide a solution to the crisis while preserving the interests of the United States.

The politicoeconomic crisis of the 1930s meant a breakdown of the traditional political order and the consensus inside the power bloc. That is, it broke down the consensus between the classes that exercised power by control over the means of production and the colonial state, whose common interests were the preservation of capitalist relations of production (i.e., private property and the subordination of wage labor to capital) and the colonial relation. As a consequence of the crisis, the political forces in Puerto Rico were realigned into four major groups. The two sectors outside of the power bloc were (1) the traditional petty bourgeoisie (primarily rural), who assumed a nationalist position when faced with the threat of economic and social extinction, and (2) a militant fraction of the working class, led by disgruntled members of the PS and the FLT, in search of a new political alternative and leadership, which led to the formation of the Partido Comunista Puertorriqueño (PCP) and, later, the CGT. On the side of the power bloc were a conservative group, represented by those closely tied to sugar production, who opposed any structural change as a solution to the crisis, and a reformist group, represented by those within the power bloc not directly linked to the sugar sectors, who understood that the solution to the crisis must involve structural changes at the expense of the sugar sector.

The first clear manifestations of this division within the power bloc were expressed in the debates about an alternative economic strategy. Since the notion of "development strategy" was not part of the lingo of economics at that time, the alternative strategy was conceptualized in terms of a program for economic reconstruction.

The Solution to the Crisis and
the Roots of Developmentalism

The most important proposal for the economic and social reconstruction of Puerto Rico was known popularly as the Chardón Plan, which resulted from a series of discussions and exchanges between members of the Roosevelt administration and members of the colonial government. The basis of the plan had been proposed by the chancellor of the University of Puerto Rico, Carlos Chardón, who would later be selected to head the Puerto Rico Policy Commission, appointed by President Franklin D. Roosevelt to design a program for the use of the funds collected from a special federal government tax on sugar refining for economic reconstruction purposes.[24] The Chardón Plan proposed a series of long-term economic measures for restructuring the Puerto Rican economy at the expense of the sugar interests. The fundamental reforms were aimed at reducing sugar production; diversifying agriculture; creating a state-controlled sugar-producing sector; developing an industrialization program using local raw materials and producing for the local market; and, in the long run, reducing overpopulation and unemployment through migration.[25] These changes would be accomplished by means of a land distribution program and government intervention in the process of production. According to the plan, marginal sugar lands were to be purchased with the special reconstruction funds and distributed to landless peasants and unemployed workers of the sugar industry. Another idea was to create cooperatives of small *colonos* who would grind their sugarcane in government-owned mills. In addition, private mills would be pressured to pay better prices for the *colonos'* sugar. Other plans were drawn up for the rehabilitation of coffee, tobacco, and citrus fruit production and for a limited program of industrialization. The implementation of this program would be in the hands of a public corporation funded by the sugar refining tax.

This plan generated great opposition from U.S. sugar companies, the local sugar bourgeoisie, and their allies within the United States, particularly in Congress. This opposition was the main reason why the Chardón Plan gained a reputation among the working classes as being in the interests of "the people." In reality, the measures proposed by the plan were framed along the lines of the New Deal policies and represented the solution to the politicoeconomic crisis put forth by the antisugar sector within the colonial power bloc. This sector coincided with, and was allied to, elements within the U.S. government connected to the executive branch (the president and the secretary of the interior) who were aware of the need for structural reforms. The following statement from the introduction of the report containing the plan substantiates this contention:

> The suggestions and recommendations contained in this report are predicated upon our conviction that the United States, under the present administration, will at all times place the welfare of the

Puerto Rican people above the interests of particular groups and that the only interests that must be recognized as deserving special preference in the premises is the prestige of the American nation as a whole in connection with the development of a rational and equitable economic policy in the Caribbean. As a result of the plans suggested, it is probable that the United States would temporarily lose perhaps as much as 15 percent of its trade with Puerto Rico. This would mean, by present figures, a loss of perhaps 10,000,000 dollars a year to American exporters. An increase in employment and prosperity in Puerto Rico would be likely to more than cover this temporary loss in a number of years, through an increase in our purchasing power which will immediately result in increased trade with the mainland. But even assuming that it would not be covered, it must be borne in mind that Puerto Rico is headed toward a major social catastrophe, which can hardly be postponed for more than twenty years unless something fundamental is accomplished. The issue, therefore, is between the possible loss of several millions to American exporters and the practical certainty of social chaos in Puerto Rico. Quite independent of the fact that such chaos would entail a much greater loss to the United States, but purely as a problem in responsibility and humanity, there can be little doubt as to how the American people would wish such an issue to be decided, or as to how a high order of American statesmanship, once convinced of its reality, will decide it.[26]

However, the Chardón Plan could not be implemented for two reasons. First, it was opposed by the sugar interests that controlled a part of the colonial state apparatus and managed to get the support of the majority of the U.S. Congress, which prevented the approval of the funds and the necessary legislation to implement the plan. Second, the confrontation between the Nationalists and the colonial regime culminated in the assassination on 23 February 1936 of Colonel Riggs, chief of the colonial police. This incident created a wave of anti-Puerto Rican sentiment in Washington and anti-Americanism in San Juan, which temporarily distanced the elements that intended to solve the crisis through implementation of the plan.[27]

Instead of going ahead with the Chardón Plan, a compromise was reached. The PRRA was created by executive order of President Roosevelt to implement the least controversial aspects of the plan. With the backing of the U.S. executive, control over the PRRA settled in the hands of the antisugar sector. The control that this group had over the PRRA and its multimillion budget, as well as over PRERA (the other major federal relief agency), provided it with the material basis to organize a political machine based on a system of patronage as large as that of the local government. For example, between 1935 and 1938, the PRRA employed nearly sixty thousand persons and paid close to a million dollars per month in salaries.[28] The bureaucrats and technocrats who ran PRRA and PRERA were associated with the faction within the Partido Liberal (PL) led by Luis Muñoz Marín, who was a personal friend of President Roosevelt. The PL had been created in

1931 by the PUP's component of the Alianza, after the latter disintegrated. Muñoz had become the leader of the proindependence faction of the PL, a group known as Acción Social Independentista (Pro-Independence Social Action). It was common practice for the PL to ask PRRA employees for regular "donations" to the party in return for having found them jobs. The control of these programs provided this group with a means to reach and attract sectors that were not organized politically, such as the peasants and the unemployed.

In a sense, the creation of a parallel welfare apparatus by the federal government in Puerto Rico reflected the political divisions not only within the colonial power bloc but within the metropolis itself. Yet despite these divisions, the groups within the metropolitan state that favored reform in the colony achieved two things. First, the federal relief programs managed to alleviate somewhat the depressed social and economic conditions of working people; this helped to contain political protest among the popular sectors. Second, the programs facilitated the formation of a political force whose political project was neither anti-imperialist, nor nationalist, nor communist. The faction of the PL led by Luis Muñoz Marín split in 1938 to create the PPD, which quickly became a major political force. The political program of the PPD was patterned along the lines of the Chardón Plan, which did threaten the immediate interests of the sugar sector but not U.S. strategic interests on the island.

By the end of the 1930s, it was impossible to make any attempt at economic recovery based on the sugar sector. Classes and social sectors that previously formed part of or were identified with the power bloc had been displaced from their positions of power and economic privilege. Thus, the sugar interests and the political sectors that supported them saw their politicoeconomic power base eroded. This led to the realignment of social and political forces, creating the conditions for the development and diffusion of the political project of the antisugar sector.

The Chardón Plan clearly expressed the key ideas associated with developmentalism in Latin America. First, it introduced the Keynesian notion of state intervention to stimulate economic development. Second, it proposed agrarian reform and the restructuring of agricultural production as a necessary condition to overcome the crisis. Third, it advocated industrialization as a means of economic growth. Finally, it predicated the desirability of increasing wages and thus the purchasing power of the population. Clearly, the developmentalist formula was firmly rooted in the attempts of certain groups to deal with the adverse effects of the Great Depression. It was not produced by a group of neutral bureaucrats, but by a commission of U.S colonial government officials headed by Carlos Chardón, a member of the PL. The application of modern Keynesian concepts did not occur in a political vacuum. The plan clearly acknowledged, as shown in the earlier quotation, that its aim was to avoid "social chaos" and a greater economic loss to the United States. The origins of developmentalism are thus firmly grounded in class struggle. As an ideology, it expressed the interests and ideas about solving the crisis of a particular class alliance.

From the Crisis to World War II:
The PPD's Populist Developmentalism

Attempts to provide a solution to the economic crisis by using federal relief programs as the basis for social reforms were hindered by the resistance of the sugar interests, the opposition of the Nationalists, and the mistrust between the New Deal bureaucrats in Washington and the local bureaucrats administering federal programs. The Chardón Plan had been diluted to the PRRA, and the structural reforms it proposed were never implemented. Poverty, unemployment, poor health conditions, and excessive land concentration were still major problems in the late 1930s.

Anti-Americanism had not diminished and still constituted a potential political force, even though the imprisonment of the Nationalist leadership in 1936 had certainly prevented this sentiment from becoming articulated into a major political movement. The potential explosiveness of the situation is expressed in Rexford G. Tugwell's observation when he became governor (1941) that "the materials for a class war were all present."[29] It is within the political vacuum created by the collapse of the sugar economy, the failure of the traditional parties, and the inability of the metropolitan government to provide a durable solution to the crisis that the PPD emerged as a serious political alternative and drew widespread electoral support for its reformist political project. The bulk of the support came from the discontented working classes (landless peasants, rural proletariat, unemployed) who were in search of a political alternative that would articulate their interests.

Other structural and political factors facilitated the electoral triumph of the PPD in 1940 and the development and implementation of the reformist development project, despite the tenacious opposition of the sugar interests and conservative groups within the metropolis and the colony. These elements were:

1. The inability of the metropolis to fill the political vacuum due to its involvement in World War II, coupled with the previous failure of federal programs (PRRA, PRERA), which had diminished the faith of local politicians in the ability of the U.S. government to provide a long-term solution to the crisis.
2. The growing political weakness of the local and North American sugar interests and the consequent inability of these groups to reverse sugar quota restrictions. This meant the reduction of sugar

production in Puerto Rico in favor of continental producers (Louisiana, Florida) and low-cost production areas (Cuba), and doomed the island's sugar industry.

3. The absence of a local sector, other than the sugar sector, with some control over the productive process that could articulate a viable economic alternative. The monopolistic character of the sugar economy had stunted the development of other key economic sectors (e.g., coffee).

4. The need for local production of agricultural and imported manufactured goods created by the relative isolation of the island during the war and the reduction in the land dedicated to sugar cultivation.

5. The acceptance in circles of the U.S. government of Keynesian ideas about state intervention in the economy.

6. The extraordinary expansion of the public sector's income, due to increases in taxes received from the exportation of rum to the United States (which increased due to the reduction in the production of whiskey during the war) and due to increased federal expenditures and subsidies for social relief and the construction of infrastructure and military bases.

The PPD's Ascent to Power

In 1940, the PPD rose to power under the populist slogan of "bread, land, and liberty." This slogan evoked for many, especially the colonial governor and the sugar corporations, images of the Russian and Mexican revolutions whose slogans were "peace and land" and "land and liberty."[30] The 1940 platform of the PPD began by denouncing the "state of misery," the "social insecurity," and the "regime of exploitation" existing in Puerto Rico. However, far from following the call of Lenin or Madero to armed revolution, the PPD and its leader, Muñoz Marín, called upon the people to "lend" them their votes so that once elected the PPD "could confront the public problems which derived from the state of exploitation that we [the PPD] denounced."[31]

The rhetoric and the style of the PPD made it appear as if this party expressed mainly the interests of the working classes, especially those of the landless peasant (the *jíbaro*). In fact, the PPD's denunciation of absentee capital (the sugar corporations) as the culprits of the current state of affairs and its demands for social justice and land reform, along with the direct contact that Muñoz established with the peasants and workers during the 1940 political campaign, were the basis for accusations by the sugar interests that the PPD was radical and communist. However, when this denunciatory language and populistic political style, characterized by direct contact between the charismatic leader and "the people," are translated into concrete political practice, the true class character of the PPD and its reformist political project can be seen clearly.

Although the rhetoric of Muñoz appeared on the surface to be anti-American and socialistic, the PPD had emerged as a party led by a fraction of the colonial power bloc.[32] The PPD built its popular base, however, by capitalizing on the discontent brought about by the crisis and the patronage of the federal relief agencies. It emerged as a principal political force at a juncture when the leadership of the PS had lost credibility and the PN had been badly repressed. It filled the political vacuum existing among the working classes and provided organic direction to their spontaneous political protest. The political project of the PPD was not the product of working-class participation, as was the case with the programs of the PS or the PCP, for example. Yet the PPD's political project expressed many of the aspirations of the working classes. It captured the popular protest against the sugar interests—both local and foreign—and combined it with the interests of the antisugar sector within the colonial power bloc, thus laying the political basis for the implementation of a reformist program.

The PPD's political project, however, was framed within the categories of the Chardón Plan, which aimed to restructure imperialist capitalism while maintaining the basis for U.S. colonial domination in Puerto Rico. The PPD program would finally put into effect the policies advocated by the Chardón Plan, but with a new focus and emphasis. Rather than reconstruction, the program of reforms advocated by the PPD would be couched in the discourse of *social justice*. Land redistribution would become land reform, portrayed as a battle between the people and "absentee capital." In short, the categories of developmentalism would be encompassed by populism, as was the case in Latin America. In the end, what could not be achieved through the bureaucratic politics of the federal relief programs, the PPD achieved by attaining colonial power. It would be political power, rather than superior rationality, that would enable the developmentalist alternative to become implemented.

After the 1940 elections, the obstacles facing the PPD ranged from the lack of a majority in the colonial House of Representatives to the power of the colonial governor and of the U.S. Congress and president to veto any law approved by the colonial legislature. The fact that the reform program of the PPD was carried out within the context of the colonial government, without major obstruction except from the sugar interests, is indicative of the orientation of these reforms.

The Reformist Strategy: Agrarian Reform and Industrialization

The first step in the implementation of the populist reform program was agrarian reform. The agrarian reform law was based on the five hundred-acre limitation that had been included by Congress in the Foraker Act of 1900 and the Jones Act of 1917, which replaced it as the legal framework of the colonial relation. The "500-acre law," as it became popularly known, was never enforced until 1935, shortly after Law 47 was enacted by the government of the Coalición. On 27 March 1940 the newspaper *La Democracia*, of which Muñoz was editor, reacted euphorically to the decision of the U.S. Supreme Court to uphold Law 47 in the landmark case of "The People of Puerto Rico vs. Rupert Hermanos, Inc."[33] "The Land is Ours," read the paper's headline.[34]

The Land Law of 1941, Law 26, passed by the PPD, was more radical than Law 47 but remained within the legal-political framework of the colonial regime, the "500-acre law." In the Statement of Motives this law incorporated the two extremes of a contradiction that was at the very basis of the crisis of Puerto Rican society. The first paragraph declared "that the land in Puerto Rico is to be considered as a source of livelihood, dignity and economic freedom for the men and women who till it," expressing thus the interests of the peasants and rural proletarians who constituted the mass of the PPD's electoral base. However, the following paragraphs were dedicated to praising the wisdom of the decision of the U.S. Supreme Court, which served as the framework and the political justification of Law 26. In doing this, the PPD leaders were reassuring their allies in the Roosevelt administration and Congress that they had no intention of threatening U.S. strategic interests on the island. The PPD's agrarian reform would mainly affect the sugar interests, which, in any case, were less important to the United States since the enactment of the sugar quota in 1934.

Law 26 stipulated the mechanisms for the application of the "500-acre law" to corporations ("juridical persons") and specified the procedures for the expropriation or purchase of land in excess of this amount. The law also provided for the creation of a public corporation responsible for enforcement, called the Land Authority. This corporation had the power to buy, sell, rent, own, or in any other manner possess land to operate farms; to initiate lawsuits against violators of the law; and to implement a program of agrarian reform. However, all land expropriations had to be carried out through appropriate court procedures and provide adequate economic compensation.[35] Indeed, all lands acquired by the authority were adequately compensated. The capital for buying land came from government appropriations. Initially, the colonial legislature provided $2 million for the operation of the authority. In addition to this, the authority could issue bonds up to a maximum of $5 million. Between 1940 and 1947, the authority received funds for a total of $23.5 million to carry out the agrarian reform program.[36]

The most important projects implemented by the authority were the proportional profit farms, the individual farms program, and the *parcelas* (small plot) program. The proportional profit farms were units of one hundred to five hundred acres that were leased to farmers, agronomists, and other persons with knowledge of farm administration. Administrators and workers would receive a fixed salary, and at the end of the year the net profits of the operation would be divided among the administrators (who received a fixed percentage) and the workers (who received their share in proportion to the days worked and total salary earned). This type of farm tried to combine the efficiency of large units, particularly in the production of sugar, with the principle of better income distribution. The farms were labeled as cooperatives, but in reality they were not. The decisions were made by the administrators, and the farms were the property of the government, not the workers. Moreover, the salary of the administrator and his share of the profits were greater than that of the workers, making him more of an entrepreneur than a cooperative leader interested in the socialization of the means of production. Governor Tugwell perceptively remarked that the proportional profits farms had "the possibility of preserving large-scale agriculture against its enemies and of keeping far enough away from classical cooperation to escape the 'communist' label."[37] The two main objectives of these farms were to transfer part of the sugar production from the corporations to the government and redirect to the local economy part of the profits that had previously gone to the United States and to pressure the sugar companies into paying better wages to workers and better prices to the smaller sugar growers.

The second important aspect of the law was the individual farms program under which the authority divided some of the large estates it purchased or expropriated into small farms averaging from five to twenty-five acres of land. In turn, these farms were to be sold under very favorable financial conditions to families considered eligible according to certain criteria stipulated by the law (experience in agriculture, no possession of other lands). A key objective of these units was to stimulate the cultivation of foodstuffs, thus fostering agricultural diversification and a cheaper supply of basic food products. This would also be an important step in reducing food imports at the time when the United States was entering the war.

The third program, which ended up being the most important, was the *parcelas* program created under Title Five of the law. Under this program, the authority divided farmlands into small plots of between one-fourth and three acres to be distributed among landless peasants and rural proletarians. To prevent big farmers from buying these lands, or other speculators from acquiring them, the *parceleros* were not given ownership titles, and any transactions involving these lands were subject to the approval of the authority. This program was to provide landless peasants and other rural workers with a stable dwelling and a stable means for producing some of the staples of their diet. This, it was thought, would help stabilize the labor supply in the countryside and reduce the migration of unemployed rural workers to the cities. In the long run, this program would also help to ensure the supply of cheap labor around some urban centers.

The second pillar of the reformist project was the industrialization program implemented by the Puerto Rico Development Company—popularly known as Fomento—created by Law 188 of 11 May 1942. According to this law, the main objective of Fomento was to explore the possibilities for developing Puerto Rico's resources through the creation of industrial enterprises. For this purpose Fomento received an initial funding of half a million dollars per year. Aside from these regular allocations, Fomento could borrow money from private institutions or issue bonds to finance its projects and enterprises. However, due to an extraordinary assignment of funds at the end of the war, Fomento received a total of $19 million in government funds between 1940 and 1947.[38]

Law 188 was very clear with regard to the kind of industrial development it intended to promote. Article 8 of the law provided a list of manufacturing activities that Fomento should promote, mainly light industries oriented to the local market. This local orientation in manufacturing was further stressed in Article 9, which stated that Fomento's activities "shall tend to promote the engagement in industrial enterprises of capital owned by residents of Puerto Rico and to avoid the evils of absentee ownership of large scale capital."[39]

The emphasis placed on local production by articles 8 and 9 contributed to the interpretation of the PPD's political project as being oriented toward national autonomous capitalist development.[40] Nonetheless, it should be remembered that Law 188 was conceived within the limits of the colonial relation with the United States and was in keeping with Keynesian economic ideology widely accepted by the Roosevelt administration. This economic ideology was adopted by nationalist and populist Latin American governments, but in the United States it had also served as the basis for regional development companies such as the Tennessee Valley Authority. State intervention in the economy and local orientation of industrial production are not by themselves the conditions of national autonomous capitalist development.

Following the spirit of the law and the need to substitute imports during the war period, the first industries established by Fomento were the Puerto Rico Glass Corporation and the Puerto Rico Pulp and Paper Corporation. The first produced bottles for the rum industry and the second produced cardboard for making the boxes to package and ship the rum. The glass plant used silica sand, which was found in large quantities on the island, and the cardboard plant used bagasse (sugarcane husks) and paper wastes collected locally. Other subsidiaries, such as the Puerto Rico Cement Corporation, acquired from the PRRA, the Puerto Rico Clay Products Corporation, the Puerto Rico Shoe and Leather Corporation, and Telares de Puerto Rico (which eventually was established as a joint venture between Fomento and Textron Corporation), illustrate the program's orientation toward the local market.[41]

These two key programs were complemented by a series of reforms also conceived of within the context of the New Deal legislation passed by the

Roosevelt government. An example of these reforms were the laws on minimum wages and labor conditions. These laws increased the minimum wage in the sugarcane and home needlework industries and were the result of the extension to Puerto Rico of the Fair Labor Standards Act, approved by the U.S. Congress in 1938.[42] Another measure based on federal legislation was the expropriation of all private electric and energy companies operating in Puerto Rico and their centralization under a public corporation, the Water Resources Authority. The federal government expropriated these companies under power granted to it by the War Powers Act for national security reasons and later transferred them to the colonial government's Water Resources Authority.[43] In no way were these expropriations "nationalizations"; rather they were "state takeovers" of public services for strategic reasons.

In synthesis, the development strategy implemented by the PPD between 1940 and 1947 intended an agrarian reform that would resolve the crisis in the agricultural sector that had been precipitated by the restrictions of the sugar quota. It also sought to lay the basis for the development of the industrial sector as the dynamic and principal sector of the economy. The implicit development model assumed an increase in economic production and in worker productivity that would allow a greater remuneration for the workers and thus higher living standards. But it also envisaged all this within the framework of capitalist economic relations and colonial political relations; that is, within a framework that would preserve the eminent control of private ownership over the means of production and the subordination of wage labor to capital, as well as U.S. strategic and political interests on the island. Only when we venture beyond the populist rhetoric of the PPD's programs and campaign promises and look into the implementation and impact of their policies does the actual class character of the PPD's developmentalist project become clear.

The Impact of the Reformist Strategy on the Socioeconomic Structure

The PPD's reform program had limited success in transforming the Puerto Rican economy. The agrarian reform law set in motion a limited restructuring in the patterns of land tenure, but the changes after 1930 were caused more by the crisis of the sugar economy than by the agrarian reform program, as Table 2.1 shows. Economist José A. Herrero pointed out the relative inefficiency of the PPD reforms, arguing that there was greater improvement in land distribution during the 1930s than during the 1940s.[44]

There are several explanations for this limited impact. First, a great part of land distributions took place under the *parcelas* program. By 1945, a total of 13,103 *parcelas* had been distributed for housing units and some 1,159 for communal facilities (churches, schools) for the *parceleros*.[45] This is important because the small plots distributed under this program did not constitute productive units (note that in Table 2.1, farms of three acres or less are excluded from the accounts of farmland area in 1950).

It is also worth noting that between 1940 and 1950 total cultivated land declined by 57,368 acres, most of which came from the farms of over 260 acres (a total reduction of 45,990 acres). It could be argued that many of these lands were marginal sugar lands discarded as agricultural lands and then partially distributed in *parcelas*. Nonetheless, this did not substantially alter the distribution of productive farmland, which was still dominated by large landholders.

There is a third reason why there was relatively little change in the land tenure structure during the 1940s. As was noted above, the "500-acre law" was applied to corporations ("juridical persons") according to the stipulations of Law 26. This meant that many large *colonos* (who were individual owners, not corporations) were able to own lands without having to fear action from the Land Authority. Thus the large *colonos* became beneficiaries of a law that allowed the relative concentration of lands into their hands. Harvey Perloff noted that in 1948 of the four large North American sugar companies, two did not own any land, which meant that all of their sugarcane supply was grown by *colonos*. In all, 75 percent of the sugar ground by the U.S. corporations that year was grown by *colonos*.[46] Clearly, the main beneficiaries of the limited land redistribution effected by the law were the large *colonos* and the *parceleros*.

The other effect of the agrarian reform was to reduce the economic and political power of both the North American and the local corporate sugar sector. This allowed the PPD to consolidate its power vis-à-vis the PR, whose dominant social component, the sugar bourgeoisie, was in retreat. Aside from this, the agrarian reform, particularly the *parcelas* program, was a step toward stabilizing the rural labor supply and reducing migration into the cities, which aggravated problems such as unemployment, urban poverty, and housing in urban centers. This stabilization was also favorable to landowners who could now count on a stable and subsidized source of labor.[47]

The agrarian reform was unable to halt the decline in agriculture's share of the national income that began in the 1930s and continued throughout the 1940s, as shown in Table 2.2. War conditions may have stimulated an increase in the dollar value of agricultural production but its relative economic importance declined substantially. In terms of the objective of agricultural diversification, agrarian reform had limited impact as well. By 1950, sugar continued to be the principal product in terms of value of production as well as value of exports. In 1949/50, sugar production represented 52 percent of the total farm value of agricultural products, which was identical to the 1939/40 figures. Also, sugar constituted 59 percent of the total value of exports in 1949/50, while in 1939/40 it had constituted 62 percent. The products that experienced major growth were animal products (meat, milk, and eggs), which increased from 22 percent of farm value in

Table 2.1 Cultivated Land by Farm Size: 1930, 1940, and 1950

	Total Acres 1930	%	Total Acres 1940	%	Total Acres 1950	%
3 acres or less	3,909	0.2	2,154	0.1	—	—
4-9 acres	127,523	6.4	143,284	7.6	143,008	7.8
10-19 acres	147,503	7.4	151,510	8.1	144,449	7.9
20-49 acres	264,712	13.4	258,563	13.7	263,720	14.4
50-99 acres	226,464	11.4	215,540	11.5	216,148	11.8
100-174 acres	201,928	10.2	191,678	10.2	186,539	10.2
175-259 acres	143,888	7.3	135,568	7.2	133,055	7.3
260 or more acres	863,531	43.6	783,557	41.6	737,567	40.4
Total	1,979,458	100	1,881,854	100	1,824,486	100

Source: Herrero, "La mitología del azúcar," p. 29.

Table 2.2 Share of National Income Generated by Agriculture: 1929-1949 (million dollars)

	1929	%	1934	%	1939	%	1949	%
National income	176	100	164	100	196	100	597	100
Agriculture	87	49.4	71	43.3	59	30.1	152	25.4

Sources: Smith, *Puerto Rico's Income*, p. 19; Junta de Planificación, *Ingreso y producto, 1978*, p. 26.

1939/40 to 25 percent in 1949/50, and starchy vegetables, which increased from 5 percent of the farm value in 1939/40 to 7 percent in 1949/50. Conversely, tobacco and coffee declined during this same period.[48] Despite some changes brought about by land reform, sugar, although declining, remained the most important crop and export in the Puerto Rican economy.

The history of the industrialization program is also one of limited success in the short run. Even though industrialization had become a major goal of government policy, the reality was a rather slow development of this economic sector. The reduction in manufacturing's shares of total employment and wages, shown in Table 2.3, indicates a minimal impact on the expansion of the economy, as does the small increase in the share of national income. The decrease in employment and wages can be attributed in part to the decline in the demand for sugar and rum immediately after the war. However, this shows the importance that sugar processing and its derivatives still had for the manufacturing sector after the war, and the incapacity of the industrialization program to counterbalance the negative effects of the decline of this industry.

Table 2.4 demonstrates that relatively little change occurred in the industrial structure between 1939 and 1949. The sugar industry (its manufacturing component) continued to be the most important sector in spite of its declining trend. It should also be noted that the sector that advanced the most was stone, clay, and glass products, which included three of the largest production plants in the country owned by the state.

Table 2.3 Manufactures Shares of National Income, Total Employment, and Wages: 1940 and 1949 (percent)

	1940	1949
National income	11.8	13.6
Employment[a]	10.9	9.1
Wages	15.9	14.1

Sources: Junta de Planificación, *Ingreso y producto, 1978*, p. 26; Planning Board, *Economic Development*, pp. 153, 160.
[a]Does not include the home needlework industry.

While it is true that the reformist industrialization program did not fundamentally alter the industrial structure, the construction of infrastructure (buildings, roads, electrical installations, etc.), the training of industrial workers and administrators, as well as the creation of new jobs (albeit in very limited quantities), may well be the most important achievements of the PPD's industrialization program in the short term. Yet, beyond these, there was a qualitative achievement of even greater importance: the creation of an economic and ideological climate favorable to private industrial capital. As a Fomento report stated: "[T]he intention [of Fomento's industrialization program] has been and continues to be to show private capital the road to productive investments, to stimulate it in the selection of feasible projects, and to share the risks and labors in cordial cooperation with it."[49] The specific sector of private industrial capital to which Fomento was willing to show the road to productive investment will be discussed below.

The agrarian reform and the industrialization programs provided a temporary and incomplete remedy to the crisis of the sugar economy while at the same time laying the groundwork for the coming of private industrial investments. But this raises some important questions. What was then the main achievement of the PPD's reformist project during the 1940s? What did the party accomplish that earned it a sweeping electoral victory in 1944 and thereafter for two decades? What did the PPD do to weld its popular support while articulating the interests of the dominant sectors of the colonial society?

A study by the Economic Division of the Puerto Rico Planning Board published in 1951 suggested that government and other services expanded during the war and leveled off afterward.[50] The figures show that between 1940 and 1946, the government share of national income grew from 17.5 to 29.5 percent and declined to 18.8 percent by 1949. The government shares of total employment and wages grew from 2.5 to 8.1 percent and from 31.3 to 46.3 percent, respectively, during the war, dropping to 7.2 and 36.2 percent in 1949. Other sectors where the share of total employment grew significantly during the war were transportation, communications and utilities, trade, and construction.[51]

Table 2.4 Ten Leading Manufacturing Industries: 1939 and 1949

	% of Total Value Added		Rank		% of Total Production Employment		Rank		% of Total Wages		Rank		% National Income[b]		Rank	
	1939	1949	1939	1949	1939	1949	1939	1949	1939	1949	1939	1949	1940	1949	1940	1949
Sugar	53	41	1	1	43	31	1	1	N/A	40	—	1	35	36	1	1
Apparel	20	11	2	2	26	22	2	2	N/A	15	—	2	22	20	2	2
Beverages	7	10	3	3	4	5.5	4	3	N/A	5.5	—	5	8	4.2	3	5
Bakery products	3	4.5	4	6	6	5.5	3	3	N/A	6	—	4	4.4	4.2	4	5
Printing & publishing	2.9	4	5	7	3	2	6	8	N/A	4	—	6	3.3	3.5	6	8
Chemicals	2.1	5	6	5	1.7	2	8	8	N/A	3	—	8	4.1	3.9	5	7
Non-electrical mach.	1.9	1.5	7	10	2.1	1	7	10	N/A	2	—	10	N/A	N/A	—	—
Furniture	1.5	3	8	8	3.4	4	5	6	N/A	3.7	—	7	2	4.4	8	4
Manufactured ice	1	a	9	a	1	a	10	a	N/A	a	—	a	N/A	N/A	—	a
Tobacco manufactures	0.8	a	10	a	1.7	a	8	a	N/A	a	—	a	N/A	a	—	a
Stone, clay, glass, and cement	a	7	a	4	a	5	a	5	N/A	7	—	3	3.3	6	6	3
Costume jewelry	a	1.6	a	9	a	4	a	7	N/A	2.4	—	9	N/A	N/A	—	—

Sources: U.S. Bureau of the Census, Census of Manufactures, Puerto Rico, 1949; Junta de Planificación, Ingreso y producto, 1978.
[a] Out of the top ten.
[b] There are no detailed figures for national income before 1940.
N/A = not available.

The economic expansion experienced in the 1940s was mainly due to the extraordinary expenditures of the U.S. federal government in military projects and infrastructure (military bases, roads, communications). Between 1942 and 1946, the expenses of the federal government in Puerto Rico directly related to war activities represented a minimum of 9.3 percent of the gross national product in 1942 and a maximum of 18.2 percent in 1945. Total expenditures of the federal government exceeded the $100 million mark from 1943 to 1946.[52] In addition to these extraordinary revenues from direct war expenditures, the federal government gave some $168 million in collected taxes to the colonial government between 1942 and 1946, much of which came from the return of excise taxes on rum.[53]

These two sources of revenue permitted the colonial government to expand its economic activity. While the expenditures of the federal government were directed to the construction of infrastructure, roads, and sanitary facilities, the colonial government could channel the other revenues into its developmental and social welfare programs. The expenditures of the colonial government for administration and social welfare programs increased from $18.3 million in 1939/40 (65 percent of all government expenditures) to $91.2 million in 1949/50 (78.3 percent of all expenditures). In social welfare, the specific areas that received increases were education, whose share increased from $7.3 million (26 percent of all government expenditures) to $33.1 million (28.4 percent of expenditures); public aid, which jumped from $0.5 million in 1939/40 (1.8 percent of total expenditures) to $8 million 1949/50 (6.9 percent of total expenditures); and public health, which increased from $1.1 million (3.9 percent of total expenditures) to $6.7 million (5.7 percent of total expenditures). Also, government expenditures in industrial development increased from $99 thousand in 1939/40 to $8.3 million in 1945/46, but were reduced to $2.1 million by 1949/50; expenditures in agricultural development for these same years were $1.5, $4.5, and $4.2 million, respectively.[54]

Thus, wartime conditions actually enabled the PPD government to fulfill many of its promises and to consolidate its popular base of support. The expansion of government services, employment, and national income, as well as the implementation of some income redistribution measures, were relatively successful in improving the living conditions of many Puerto Ricans. Besides social services, one key improvement was in wages. Real wages increased by 47 percent in the agricultural phase of the sugar industry, and they increased in every other industry except the home needlework and sugar processing industries.[55] The share of the national income corresponding to wages increased from 55.5 percent in 1940 to 60.4 percent in 1947. Conversely, the share corresponding to profits and interests declined slightly from 37.1 percent to 36.6 percent during this period. National income as a whole increased by 142 percent, the wage component of the national income increased by 163 percent, and the profit and interest component increased by 138 percent.[56] That is, wages grew at a higher rate than profits and interest during this period.

In addition to all of these improvements, it should be remembered that the PPD had literally given away thousands of *parcelas*. If it is true that these were only a small number in comparison to the many thousands of peasants who remained landless, it was still an important political gesture. The hope of receiving a *parcela* was not a mere dream but a real possibility as long as the PPD was in power. This was certainly important also in the consolidation of the electoral base of the PPD.

Class Basis and Contradictions of the Reformist Strategy

The reform program of the PPD was established and implemented within the legal-political framework of the colony. Even though these reforms were directed against the sugar interests, the existing legal-political order was not questioned by the PPD leadership. In fact they made it clear that the resolution of the colonial question was not a campaign issue in the 1940 and the 1944 elections. They stressed that their immediate commitment was to solve economic problems, the "problems whose solution will be within the realm of their power as a majority party."[57] The question is, why did the PPD's reformism remain within the boundaries of the colonial juridical framework and within the framework of imperialist capitalism? And how did they consolidate their popular support while articulating the interest of the dominant classes?

The crisis of the 1930s contributed to the formation of a populist alliance around the PPD. A great number of rural proletarians and peasants had been displaced and now formed a mass of unemployed people migrating to the cities; these workers defined their immediate interests in terms of a job and a place to live. The rupture resulting from the crisis allowed the emergence of a subordinate fraction of the power bloc as the leading force in the political opposition to the continuation of the sugar economy. Other elements integrated into the PPD were the displaced *hacendados* and the *colonos*. As Angel Quintero Rivera points out, the former had lost or sold their lands and were now in the service sectors of the economy; the latter saw in the PPD the opportunity for changes in the sugar sector that would reduce the power of the corporations and benefit them.[58] The leadership of the PPD was formed by a state-based technobureaucracy made up of intellectuals, professionals, and technicians. Some of this group had been part of the colonial bureaucracy but were not directly linked to the dominant sugar sector; many came from the ranks of the federal relief agencies. The heterogeneity of this alliance made it necessary to reconcile diverse and often opposed interests into the PPD political project.

The agrarian reform benefited the small and medium farmers, stimulating their growth and improving their economic condition. It also benefited agronomists, foremen, and farm administrators, displaced by the decline of export agriculture, who now had a chance to get good jobs on the proportional profit farms and in other programs of the Land Authority. The PPD also did not enforce the "500-acre law" against the large *colonos* and favored the distribution of sugar quotas in such a way as to benefit local sugar growers and producers and to improve the terms for financing the *colonos'* crops.[59] Other large landowners were also benefited indirectly by the reform since the *parcelas* communities stabilized labor supply in rural areas by reducing migration and subsidized wages by providing rural workers land on which to grow a portion of their food. Finally, the individual farms and the *parcelas* program opened the possibility for landless peasants and rural proletarians to secure their basic subsistence, while the incentives and projects for agricultural diversification brought hope back to coffee, tobacco, and fruit growers.

While the reformist program favored the interests of the elements that made up the populist alliance, the reforms did not affect the strategic interests of the United States in any fundamental way. Agrarian reform directly affected the corporate sugar interests, but the importance of Puerto Rican sugar to the United States had been declining since the imposition of the 1934 quota. In fact, U.S. corporations adapted to the reform by restructuring their operations, reducing sugar growing, and concentrating on grinding, processing, and marketing, and thus were able to maintain their profitable status.[60] Moreover, during the war the Agricultural Adjustment Administration (a federal agency created by the Roosevelt administration) paid subsidies to sugar growers (including the large U.S. corporations) to stimulate reductions in sugar cultivation and increases in food crops. Thus, the agrarian reform policies of the PPD coincided with the policies of self-sufficiency encouraged by the U.S. government during the war.[61]

The industrialization program was presented as a permanent solution to the socioeconomic crisis and was successfully portrayed to the working classes by the PPD leadership as having unlimited possibilities to provide stable and well-paid jobs. This explains in part the enthusiastic support given initially to the PPD's industrialization program by the CGT and the PCP.[62] The professionals and technicians who formed the core of the PPD leadership had developed as a coherent group and a social force through their participation in institutions like PRERA and PRRA. They, too, saw in state-based industrial development the opportunity to occupy positions of leadership in society because they would control the institutions linked to the industrialization process.

Elements within the local bourgeoisie also participated actively in the process of state-based industrialization, although they were not a highly visible part of the populist alliance. Their participation was more at the level of policymaking than political activism. Puerto Rican entrepreneurs from private banks and industries were incorporated into the board of directors of Fomento and of all of its subsidiaries. According to David F. Ross, they provided a measure of conservatism and "respectability" to the state's industrialization program.[63] Indeed, their participation ensured that the interests of the local bourgeoisie were a part of the development program.

For their part, the U.S. officials in charge of Puerto Rican policy and the U.S. colonial administrators on the island saw clearly that the establishment of government industries could fulfill a double purpose: import substitution during the war, when freight ships operating between Puerto Rico and the United States had been necessarily reduced, and providing the basis for a long-term solution to the socioeconomic crisis of the colony. President Roosevelt was quoted in Fomento's *First Annual Report* as saying, "the situation in Puerto Rico calls for the encouragement of industrial enterprises which will create employment." In this same report President Roosevelt's remarks were joined by those of conservative Senator Robert H. Taft, who was quoted as saying, "I believe that the only possibility of a decent standard of living lies in the industrialization of the island."[64]

Most certainly, the PPD's industrialization program coincided with the long-term interests of the North American bourgeoisie. Indeed, the technocrats leading Fomento were aware of this convergence and utilized it to legitimize their program in the eyes of the metropolitan government. In its *Third Annual Report* Fomento appeals for U.S. support for its program, arguing that it is consistent with emerging foreign policy.

> Management [that of Fomento] is confident that the federal government will give the island the same opportunities to develop industries as is apparently the established policy with respect to foreign countries. This may be judged by the following statement of Honorable Spruille Braden, Assistant Secretary of State, published on December 8, 1945, in *Foreign Commerce Weekly*, an official publication of the U.S. Department of Commerce. "Lest there be misunderstanding on this score, I wish to emphasize that the United States Government rejects the view that the industrialization and diversification of the Latin American economies are threats to the maintenance of our export markets in that area. The ancient mercantilist fallacy that an industrial exporting nation should strive to impede the industrialization of its overseas markets was ridiculed and exploded nearly 200 years ago by Adam Smith; but like many mistaken theories, this one dies hard.
> Self-evidently, countries with low productivity have low living standards: life among the masses is a bitter struggle for rudimentary needs, and so the market for imports is narrow and limited. This axiom is witnessed in the significant fact that we normally export more goods to Canada, an industrialized nation, than to the whole of

South America; although the latter has nearly 10 times the population of the former."[65]

Obviously, the most advanced sectors of the industrial fraction of the imperialist bourgeoisie were foreseeing the advantages (for them) of industrialization in Latin America after the war. The increased capacity of U.S. industry, particularly in the production of machinery, consumer durables, and other capital goods, was beginning to prompt a redefinition of the role of U.S. capital in Latin America. Instead of the traditional role of producer of primary goods and consumer of finished manufactured goods, Latin America now was seen as a market for surplus capital and a consumer of capital goods. As a result of the extraordinary technological developments during the war and the increased productive capacity of industry, the imperialist fraction of the North American bourgeoisie looked for new horizons. Industrial development in Latin America could be part of the answer to a possible postwar crisis created by excess productive capacity and idle capital. The most advanced elements of the imperialist bourgeoisie and its strategists in government were beginning to see with relative clarity the need for a redefinition of the international division of labor after the war. To their credit, the PPD cadres in Fomento also perceived this emerging trend and were trying to insert Puerto Rico into this new international capitalist order.

Clearly, the reform programs of the PPD in the areas of agriculture, industry, public works, and social welfare coincided with the strategic interests of the metropolitan state, which at that time were politicomilitary. For Tugwell, for example, his main duty as colonial governor was to maintain political stability to prevent internal attacks (sabotage) to the military bases being built during the war. Economic and social reform were crucial to achieve stability. Hence, the agreement of Tugwell and the Roosevelt administration with the reformist policies of the PPD.[66]

Thus the PPD managed to articulate a broad alliance with a wide popular base by presenting its reformist project as the alternative to the crisis of the sugar economy in which everyone gained something. After the colonial government suppressed the possibility of a radical nationalist alternative through repression of the PN, and after the PS-PR coalition proved its incapacity to provide a durable solution to the crisis, the reformist project became the most appealing alternative for both the dominant and the subordinate classes. The PPD leadership was also a social category in the sense that Nicos Poulantzas defines it: a group whose identity and position in society are defined by its relation to the political and ideological structures.[67] The technocrats and bureaucrats who led the PPD enjoyed a degree of political autonomy vis-à-vis other groups and classes by virtue of the existing political vacuum left by the crisis of the 1930s and their relative independence from the preceding colonial regime and the sugar interests.

Their technocratic character enabled them to appear as honest brokers with a popular solution to the crisis.

The Importance of Developmentalism

In addition to the structural and social elements propelling the reformist development strategy there was a crucial ideological dimension. In order to articulate diverse class interests, the PPD resorted to ambiguous nonclass discourse typical of populist movements and "condensed" class contradictions by expressing them as the people/power bloc contradiction.[68] The political campaign of 1940 revolved around the issues of agrarian reform, the elimination of the sugar monopoly, and the pursuit of social justice. These issues attracted the peasants, elements from the rural and urban proletariat, and the unemployed to the political sphere of the PPD. These groups identified their most immediate interests with the PPD's promise of "bread, land, and liberty." To them "bread and land" articulated their aspirations for economic well-being and stability, while the call for "liberty" expressed their discontent with the oppression of the sugar corporations and the colonial regime associated with them. As Angel Quintero Rivera and Emilio González correctly argue, it was very unlikely that either the class rhetoric of the PS, which had been discredited by its participation in the Coalición, or the recently formed PCP would appeal to these sectors.[69] However, the PPD's nonclass slogans (bread, land, and liberty) did appeal to the immediate interests of these sectors. In other words, the process of socioeconomic displacement and political realignment of the working classes triggered by the crisis laid the groundwork for the dilution of what were basically class contradictions into nonclass contradictions at the politicoideological level. In PPD rhetoric, the displaced working classes and other sectors of the subordinate classes constituted "the people."

The PPD's discourse transformed and reduced class contradictions to a series of antinomies representing two polarities: the people, whom the PPD represented, and the enemies of the people, the power bloc, incarnated by the sugar companies and the socialist-republican coalition. The metropolis/colony antagonism was expressed in the PPD's discourse as the juxtaposition between the *jíbaro* (the Puerto Rican peasant) and "absentee capital" (U.S. sugar corporations). The first represented all that was essentially good in Puerto Rican culture and society; the second represented all that was evil. The rich/poor, exploiter/exploited antinomies were also used in the PPD's rhetoric as static concepts of social positions rather than as characterizations of exploitative relations. Rich and poor were seen as two points on a hierarchy of differential incomes, educational levels, and other social factors rather than as the expression of a relation of exploitation. Finally, the people/enemy-of-the-people antinomy served to detach class character from the terms of political struggle and to redefine the boundaries that divided political forces by transforming them into moral categories, the good versus the bad; the enemy may be the sugar corporations but it may also be the Nationalists or the communists who "oppose progress."

The agrarian reform, the "bread and land" of the PPD's slogan, did not mean the expropriation of corporations and the distribution of their lands to the peasants and workers who "tilled it"; rather it meant the establishment of state-owned farms, *parcelas* on marginal lands, and a few individual farms. Social justice did not mean workers owning the factories they worked in, or trade unions participating in policy decisions for profit distribution, as would be the case with the projects of the PCP and the CGT. What it meant was wage increases and increases in social services aimed at providing adequate conditions for the social reproduction of labor to be exploited by capital. There was no basic alteration in the private ownership of the means of production or in the colonial nature of political domination and, therefore, in who would ultimately decide what to produce, when to produce it, and how to distribute it. "Liberty," as we shall see later, would mean self-government for the colony rather than the construction of a nation-state through independence, as the Nationalists advocated.

The key achievement of the PPD's reformism was to lay the politico-economic conditions for the change of the axis of capital accumulation from North American and local capital in export agriculture to the colonial state. Thus the PPD's reformist developmentalism allowed the necessary social and political changes for reasserting the political and economic dominance of the United States in Puerto Rico.

Herein lies then the importance of developmentalism as a dominant ideology. Insofar as the economic problems of Puerto Rico were framed in a developmentalist ideology, the key issues were reconstruction, growth, and equitable distribution of income. The Keynesian framework in which the Chardón Plan was framed never attempted to consider the desirability, or even the possibility, of restructuring the Puerto Rican economy outside of the colonial relation. Moreover, the idea of an economic alternative beyond a reformed version of imperialist capitalism was not even raised. By making economic issues the center of political attention and framing those issues in the Keynesian and New Deal discourse of capitalist restructuring, first the Chardón Plan and later the PPD program managed to defuse the most sensitive issue during the crisis of the 1930s—the legitimacy of the colonial relation. By introducing developmentalism as the dominant form of discourse, the debate shifted away from the political basis of any new social order and focused on how to make the existing order work. Capitalism within a colonial framework became a premise of the reformist political discourse. By articulating the people/power bloc contradiction within the categories of developmentalism, an ideological terrain was successfully created that blurred class antagonisms, permitting the convergence between the working classes and a fraction of the power bloc around the developmentalist project of the PPD. In time, this convergence would allow the dominant classes to prevent the antagonistic classes (the Nationalist petty bourgeoisie or the communist working class) from developing an independent political project and thus resolve the crisis of colonial domination by reasserting their political power in a new manner.[70]

By establishing developmentalism as the dominant ideology and removing class content from issues of economic development, the PPD laid the basis for restoring the dominance of U.S. economic interests in Puerto Rico after the war. The despised "absentee capital" embodied in the sugar corporations would become the collaborator in development, embodied by industrial capital.

Notes

1. For a detailed analysis of this process see Quintero Rivera, *Patricios y plebeyos*; Mattos Cintrón, *La política y lo político*, Chaps. 1–2.
2. Quintero Rivera, "Background," pp. 97–127.
3. Perloff, *Economic Future*, p. 407; Diffie and Diffie, *Porto Rico*, pp. 45–59; and Gayer, Homan, and Jones, *The Sugar Economy*, pp. 21, 63, 97–146.
4. Diffie and Diffie, *Porto Rico*, pp. 52–65.
5. Two Canadian banks, the Royal Bank of Canada and the Bank of Nova Scotia, controlled 17 percent of total bank assets. Besides this, about 25 percent of the assets of local banks were controlled by foreign interests. Diffie and Diffie, *Porto Rico*, pp. 100–117; Perloff, *Economic Future*, p. 136; Quintero Rivera, "El desarrollo de las clases," p. 178.
6. In 1899, 42 percent of the land was dedicated to food crops for local consumption; by 1929 only 28 percent was dedicated to this. By the 1930s, about 33 percent of Puerto Rican imports were food. Gayer, Homan, and Jones, *The Sugar Economy*, p. 30.
7. Cardoso and Faletto, *Dependencia y desarrollo*, p. 53.
8. Quintero Rivera, "Development of Social Classes," pp. 217–219.
9. Tugwell, *The Stricken Land*, pp. 37–38.
10. Acevedo, "American Colonialism," pp. 79–89; Pagán, *Partidos políticos*, 1, Chaps. 10 and 11.
11. Herrero, "La mitología," pp. 49–50.
12. Ibid., pp. 41–51; LeRiverend, *Historia*, pp. 232–233.
13. Acevedo, "American Colonialism," pp. 109–110.
14. Bird, *The Sugar Industry*, pp. 40, 129.
15. Mathews, *Puerto Rican Politics*, p. 137; Quintero Rivera, "La base social," pp. 43–45.
16. Puerto Rico Policy Commission, *Report*, pp. 8–9. Hereafter quoted as "Chardón Report."
17. Ibid., p. 9.
18. Corretjer, *Albizu Campos*, pp. 9–12; Acevedo, "American Colonialism," pp. 140–144.
19. Fromm, "La historia ficción (V)," pp. 6–7; and "La historia ficción (VI)," pp. 4–5.

20. Gayer, Homan, and Jones, *The Sugar Economy*, p. 223.

21. Corretjer, *La lucha*, p. 69; Acevedo, "American Colonialism," p. 148.

22. The problem of forming an anti-imperialist popular movement presents complexities that go beyond the ideological differences between the PN and the workers. The Partido Comunista Puertorriqueño (Puerto Rican Communist Party), which had emerged from within the membership of the FLT in 1934 and whose class origin was clearly proletarian, could not capitalize on the crisis either. The crisis, instead of facilitating the development of a political alternative for the working classes, had the immediate effect of dividing them. Fromm, "La historia ficción (V)" and "La historia ficción (VI)"; and Corretjer, *El líder*.

23. Acevedo, "American Colonialism," pp. 167–176; Torres, *El proceso*; Corretjer, *Albizu Campos*.

24. Mathews, *Puerto Rican Politics*, pp. 154–165.

25. Chardón Report, pp. 1–7.

26. Ibid., p. 7.

27. Mathews, *Puerto Rican Politics*, Chaps. 6 and 7.

28. Acevedo, "American Colonialism," p. 160.

29. Tugwell, *The Stricken Land*, p. 7. For an account of the anti-Americanism during the 1930s and its persistence at the beginning of the 1940s, even within the ranks of the PPD, see Brown, *Dynamite*. This view may be somewhat exaggerated due to the author's prejudices, but it illustrates the existing tensions.

30. Tugwell, *The Stricken Land*, p. 7. According to Juan A. Silén, "pan, tierra, y libertad" (bread, land, and liberty) had been the slogan of PCP's newspaper, *Lucha Obrera*, in 1935. Silén, *Apuntes*, p. 92.

31. Partido Popular Democrático, *Compilación de programas*, p. 1. Hereafter, PPD, *Compilación*.

32. In the 1920s Muñoz had flirted with the PS and in the 1930s he declared to be for independence. Nonetheless, anyone who reads carefully Mathews' or Tugwell's books would see that Munóz's socialist background and proindependence stance were more posturing than a political project. In fact, after some years in power Muñoz declared that his proindependence past was a "youthful mistake." See Mathews, *Puerto Rican Politics*, Chaps. 5–7, and Tugwell, *The Stricken Land*.

33. Villar Roces, *Reforma agraria*, pp. 42–43.

34. As quoted in Edel, "Land Reform," Pt. 1, p. 30.

35. "Ley Número 26," in Puerto Rico, *Leyes* (1941), pp. 389–457; Edel, "Land Reform," Pt. 1, p. 38.

36. Puerto Rico Planning Board, Economic Division, *Economic Development*, p. 176, Table 30. Hereafter referred to as Planning Board.

37. Tugwell, *The Stricken Land*, p. 87.

38. Planning Board, *Economic Development*, p. 176, Table 30.

39. Puerto Rico, *Leyes*, (1942), p. 942.

40. See Quintero Rivera, "La base social" and "The Socio-Political Background"; González, "Class Struggle"; Navas Dávila, *Dialéctica*; and Villamil, "Puerto Rico."

41. For a detailed account of the Fomento's early programs and its subsidiaries see Ross, *The Long Uphill Path*, and Dietz, *Economic History*, Chap. 4.

42. Puerto Rico Planning, Urbanizing and Zoning Board, *A Development Plan*, p. 44.

43. This was the case with the expropriation of the Porto Rico Railway Light and Power Co. and the Mayaguez Light, Power, and Ice Co. See Puerto Rico, Governor, *Forty-Third Annual Report*, pp. 40–41.

44. Herrero, "La mitología," pp. 20–30.

45. Puerto Rico, Governor, *Forty-Fifth Annual Report*, p. 98.

46. Perloff, *Economic Future*, pp. 74–76.

47. Quintero Rivera, "La base social," pp. 68–69; and Wolf, "San José," p. 250.

48. Planning Board, *Economic Development*, pp. 28, 48, 101, 163.

49. Puerto Rico, Compañía de Fomento de Puerto Rico (CFPR), *Informe anual; 1944*, p. 7.

50. Planning Board, *Economic Development*, pp. 7, 28.

51. Puerto Rico, Junta de Planificación, *Ingreso y producto, 1978*, pp. 26, 30, 34. Hereafter, Junta de Planificación. Planning Board, *Economic Development*, pp, 18, 153, 160; and Perloff, *Economic Future*, pp. 398–399.

52. Planning Board, *Economic Development*, p. 126.

53. Cestero, *Balance of Payments*, p. 13.

54. Planning Board, *Economic Development*, p. 71.

55. Planning Board, *Economic Development*, p. 156, Table 7.

56. Calculated from Junta de Planificación, *Ingreso y producto, 1978*, p. 43.

57. PPD, *Compilación*, p. 2.

58. Quintero Rivera, "La base social," pp. 73–79.

59. Jesús T. Piñero, who had been president of the Puerto Rican Farmers Association, is probably the best illustration of the influence of the large *colonos* within the PPD. Piñero was elected to the Puerto Rican legislature for the PPD in 1940, and in 1944 was elected the PPD's resident commissioner for Puerto Rico in Washington. In 1946, President Truman appointed him governor of Puerto Rico, and he thus became the first Puerto Rican governor appointed by a U.S. president. On the benefits of the PPD's legislation to *colonos* see Navas Dávila, "Surgimiento y transformación," pp. 24, 27, and passim.

60. Between 1942 and 1948 the profits declared by the U.S. sugar corporations amounted to a total of $19.7 million. In 1942 profits were $4.5 million; they declined to $1 million in 1946 before rising again to $4.1 million in 1948. Cestero, *Balance of Payments*, p. 18; Tugwell, *The Stricken Land*, p. 91.

61. Puerto Rico, Governor, *Forty-Third Annual Report*, p. 3; Puerto Rico Planning, Urbanization and Zoning Board, *A Development Plan*, p. 19; and Goodsell, *Administration*, pp. 22–26.

62. Mattos Cintrón, *La política y lo político*, pp. 13, 200, and notes 143 and 145.

63. Ross, *The Long Uphill Path*, p. 85. A list of the private entrepreneurs that formed part of the board of directors of Fomento and its subsidiaries appears in Puerto Rico Development Company (PRDC), *Third Annual Report, 1945*, p. 7.

64. PRDC, *First Annual Report, 1943*, p. i; see Puerto Rico Planning, Urbanization and Zoning Board, *A Development Plan*, p. 5.

65. PRDC, *Third Annual Report*, p. 35. A similar quotation from the U.S. National Association of Manufacturers had appeared also in CFPR, *Informe anual, 1944*, p. i.

66. Tugwell, *The Stricken Land*, p. 148; see also pp. 69 and 137.

67. Poulantzas, *Political Power*, pp. 84–85.

68. Here I am following the arguments of Laclau, *Politics and Ideology*, Chap. 4.

69. Quintero Rivera, "La base social," pp. 73–79; González, "Class Struggle," pp. 50–51.

70. As Laclau suggests, the people/power bloc contradiction can be articulated by a fascist as well as a socialist movement. It is precisely the ambiguity intrinsic in populist discourse (the demagoguery normally associated with these movements) that permits the conciliation of contradictory interests. Laclau, *Politics and Ideology*, pp. 170–176.

3

The Capital-Importation/Export-Processing Strategy: The First Stage

The end of World War II brought with it a shift in the development strategy and the axis of accumulation. The PPD's development program shifted from the promotion of state-owned industries to the attraction of U.S. capital in light export-oriented manufacturing industries. The axis of accumulation would shift from the colonial state to a fraction of U.S. capital. The restructuring of imperialist capitalism will be taken one step further through what I shall call the capital-importation/export-processing (CI/EP) strategy.

The CI/EP strategy is a variation of what neoclassical economics now calls the export-promotion development model. The basic premise of the export-promotion model is that exchange rates do not discriminate against exports. But the neoclassical economists do not discuss its sociopolitical premise: that adequate exchange rates need to be accompanied by other incentives and favorable political conditions. That is, this model needs to be part of a wider strategy that includes incentives above and beyond adequate exchange rates. The incentives associated with export-promotion strategies, such as tax holidays, wage and rent subsidies, and so on, were developed in Puerto Rico under the industrialization program known as Operation Bootstrap, initiated between 1947 and 1948. This was the first time that such incentives were developed as part of a comprehensive development strategy based on export-oriented industrialization in the capitalist periphery. The industrial incentive laws of Puerto Rico and the investment-promotion programs of Fomento were the first designed to provide the "adequate incentives" needed to attract the investment for this type of development. Since foreign investment became the fuel for export-led industrialization strategies, I have included the label "capital importation." Today these strategies are known as the Puerto Rican model, the industrialization by invitation model, the Asian model, or the *maquiladora* model. But it all started with Operation Bootstrap.

This early stage of the CI/EP strategy extends from the end of the war to the mid-1960s. More specifically, it could be argued that this stage runs from the passage of the first industrial incentive law in 1947 to the passage of the 1963 Industrial Incentive Act, which shifted economic development in yet another direction. These dates will be used as demarcation points and should not be taken to mean that the incentive laws were the driving force or the cause of the process of development.

The Redefinition of the Reformist Strategy: Political and Ideological Conditions

After a sweeping victory in the 1944 election, the PPD leadership began to show more openly their convergence with the politicoeconomic interests of the metropolis. In the 1944 election, the PPD received 64.7 percent of the total vote, taking seventeen of the nineteen Senate seats and thirty-seven of the thirty-nine seats in the House of Representatives. It also elected seventy-three of the seventy-seven mayors of the country.[1] Having defeated their principal political enemy—the PR/PS coalition—the PPD's leadership moved against their secondary enemies—the most militant elements within the labor movement, particularly the Confederación General de Trabajadores (CGT), and the proindependence faction within PPD, which formed the Congreso Pro-Independencia (CPI). At the same time, the PPD also announced the abandonment of its state-based industrialization program, gave a low profile to the agrarian reform program, and passed an industrial incentives law that opened the door to U.S. investment in manufacturing industries. This process of political reshuffling also included a renegotiation of the colonial pact with the metropolitan ruling classes that gave the PPD's technobureaucracy greater participation in running the internal affairs of the colony.

The ambiguity and evasiveness of Luis Muñoz Marín and the PPD top leaders on the issue of independence and other issues related to the colonial question posed a potential threat to the PPD's newly acquired political dominance in 1944. This threat had become tangible in 1943 when the CPI was organized to push for proindependence positions within the party. Pressures from the CPI had forced Muñoz and the rest of the PPD leadership to reaffirm their commitment to a resolution of the colonial question through a referendum once the war was over. Muñoz had even expressed concern that these pressures would undermine or even cost him his leadership of the party. Nonetheless, throughout the 1944 election campaign, party publicity made clear that it was not for independence. The election results did away with all the worries of the leadership and paved the way for a campaign to either co-opt or expel these radical elements from the PPD.[2]

The first step in this direction came in March 1945 when the PPD labor leaders managed to divide the CGT into two groups. The first, called the "governmental" CGT, was controlled by PPD labor leaders (one of them was the vice-president of the House of Representatives and the other a senator). The other group, called the "authentic" CGT, was controlled principally by leaders of the recently dissolved PCP. The issue that provoked the split was the question of whether the labor movement should assume political positions or limit itself to economic bargaining issues. The governmental CGT favored the latter. This faction reflected the PPD's desire to control and restrict the labor movement by making it only an agent for economic bargaining. The authentic CGT wanted a nonpartisan yet politicized movement. They proposed that the CGT should support "the struggle against colonialism and for national liberation."[3]

The PPD leadership within the CGT was trying to capitalize on two key elements of the political juncture following the 1944 election. The first was the popularity and strength of the PPD as shown by its sweeping victory. The second was the weakness of the PCP within the CGT and the country at large. This weakness had been deepened by the decision of the PCP leadership in 1944 to dissolve the party and support the PPD, thus following the lead of the Communist party of the United States and other communist parties in the hemisphere that adopted the politics of "popular fronts," supporting populist "progressive" parties. In the analysis of the PCP leaders, the PPD was a progressive popular movement that should be supported by the workers' organizations. They also argued that, given the historical conditions at the time, there was no need for a party of the proletariat to exist.[4] Thus the PPD found it relatively easy to attempt a takeover of the labor movement at the expense of the communists.

With the division of the CGT, the PPD killed two birds with one stone. On the one hand, they weakened the labor movement in general and undermined the leadership of radical labor leaders by isolating them. On the other hand, their control over a faction of the labor movement allowed the PPD to continue to present itself as a faithful ally and representative of the interests of the working classes. In the long run, the weakness of the labor movement and the control of a faction of it by the PPD would be used as an enticement to attract U.S. capital.

The assault of the PPD on the labor movement was complemented by further actions from the metropolitan government and the U.S. labor movement. The passage of the Taft-Hartley Law by the U.S. Congress in 1947 and the introduction to Puerto Rico of North American unions were also instrumental in weakening labor's militant positions. The application to Puerto Rico of the Taft-Hartley Law made solidarity strikes illegal and made the unions subject to federal government arbitration. For its part, the coming to Puerto Rico of U.S. unions added an element of conservatism to the labor movement and furthered the alienation of workers from their representatives.[5]

The second move of the PPD leadership against their antagonistic allies came in 1946 with the expulsion of CPI members from the party. Among the members of the CPI there were some middle-ranking leaders of the PPD who held legislative seats. They had been pressuring the top leadership of the PPD to assume a clear proindependence position so that under the PPD's pressure the United States would be forced to resolve the colonial question by conceding independence to the island. Until 1945, Muñoz had managed to keep the CPI faction under control by convincing them that he was for independence, but that pushing for it during the war was not a wise tactical move. Muñoz's reasoning was that it was better to wait for the war to end because the U.S. government would be more receptive then to any proposal for independence. Meanwhile, argued Muñoz, the main priority was to initiate social and economic reforms that would pave the way to freedom.

However, in praxis the reformist program never intended to lay the basis for independence but rather was geared toward restructuring imperialist capitalism. Hence, the very logic of the PPD's political project ran against independence. If the top leadership of the PPD never expressed its opposition to independence clearly before the 1944 election, it was because the anti-Americanism of the 1930s was still an important ideological force. However, after the war the United States appeared as the defender of democracy against the abhorrent fascists. Puerto Ricans were fighting for democracy as U.S. soldiers, and a "benevolent" U.S. governor (Tugwell) had contributed to the implementation of the PPD's program of "social justice."

Within the context of these favorable circumstances, the PPD launched a campaign to discredit the members of the CPI by accusing them of sabotaging the party. This campaign culminated in February 1946 when the party leadership declared it incompatible to be a member of the CPI and of the PPD. Only two persons were opposed to this decision, a fact that indicates there were few PPD leaders who actively supported independence.[6] Eventually, most members of the CPI were expelled from the PPD. They went on to create the Partido Independentista Puertorriqueño (PIP) in October 1946 and participated in the 1948 election with a political program that was mainly concerned with the achievement of independence; all other issues were considered secondary.[7]

Another element that strengthened the position of the PPD leadership vis-à-vis the proindependence sectors was the passage by the U.S. Congress of Public Law 362, on 5 August 1947. This law, which amended the Jones Act of 1917, gave the people of Puerto Rico the right to elect their governor and the elected governor the right to appoint all members of the colonial executive branch with the approval of the colonial Senate. However, the U.S. president continued to appoint the attorney general and the judges of the Puerto Rican Supreme Court. Also, the law provided for a coordinator of federal agencies who would play the role of political overseer of the colonial government, to make sure that its policies did not conflict with U.S. interests.[8]

The approval of Law 362 was presented by the PPD as a partial fulfillment of their promise of "liberty" and strengthened their argument that it was unnecessary to demand independence when colonialism was gradually disappearing. In his annual message to the legislature, Governor Jesús T. Piñero referred to Law 362 as a "democratic conquest" and an enhancement of "our political and social path."[9] Speaking of this law at his inauguration as the first elected colonial governor, Muñoz echoed Piñero's views, arguing that the colonial system was disappearing with great rapidity, as the election of a Puerto Rican governor demonstrated.[10] Most certainly, Law 362 became an important political weapon against the supporters of independence. The concession of limited political freedoms would allow the PPD leadership to back down from their anticolonial rhetoric while saving face on the issue of achieving "liberty."

In 1948, the PPD obtained another sweeping electoral victory. This time it received 61.2 percent of the votes, 3.5 percent less than in 1944. However, it again won seventeen out of the nineteen seats in the Senate; thirty-eight out of the thirty-nine seats in the House of Representatives, one more than in 1944; and seventy-six out of the seventy-seven mayoral posts, three more than in 1944. All the participating parties reduced their share of the vote in comparison to the 1944 elections. This is attributable in part to the emergence of the PIP, which got 10.2 percent of the vote.[11] The annexationists, now running under the Partido Unión Republicana Progresista, the PS, and the PL all lost to the PPD for the third consecutive time. The only emerging force at this time was the PIP, which captured most of the proindependence vote.

The period between 1948 and 1952 saw a revival of nationalism in a broad sense. Pedro Albizu Campos returned from his imprisonment in December 1947, triggering a revival of Nationalist militancy. Denunciations of the PPD as a colonialist party increased. In 1948, proindependence students went on strike at the University of Puerto Rico to protest the suspension of five students who had raised the Puerto Rican flag to salute the return of Albizu Campos. Nationalist protest achieved its high point in 1950, when the PN led an insurrection to denounce the approval of Law 600, a bill to renegotiate the colonial pact, as a perpetuation of colonialism.[12]

To counter this protest movement, the PPD government began a campaign of harassment and repression against the sympathizers and members of proindependence groups. The first major step in this campaign was the approval of Law 53 in 1948. This law, popularly known as the "law of the muzzle" or the "gag law," was patterned after the antisubversive "Smith Law" of the United States. Law 53 declared it a felony to "promote, advocate, advise or preach" violent subversion. The penalty for violating this law was up to ten years in prison. It was first used to incarcerate the leaders of the 1948 student strike and, in the aftermath of the failed insurrection, to incarcerate or blacklist persons known to be Nationalist sympathizers. Using this law the local police and the U.S. Federal Bureau of Investigation established a constant surveillance of anyone identified with the PN.[13]

Repression of the Nationalists became a condition for legitimizing the renegotiation of the colonial relation.

In order to counterbalance the accusations of colonialism from the proindependence groups as well as from the signatories of the Atlantic and the United Nations charters, something more had to be done. Here, once more, the political changes taking place around the colonial state were determined by both internal and external conditions. On the one hand, the metropolis/colony contradiction and the contradictions between different metropolitan centers (i.e., the contradictions created with the Europeans by the U.S. postwar anticolonial policy) forced the United States to make changes in the colonial relation. On the other hand, the class contradictions inside the colony (i.e., the contradictions that led the working classes to support the reformist project's libertarian rhetoric) made it necessary to bring about a political change that would fulfill the promise of liberty and legitimize the process of restructuring imperialist capitalism in Puerto Rico.

The political alternative proposed by the PPD leadership and supported by the U.S. Congress was the creation of a new colonial formula that, literally translated, would be called the Free Associated State of Puerto Rico. The official translation, however, was the Commonwealth of Puerto Rico. This formula was sanctioned by Public Law 600 of 1950, also known as the Federal Relations Act. This law was passed by the Congress to represent a compact between the people of Puerto Rico and the United States. The Puerto Rican people would vote in a referendum to either accept or reject the law. No modifications to the law could be made by the people of Puerto Rico. The law provided that the people of Puerto Rico, once they accepted the law in a referendum, could form a Constitutional Assembly to write their own constitution within certain limits stipulated by the U.S. Congress. Law 600 was approved by the people of Puerto Rico in a referendum held in July 1951. The Constitutional Assembly was convened and wrote the Constitution of the Commonwealth of Puerto Rico. In turn, the constitution was submitted to the U.S. Congress, which made three amendments to it. The Constitutional Assembly had to be convened again to consider the amendments under the threat that if they were not accepted there would be no constitution at all for the commonwealth. The symbolic importance of the constitution for the legitimacy of the PPD dominance was such that its delegates in the assembly, who were in the majority, accepted the amendments with resignation.[14]

But the constitution did not make any substantial changes in the colonial relation. Because of this the PPD leadership developed two interpretations of the commonwealth formula, one for the consumption of the U.S. Congress and another for the consumption of its electoral base. In Congress, Muñoz asserted "that if the people of Puerto Rico became crazy Congress could always find a way to pass new legislation,"[15] thus implying that if the people of Puerto Rico wanted to go beyond the colonial limits the U.S.

Congress had the power to revoke the concessions given. Meanwhile, in Puerto Rico, Muñoz gave a different interpretation of the meaning of Law 600, arguing that in the decade between 1940 and 1950 the colonial period had ended in Puerto Rico.[16]

A look at the transcripts of the *Congressional Record* and other accounts of some of the protagonists in the approval of Law 600 reveals that the PPD accepted Congress' interpretation without question. According to this interpretation, Law 600 did not change the fundamental political, social, and economic relations between the United States and Puerto Rico. Furthermore, the fundamental sections of the Jones Act regarding relations between the United States and Puerto Rico would remain in force.[17] As Harvard professor of international law Rupert Emerson put it in 1953:

> [T]he most distinctive element is that they now have for the first time in their history given themselves a constitution and given their free consent to their relationship with the United States. . . . It is arguable that the status which they now have does not differ greatly in substance from that which they had before; but to press that argument too far would be to ignore the great symbolic effect of entering into a compact with the United States and governing themselves under an instrument of their own fashioning.[18]

The PPD technobureaucracy was caught in a contradiction that needed to be resolved in order to assure the orderly continuation of the restructuring process and the maintenance of their dominant position in the colonial power structure. On the one hand, the PPD's strategic alliance with the metropolitan state and bourgeoisie committed them to the preservation of the colonial relation. On the other hand, their tactical alliance with the working classes (their electoral base of support) forced them to fulfill their promise to put an end to colonialism. The dual interpretation of the commonwealth formula as both a continuation of the colonial relation and as the achievement of "liberty" reflects the attempt of PPD technobureaucracy to reconcile its contradictory political alliances.

Even though the creation of the commonwealth did not resolve the political contradiction inherent in the colonial relation, it certainly redefined its terms in a significant manner. The colonial relation took on the appearance of a compact, giving greater participation to the colonized in the running of their internal affairs while maintaining intact the key structural features of the colonial relation. The politicoideological impact of this change was crucial: it reestablished the legitimacy of U.S. dominance in Puerto Rico. The process of restructuring after the crisis of the thirties had led to colonial domination by consent; metropolitan hegemony had been reestablished. The redefinition of the colonial pact through the creation of the commonwealth completed the formation of what Gramsci would term a new historic bloc, a new order in which economic structure and the ideological and legal-political superstructure correspond.[19] The commonwealth would pave the way for the implementation of a new development strategy that articulated the postwar interests of the metropolitan bourgeoisie.

By the end of World War II, the PPD had divided, weakened, and taken partial control of the labor movement; it had repressed and isolated the proindependence sectors; and it had succeeded in creating a new colonial formula that consolidated the position of power of the technobureaucracy, guaranteed the dominance of the imperialist bourgeoisie, and legitimated the PPD in the eyes of its popular base of support.

The New Development Strategy

By 1950, the agrarian reform program had become mainly a land distribution program for peasants and rural workers. The *parcelas* program was transferred from the Land Authority to the Social Programs Administration, an agency created in 1950 within the Department of Agriculture and Commerce. For all practical purposes, the Land Authority had become a government-owned sugar corporation, concentrating its activities on the sugar-producing proportional profit farms. After 1952, the Land Authority did not expand its activities and dropped all efforts to enforce the "500-acre law."[20]

The alleged reasons for this change were that using public funds to purchase productive land was a misuse of resources, that there were many labor problems on the government farms, and that sugar prices were constantly falling.[21] However, the key reason was that by 1950 the power of the PPD vis-à-vis the sugar sector and their representatives, the PR, was well established and consolidated. In political terms, the most important aspect of the agrarian reform was the *parcelas* program, which got many votes for the PPD; hence, the continuation of this program while the others were eliminated or remained stagnant. Yet another possible reason for the PPD's abandonment of agrarian reform was the negotiations in Congress about Law 600, which compelled the PPD to act cautiously. Agrarian reform had never been to the liking of U.S. congressmen, and it was not wise then to push the issue any further.

The abandonment of the agrarian reform policy did not constitute a drastic change or a rupture in the continuity of capitalist development. Rather, it was a necessary adjustment.[22] The reformist strategy had already fulfilled its function: overcoming the crisis of capitalism by shifting the axis of accumulation from export agriculture to the colonial state, thus preserving the strategic interests of the metropolis during the war. Having used state intervention successfully, the strategy could be redefined to make possible the realization of the new economic interests of the metropolitan bourgeoisie. After the war, the convergence of interests of the PPD, looking for a way to sustain the economic improvements achieved during the war, and the industrial fraction of the North American bourgeoisie, searching for investment opportunities, dictated the direction of the development strategy. In the period between 1940 and 1947, the PPD technobureaucracy had articulated an alliance with the New Deal state bureaucracy through a development strategy aimed at preserving the general strategic interest of the United States in Puerto Rico. After the war, the alliance took on a new character.

Since 1944, Fomento had been pressing for legislation to attract U.S. investment by providing tax exemptions to new industries. But the first attempt to pass a tax exemption law for industrial activities was vetoed by Governor Tugwell.[23] This forced Fomento to change its plans. In 1945, they created a program named AID (Aid to Industrial Development), designed to provide locational incentives to industries coming to Puerto Rico, principally in the form of low-rent factory buildings. At the same time as the AID program began, Fomento opened a promotional office in New York to publicize the advantages of Puerto Rico as a site for industrial investment.[24] But these programs were not very successful and did not show in a clear manner what direction the redefinition of the reformist strategy was going to take. The first concrete steps had to wait until the approval of an industrial incentive law in 1947.

On 12 May 1947 Law 346 was approved. It defined forty-one industrial activities that were eligible for tax exemption (most were light industries, e.g., food, textiles, toys, etc.), and provided for 100 percent tax exemption on industrial income, property, licences, and most other taxes normally paid by businesses. The period of exemption was to begin on 1 July 1947 and end on 30 June 1954. For the following three fiscal years, there was to be a gradual reduction of the tax exemption to 75 percent in 1954/55, 50 percent in 1955/56, and 25 percent in 1956/57. After 1957, all industrial establishments were to be taxed according to the applicable laws. In order to be eligible for tax exemption, the industries planning to establish operations in Puerto Rico had to file a petition with the Government Executive Council.[25]

However, Law 346 was amended just a year after its approval by Law 184 of 13 May 1948. This law expressed a clearer concept of the direction toward which industrial development ought to move. Law 184 had a "Statement of Motives" that established the needs and reasons for a tax exemption policy and reaffirmed the government's commitment to industrial development. The new law had a list of forty-one industrial activities eligible for exemption that was similar to the list of Law 346. However, unlike its 1947 counterpart, items 40 and 41 of Law 184's eligibility list defined in a very broad manner most areas related to the apparel and textile industries. This new emphasis was not accidental. In 1948, Donald J. O'Connor, an economist for the Office of the Government of Puerto Rico in Washington, D.C., had conducted a study on the advantages for U.S. textile industries to establish operations in Puerto Rico. The study, published as a brochure to provide information for "potential investors," pointed out thirteen competitive advantages for Puerto Rico over other locations in the United States; among the most important were tax exemption, low wages, good labor relations (industrial peace), and free access to the U.S. market.[26]

Law 184 granted 100 percent tax exemption on all taxes between 1 July 1947 and 30 June 1959 to eligible industries (twelve years of exemptions for those companies that had been established under Law 346). For the three following fiscal years, there was to be a gradual reduction of the tax exemption to 75 percent in 1959/60, 50 percent in 1960/61, and 25 percent in 1961/62. The law would expire in 1962 and all exemptions would end. Since the exemption period was fixed, the earlier a company established operations in Puerto Rico the greater the benefits (tax exemptions also were extended to tourist and commercial hotels under both laws).[27]

In 1950, the colonial government was reorganized and Fomento's role as the main coordinating agency of economic development was strengthened. The head of Fomento was given ministerial rank, formally becoming a member of the colonial cabinet.[28] By this time, Fomento had sold its industrial subsidiaries and liquidated the last vestiges of state-based industrialization. Part of the equipment of the government-owned Puerto Rico Shoe and Leather Co. was sold to Joyce Inc., an American company that also rented the building where the former was located. The cement, cardboard, clay, and glass plants were purchased by the Ferré family of Puerto Rico, giving them a monopoly on cement production that would form the basis for Puerto Rico's largest industrial-financial empire. Finally, the textile mill (Telares de Puerto Rico) came to be operated as a joint venture between Fomento and Textron Inc., with Fomento footing over $4.3 million in overhead and fixed capital and Textron purchasing about $500 thousand of stock and covering operational expenses. By the mid-1950s the venture had failed; eventually it was taken over by another U.S. firm.[29] With the sale of the government industries to private capital, the fate of state-based industrialization was sealed.

Law 184 began to attract labor-intensive industries, especially apparel and textiles, food processing, electrical machinery, furniture, and metal products. Most of the production of these industries was for export to the United States. It was amended by Law 6 of 15 December 1953, known as "The Puerto Rico Industrial Incentive Act of 1954," which changed the terms of tax exemptions in two ways. First, instead of the fixed period of exemption granted by Law 184 (from 1947 to 1959), Law 6 granted a ten-year, 100 percent tax exemption to eligible industries on an individual basis, provided that the industry opened operations no later than 31 December 1963, when the law expired. Second, exemption from property taxes would be given in proportion to the magnitude of the investment. For example, if investment in real estate and tangible capital assets (machinery and equipment) was one million dollars or less, the period of exemption from property taxes was only five years; if the investment was ten million dollars or more, the period of tax exemption was the maximum of ten years. Between these lower and upper limits, there were various classifications.[30]

The list of eligible industries under Law 6 was similar to that of the two previous laws. However, this law expanded the qualifying branches of the textile and food and agricultural processing industries. According to the 1953/54 annual report of Fomento, Law 6 was aimed at stepping up the rates of investment and job creation and countering the recessionary effect of the end of the Korean War and its negative impact on the influx of U.S. investments to Puerto Rico.[31]

Aside from these changes in the law, the legal-political framework laid to foster the CI/EP strategy was complemented by a sizeable campaign, organized and coordinated by Fomento's Division of Public Relations, which involved contracting New York-based public relations companies McCann-Erickson and Hamilton Wright. The object of this campaign was to sell Puerto Rico to U.S. investors as an industrial and profit paradise. Much of this publicity took the form of carefully prepared brochures, films, articles, and advertisements in business publications such as *Fortune, Baron's,* and *The Wall Street Journal.* Every propagandistic resource available was used to attract U.S. capital. Fomento developed an aggressive campaign of selling Puerto Rico to U.S. investors, opening promotional offices in New York, Chicago, and Los Angeles during this period.[32]

Probably the most interesting aspect of the public relations measure was the local campaign aimed at presenting the CI/EP strategy as the fulfillment of the people's will and aspirations. In 1950 Fomento's Division of Public Relations organized a public ceremony for the inauguration of the hundredth Fomento-promoted plant. The propagandistic success of this event prompted their proliferation. Every time a new plant was opened, Fomento organized a public ceremony in which the mayor of the town, the priest, the Protestant minister, the firm's executives (almost always North Americans), and high-ranking Fomento and government officials took part. According to a Fomento annual report, "The purpose of this program is to make the citizens familiar with the industrial enterprises established in their communities, so that they may have an objective idea of what industrialization means for the people of Puerto Rico."[33] In this, Fomento was most certainly assuming the role of an Althusserian ideological state apparatus. It was not only coordinating and implementing the economic policy of the government in the administrative sense, it was also directly active in the representation of this policy as being in the interest of society at large. Fomento was articulating at the ideological level the interests of the ruling classes (expressed in the CI/EP strategy) and presenting them as beneficial to all society, thus "inscribing" the working classes in the ideological practice of the ruling classes (i.e., in the categories of developmentalism).

There were other economic enticements widely publicized in the Fomento propaganda campaigns. Of a total of $3.4 million granted by Fomento in subsidies to industries, 88.6 percent, almost $3 million, were given to U.S. firms between 1952 and 1959. In this same period, between 90 and 100 percent of the low-rent industrial buildings owned by Fomento were occupied by foreign firms. Finally, of the $24 million in loans to industry approved by the Government Development Bank between 1952 and 1959, $14.6 million (just over 60 percent) were loaned to U.S. industries.[34]

Other advantages stemming from the colonial relation were the common currency (the U.S. dollar) and the absence of federal taxes; the availability of abundant cheap labor with a low degree of unionization (or with unions controlled by the government or U.S. unions); the free trade between Puerto Rico and the United States that made the island an ideal location for companies interested in producing for the U.S. market; and "political stability," which meant that the presence of U.S. military bases in Puerto Rico and the very fact that the only army in Puerto Rico was the U.S. Army was the ultimate guarantee against any political upheavals that might threaten U.S. interests. These and the tax exemptions became the pillars of the CI/EP strategy. Fomento's message was that the colony had all the advantages of the Latin American republics but none of the risks because the companies' interests were protected by the U.S. government itself. The colony was the best of both worlds, high profits in a protected environment.

These are the fundamental elements that made possible the redefinition of the reformist strategy and the deepening and consolidation of the strategic alliance between the technobureaucracy and a fraction of the imperialist bourgeoisie. The key components of the ideological praxis articulated by this version of developmentalism began to change, and the CI/EP strategy was presented as the struggle of the people for progress, as "the battle of production," as the vehicle to achieve "integral freedom," and as a policy in which "industrialization [was] for the people."[35]

The Impact of the CI/EP Strategy on the Socioeconomic Structure

In economic terms, the CI/EP strategy was characterized by a rapid growth in the manufacturing sector, the expansion of the tertiary sector, and the continued decline of agriculture. Corollaries of this strategy were the emergence of U.S. capital as the dominant element in the manufacturing sector, the orientation of industrial production for export to the U.S. market, and the increased dependency on the importation of capital and raw materials. These tendencies in the manufacturing sector were reflected in the rest of the economy, resulting in the external control of the leading sectors of economic development.

The CI/EP strategy was accompanied by many social changes. In terms of this study, there are six important processes associated with the adoption of this strategy. First, there was a restoration of the dominance of U.S. capital, only now the dominant fraction would be small and medium competitive capital in light industries. Second, the expansion of the manufacturing sector accelerated the process of urbanization and proletarianization that started earlier with the U.S. invasion. These two processes were accompanied by the progressive displacement and marginalization of sectors of the working classes, which resulted in persistent high rates of unemployment and the massive emigration of working people to the metropolis. These three associated processes (urbanization, proletarianization, and marginalization) resulted from the incapacity of the reformist as well as the CI/EP strategies to stem the decline of agriculture or stimulate an industrial expansion capable of absorbing the labor force displaced from the agricultural sector. A fifth process was the expansion of the urban middle sectors. This was strongly linked not only to the rapid growth of manufacturing but to the expansion of the tertiary sector (services, government) and other bureaucratic nonmanual forms of labor. The middle sectors constituted the basis for the expansion of the domestic market, particularly in the area of durable consumer goods. They also became the basis of support for the continuation of the developmentalist project within the colonial relation. The sixth process was the adaptation of a sector of the local bourgeoisie to the process of industrial expansion led by U.S. capital, in effect creating a division of labor between local and U.S. capital.

Industrial Growth and Foreign Control

Figure 3.1 illustrates the patterns of growth of the principal economic sectors in terms of the shares contributed to the gross domestic product (GDP). The most salient feature is the sharp decline in the share of agriculture; this decline was compensated for by the growth of the manufacturing and the service sectors. After World War II, agricultural investment in the periphery was an area of secondary importance for U.S. capital in relation to direct investment in manufacturing.[36] North American interests in export agriculture had been declining in Puerto Rico since the 1930s. The low level of development of the economic infrastructure in Puerto Rico now made light industry the only feasible investment for U.S. capital.

Tables 3.1 and 3.2 illustrate the process through which U.S. capital became dominant in the manufacturing sector in Puerto Rico, while the local sector's relative importance was reduced to a secondary position. In analyzing these tables, it should be noted that the label "foreign" corresponds to both U.S. and non-U.S. foreign capital. However, in 1954, there were 250 foreign industries in Puerto Rico, of which 242 were U.S.-owned; in 1958, there were 407 foreign establishments, of which 396 were U.S.-owned; and in

Figure 3.1 Shares of GDP by Sector, 1948–1963

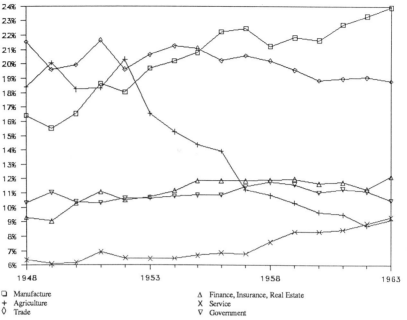

Source: Departamento del Trabajo, "Series de empleo."

Table 3.1 Local and Foreign Manufacturing Industries Shares of Total Value Added, Employment, and Wages: 1954, 1958, 1963

	Value Added ($000)	%	Production Employment	%	Wages ($000)	%
1954						
Local	117,472	62.4	41,312	68.5	39,008	65.8
Foreign	70,859	37.6	19,024	31.5	20,281	34.2
1958						
Local	145,904	49.9	30,000	49.9	43,529	46.6
Foreign	146,238	50.1	30,047	50.1	49,791	53.4
1963						
Local	239,815	38.6	31,631	37.7	64,097	35.8
Foreign	380,987	61.4	52,309	62.3	114,798	64.2

Sources: PREDA, *Locally and Nonlocally*, pp. 16–17, 85, 95; U.S. Bureau of the Census, *Census of Manufactures: 1963*, p. 155.

1963, there were 589 U.S.-owned establishments and only 43 non-U.S. foreign establishments. In other words, over 90 percent of the foreign capital in Puerto Rico was North American.[37]

Table 3.1 shows growth for both local and foreign industries in value added and wages. Employment decreased in local industries between 1954 and 1958, and then leveled off; it continued to grow in foreign industries. By 1963, the proportions had been reversed, with foreign industries contributing nearly two-thirds of total value added, production employment, and wages in manufacturing.

Table 3.2 shows the specific industries where foreign capital became dominant. As early as 1954, foreign capital had overwhelming control of production in textiles, women's clothing, women's and children's underwear, leather products, and petroleum and other products, with less than half of the establishments in those industries. Foreign dominance in electronics and scientific instruments was in all areas. The dominance in these industries increased by 1958, and expanded to tobacco, paper, and chemicals by 1963. Preserved foods was the only area where foreign industry did not gain ground.

In the period between 1947 and 1957, foreign capital investment averaged 38.6 percent of the capital funds used on the island; between 1958 and 1963, these averaged 52.7 percent.[38] In the period between 1952 and 1961, total external direct investment was $491.6 million. Of this total, $309.3 million, 63 percent, were invested in manufacturing. Of this $309.3 million, $284.7 million, 92 percent, were invested in tax-exempt industries. In all, 58 percent of the total external direct investment went to tax-exempt industries between 1952 and 1961. During the second half of the 1950s foreign investment began to move toward the service sector, particularly tourism, and wholesale and retail trade. Between 1958 and 1961, of a total $16 million of foreign investment in services, $13.2 million were in hotels. In 1960 and 1961, one-quarter and one-third of all foreign investment went to trade.[39] By 1963, the value of direct external investment in Puerto Rico was $1,106.7 million. This represented 44 percent of the total long-term external investment and 75 percent of the long-term external investment in the private sector.[40]

Contrary to the rest of Latin America in this period, production in foreign industries was mainly oriented toward export rather than import substitution. As early as 1954, only six years after the start of Operation Bootstrap, 53 percent of the industrial output of the island (measured in value of shipments) was destined for the U.S. market.[41] Most of the foreign firms imported their raw materials, processed them, and then reexported their products to the United States. This explains in part why in the period between 1948 and 1963 the import coefficient of Puerto Rico remained around 50 percent of the GDP while its export coefficient went from 27.4 percent to between 36 and 38 percent for the years 1960–1963. The areas where imports expanded most rapidly in this period were durable consumer goods (430 percent) and capital goods, raw materials, and intermediate goods (294 percent). The area that increased the least was nondurable consumer goods (103 percent).[42]

This pattern is totally different from that of early industrialization in most of Latin America, where, for example, in 1957 the highest import coefficient among the more industrialized countries was that of Chile (10.1 percent).[43] Latin American exports during this period still were dominated by

Table 3.2 Foreign Industries'Shares of Establishments, Value Added, Production Employment, and Wages in Selected Industries: 1954, 1958, 1963

	Establishments (%)	Value Added (%)	Employment (%)	Wages (%)
1954				
Canning and preserving	12.2	55.9	28.6	44.8
Textiles	45.5	71.8	64.8	71.8
Women's clothing	15.1	57.8	43.2	51.2
Women's & children's underwear	37.3	70.5	58.2	64.2
Leather products	39.3	67.2	69.0	71.1
Electrical machinery	71.0	86.9	84.7	86.3
Scientific instruments	58.3	93.6	91.5	92.1
Petroleum & coal products, rubber products, transportation equipment, miscellaneous products[a]	44.0	74.8	78.1	69.4
1958				
Canning and preserving	12.1	55.2	35.3	46.0
Tobacco products	2.8	59.5	37.7	50.3
Textiles	75.5	86.1	82.8	87.0
Apparel	30.0	68.7	58.8	68.4
Leather products	71.9	88.1	92.7	92.2
Electrical machinery	75.0	96.1	95.7	96.4
Scientific instruments	73.3	97.0	97.6	97.2
Petroleum & coal products, rubber products, transportation equipment, miscellaneous products[a]	47.5	84.6	81.6	83.5
1963				
Tobacco products	16.5	89.8	71.1	86.2
Textiles	75.5	83.5	80.0	82.2
Apparel	51.8	81.0	78.0	82.5
Paper & related products	51.7	66.2	52.8	73.1
Chemicals	32.5	81.6	58.7	65.0
Petroleum & coal products	33.3	N/A	92.4	N/A
Rubber & plastic products	54.2	62.2	65.6	67.9
Leather products	75.0	86.5	88.2	87.7
Electrical machinery	65.8	84.8	85.3	85.4
Scientific instruments	100	100	100	100
Miscellaneous products	57.7	76.0	81.6	80.8

Sources: PREDA, Locally and Nonlocally, pp. 16–17, 85, 95; U.S. Bureau of the Census, Census of Manufactures, 1963, p. 155.
[a]Separate data for these industries was unavailable.
N/A = not available.

primary products. This should not be interpreted to mean that the Puerto Rican economy was simply an enclave where all manufactures were exported and all consumption was satisfied by imports. Yet clearly there was an enclave-like character to its dynamic sector. Manufacturing was driven by external forces. By the mid-1950s, Puerto Rico had become a major export platform for U.S. capital and the archetype of what would later become known as maquiladora production.

Some further specifications must be made to better assess the impact of this strategy on the Puerto Rican economic structure. Two points are crucial: (a) the role of U.S. capital vis-à-vis Puerto Rican capital; and (b) the specific character of the fraction of metropolitan capital that assumed the dominant role in the productive process under the CI/EP strategy.

Between 1948 and 1963, there was a significant expansion of the internal market in Puerto Rico. Personal consumption of goods and services alone increased by 190 percent, from $620 million to $1,796 million. Durable goods and services experienced the greatest increases. As a whole, government and personal consumption expenditures grew by 201 percent, from $700 million to $2,109 million.[44] A share of this expanded demand was met by the production of foreign industries at the expense of the local industries.

As Table 3.1 showed, the share contributed by local industries to the total value added, production employment, and wages paid by the manufacturing sector as a whole was reduced from about two-thirds of the total in 1954 to about one-third in 1963. Though the majority of foreign industry's production was for export, an increasing share of the local supply of certain manufactured goods was satisfied by foreign industries operating in Puerto Rico. Table 3.3 shows that the share of the total value of foreign firms' shipments destined for the local market increased in every industrial branch for which there was data available.

Table 3.3 also lists four areas where the share of shipments to the U.S. market supplied by foreign firms dropped: paper, nonelectrical machinery, electrical machinery, and miscellaneous products. This implied increase in the share of shipments to the U.S. market supplied by local firms does not contradict any of the above observations about foreign industry expanding its dominance in these areas. After all, total shipments of local industries to the United States increased by 36.5 percent between 1954 and 1963, while total shipments of foreign firms increased by 358.5 percent.[45] What this increase in the shipments of local industries means is that there were elements within the local industrial bourgeoisie that adapted successfully to the new model—that is, there was a sector that not only survived the drive of U.S. capital but also articulated itself within it.

In the dialectical process of displacement and accommodation between local and U.S. capital, imperialist capital limits the possibilities of the total expansion of local capital. At the same time, it stimulates a relative growth in particular areas of local production associated with its expansion. This dialectic of peripheral development makes possible the emergence of an alliance between local capital and metropolitan capital.

The data available on industrial investment in Puerto Rico is in aggregate figures. There is little detailed information on investment, which prevents measuring the investment size of foreign firms by sector. However, there are indirect ways to characterize foreign investment in Puerto Rico. One is to compare and relate the fragmentary data that is available to what

Table 3.3 Foreign Industries' Shares of Value of Shipments to the Local and U.S. Markets: 1954 and 1963

Industry	Local Market	U.S. Market
Food		
1954	13.6%	29.7%
1963	43.6	36.6
Tobacco		
1954	8.1	20.4
1963	17.9	99.9[a]
Textiles		
1954	69.9	75.1
1963	85.3[a]	88.0
Apparel		
1954	4.1	60.2
1963	34.3	93.3
Paper		
1954	60.6	100.0
1963	62.5	87.3
Chemicals		
1954	20.9	22.3
1963	32.8	96.8
Leather		
1954	57.7	75.2
1963	65.4	92.2
Nonelectrical Machinery		
1954	2.4	97.4
1963	9.3[a]	47.9
Electrical Machinery		
1954	43.6	93.2
1963	68.4	87.0
Scientific Instruments		
1954	5.5	94.8
1963	100.0[a]	100.0
Miscellaneous		
1954	48.8	81.0
1963	56.9[a]	76.4
All Industries		
1954	20.0	78.3
1963	34.2	63.8

Sources: PREDA, *Locally and Nonlocally*, pp. 108–111; U.S. Bureau of the Census, *Census of Manufactures, 1963*, p. 156.
[a]Estimated.

Fomento said about foreign capital in its annual reports. Another is to compare the trends of capital investment in Puerto Rico with those in Latin America, thus putting Puerto Rico's position in the international division of labor in perspective and its importance to U.S. capital in a global context.

Fomento's annual reports provide the first indications of the specific character of U.S investment in Puerto Rico during this period. From the information in Table 3.2, we know that foreign investment centered around activities with low fixed investment of capital, primarily textiles, apparel, food, and electronics—industries with low capital investment per plant in operation. As a matter of fact, between 1951 and 1954 the average investment per manufacturing plant by the Fomento-promoted firms was around $300,000.[46]

The predominance of a low average investment by firm is confirmed by the requirements of one of Fomento's special incentives programs, "Operación Aprisa" (Operation Promptness), initiated in 1950 to speed up the establishment of U.S. industries. The incentives offered were free rent in Fomento-owned industrial buildings, payment of part of the cost for transportation of machinery and equipment to Puerto Rico, and reimbursement of part of the salaries paid to U.S. technicians required to begin operations. Fomento offered these on top of the other incentives provided by the Industrial Incentive Act. Interestingly, among the minimum requirements for eligibility were employing fifty persons or more for the first three months of operations and investing $200,000, of which $50,000 should be used in machinery.[47]

By 1956, there were 311 manufacturing plants operating under the Fomento program, and the investment in these plants was $163 million, an average of $524,000 per plant. However, this jump was partly attributable to $48 million invested by only three companies—two U.S. oil refineries and a chemical plant (controlled by Puerto Rican interests)—in 1955.[48] This growth continued throughout the 1950s. By 1959, there were 452 plants with an investment of $367 million, an average of $812,000 per plant.[49] This pattern is attributable to the establishment in Puerto Rico of subsidiaries of large U.S. companies, like Union Carbide, General Electric, Phelps Dodge, W. R. Grace, and others. However, despite the establishment of some larger operations, the major investors continued to be the subsidiaries of small and medium U.S. companies, which dominated the scene until the mid-1960s.[50]

If the question of what fraction of U.S. capital was dominant in Puerto Rico is approached by comparing U.S. investment on the island with that in other parts of the world between 1950 and 1959, a similar pattern is observed. Eighty-four percent of all U.S. manufacturing investment throughout the world in 1950, and 88 percent in 1959, was concentrated in the areas of chemicals and related products, transportation equipment, electrical machinery, nonelectrical machinery, food, paper products, and rubber products.[51] In Latin America, these areas represented 80 percent in 1950 and 84 percent in 1959, which closely follows the pattern for the rest of the world. The five most important areas of investment in Latin America in 1950 were chemical products, food, transportation equipment, electrical machinery, and rubber products, in that order, representing 75 percent of all U.S. manufacturing investment in Latin America for that year. In 1959, the most important areas were chemical products, transportation equipment, food, rubber products, and machinery, in that order, representing 73 percent of total U.S. investment in Latin America.[52]

Even though there is not similar information on U.S. investment in Puerto Rico, we can indirectly measure the areas where U.S. firms concentrated their production. Table 3.2 indicates where the production of foreign industry dominated vis-à-vis local capital. If this is used as a point of comparison, the production of foreign industries in 1958 was dominant in the areas of textiles, apparel, leather products, food products, tobacco, petroleum products, scientific instruments, and electrical machinery. Table 3.4 isolates the production of foreign industries in Puerto Rico and compares the shares of value added, production employment, and value of shipments generated by them. Except for the area of electrical machinery and part of the food industry, the foreign industries that predominate in Puerto Rico are areas marginal to the main drive of the international expansion of U.S. capital in the 1950s. Textiles, apparel, leather products, and tobacco provided 39 percent of the value added of foreign industries in 1958, 57 percent of the employment, and 32 percent of the value of shipments.

In light of this evidence, it is reasonable to conclude that the forces that provided the drive for the CI/EP strategy were the small and medium fractions of U.S. capital, and it is the interests of this class fraction and of the PPD technobureaucracy that are articulated in its first stage. Moreover, it can be said that the adoption of this strategy led to a process of displacement and reaccommodation of the local bourgeoisie vis-à-vis the imperialist bourgeoisie, and to the consolidation of a new form of integration of Puerto Rico into the international economy within the orbit of U.S. capital.

Social Changes

The adoption of this strategy of development accelerated the processes of urbanization, proletarianization, and marginalization. The process of urbanization in Puerto Rico began with the development of agrarian capitalism after the U.S. invasion. Between 1940 and 1960, this process accelerated, but it assumed a new variant, the displacement and marginalization of large numbers of workers and their emigration to the United States. The "explosion" of the urbanization process in Puerto Rico, as in most of Latin America, was the result of two related processes of peripheral capitalist growth: the expulsion of peasants and rural workers from the countryside as a consequence of the crisis of the primary export economy, provoked by the redefinition of the international division of labor after the Great Depression and World War II;[53] and the inability of the industrialization program to create enough jobs to absorb the displaced workers. The sharp decline in agricultural employment between 1948 and 1963 was not fully compensated for by growth in other sectors of the economy. Table 3.5 shows a sharp decline in total employment between 1948 and 1953, with only a slight recovery thereafter. Overall, there were 28,000 fewer jobs in 1963 than in 1948.

Table 3.4 Foreign Industries' Shares of Value Added, Production Employment, and Value of Shipments: 1958 (percent)

Industry	Value Added	Production Employment	Value of Shipments
Apparel	21	33	14
Food products	18	10	17
Electrical machinery	14	9	10
Textiles	9	11	9
Leather products	5	8	5
Tobacco products	4	5	4
Chemicals	2	0.1	2
Others	27	23.9	39

Source: PREDA, *Locally and Nonlocally*, pp. 108–111.

Table 3.5 Employment and Unemployment: 1948-1963 (thousands)

	1948	1953	1958	1963
Adult population	1,282	1,268	1,350	1,454
Labor force	663	646	637	643
Participation rate %	51.7	50.9	47.2	44.2
Employed	589	550	555	561
Unemployed	74	96	82	82
Unemployment rate %	11.2	14.8	12.9	12.8

Sources: Planning Board, *Economic Report*, p. A-21; and Junta de Planificación, *Serie histórica del empleo, 1981*, p. 15.

Table 3.6 shows the tendencies of rural and urban population growth as well as the migration trend between 1940 and 1960. The apparent slowdown in the urban growth in Puerto Rico between 1950 and 1960, compared to the previous decade, can be explained by the sharp increase in emigration. The Puerto Rican peasants and workers expelled from the countryside ended up in the metropolitan urban centers as an abundant supply of cheap labor. The Puerto Rican workers thus became integrated into the process of internationalization of the labor market.[54]

By 1950, 48.4 percent of the Puerto Rican migrants in the United States were classified as "operatives" (i.e., machine operators and related activities) and 18.6 percent were service workers. By 1960, 51.8 percent of the Puerto Rican migrants were classified as operatives and 15.2 percent were service workers—that is, more than two-thirds of the migrant labor force were employed as semiskilled or unskilled labor. Only a minority were classified as craftsmen and foremen (7.5 percent in 1950 and 8 percent in 1960), and even fewer were professionals or technicians (4.3 percent in 1950 and 2.8 percent in 1960). By the late 1950s 10 percent of the migrants were unemployed.[55]

On the other side of this massive displacement of the working population are the persistence of high rates of unemployment and the steadily

Table 3.6 Population Changes: 1940–1960

Total Population (000)	% Change	Urban (000)	% of Total	% Change	Rural (000)	% of Total	% Change	Migration (000)	% Change	Migrants as % of Population
1940 1,869.3	—	566.4	30.3	—	1,302.9	69.7	—	18.0ᵃ	—	1.0
1950 2,210.7	18.3	894.8	40.5	58.0	1,315.9	59.5	1.0	153.7	753.9	7.0
1960 2,349.5	6.3	1,039.3	44.2	16.1	1,310.2	55.8	−0.4	430.5	180.1	18.3

Sources: U.S. Bureau of the Census, *Census of Population, Puerto Rico, 1960*, Vol. 1, Pt. 53, pp. 53-59; Friedlander, *Labor Migration*, p. 170.
ᵃ1930–1939.

declining rates of labor force participation, shown in Table 3.5. Unemployment increased from 11.2 percent in 1948 to 14.8 percent in 1953, and then leveled off around 12.8 percent. This occurred in spite of the fact that the rate of labor force participation declined from 51.7 to 44.2 percent, which meant that a larger sector of the adult population was excluded from participating in the productive process and were not counted as unemployed.

If the almost half a million people who migrated to the United States in the 1950s had remained on the island, the displacement would have taken dramatic proportions. Stanley Friedlander estimated that, by 1960, the labor force in Puerto Rico would have increased by 325,000 workers (296,665 Puerto Ricans born on the island and 28,335 Puerto Ricans born in the United States were part of the active labor force). If this figure were added to the 625,000 workers in 1960, the size of the labor force that year would have been 950,000 people. If it is assumed that employment would have remained equal and that all of these people would have been actively seeking employment, 407,000 workers (42.8 percent of the total labor force) would have been unemployed. But Friedlander argues that if all 325,000 workers had remained on the island, 50 percent would have either dropped out of the labor force or found employment in the low-productivity areas of agriculture and the tertiary sector and another 10 percent would have found productive jobs with an additional fixed investment of $10 million. This would leave a net total of 130,000 unemployed workers. This figure, added to the 82,000 workers already unemployed, would have resulted in 212,000 unemployed workers, 22.4 percent of the total labor force.[56] The question, of course, is what would have been the social and political effects of such a scenario?

Aside from the persistence of high unemployment rates and massive emigration, the only sign of steady although slow employment growth were in the public sector and trade, as Figure 3.2 demonstrates. This could be interpreted as the tendency toward marginalization of a significant sector of the working classes displaced from agriculture but not reabsorbed into the formal economy. The displaced workers that did not migrate probably went into low-productivity service jobs and the informal or marginal economy. The rapid expansion of low-productivity service and trade activities is one of

Figure 3.2 Shares of Employment by Sector: 1948–1963

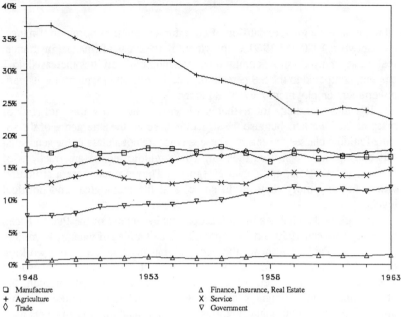

□ Manufacture   Δ Finance, Insurance, Real Estate
+ Agriculture   X Service
◊ Trade   V Government

Source: Departamento del Trabajo, "Series de empleo."

the classic signs of marginalization in peripheral capitalism. Many displaced workers take refuge in the "informal sector" (the low-productivity areas of trade and services) as street vendors, temporary domestic, or personal service workers. Between 1950 and 1960, the decade with the highest migration rate, employment in retail trade grew 7.3 percent, while total employment decreased by 8.8 percent. Likewise, nondomestic services employment jumped 23.9 percent. The area of domestic services, however, declined 42 percent, more than total employment.[57]

Although these figures tend to substantiate the argument on marginalization, they should not be construed as the key indicator of the marginalization trend in Puerto Rico during this period. The reality is that most of the displaced labor force in Puerto Rico at that time was literally "expelled" from the country through emigration. This pattern has no counterpart in any of the Latin American processes of industrialization. The colonial relation that allowed Puerto Ricans to enter freely into the United States thus provided an artificial source of stability to a structurally unbalanced economic strategy; migration became an escape valve for employment pressures.[58]

But the expansion of services does not respond only to the process of marginalization and the concomitant expansion of low-productivity activities. It also reflects the expansion of private and public services essential for industrial growth. In the case of Puerto Rico, the expansion of services has a great deal to do with the high degree of external orientation of production, which requires a great expansion of communication, transportation, finance, etc. Between 1950 and 1960, employment in the areas of finance, insurance, real estate, transportation, communication, and public utilities increased 45.1 percent, compared to the 8.8 percent decline in total employment; for its part, government employment grew 37.8 percent.[59]

It can be argued, then, that services are not only the "refuge" of marginalized workers but also the structural base for the emergence of the so-called middle classes or sectors. These sectors are not a class in the sense that this concept has been used thus far. These middle sectors are fractions of classes, social strata, and social categories. They do not share a structural unity, and any unity they might share is at the ideological and political levels.

A look at the changes in the occupational structure of the Puerto Rican economy between 1950 and 1960 provides a better idea of what these middle sectors are. Table 3.7 shows the occupational distribution of the working population according to the classifications of the 1950 and 1960 censuses. The sectors that increased the most were the craftsmen and foremen, the professionals and technicians, clerical workers, and service workers, in that order. If these occupational categories were translated into the concepts used here the craftsmen and foremen would be included in the labor aristocracy; the professionals and technicians as part of the category that has been called the technobureaucracy; and the clerical workers and service employees, as well as some professionals and technicians, as intermediary elements mainly linked to nonproductive activities. They would constitute, in an embryonic form, what Poulantzas calls the new petty bourgeoisie.[60]

So it can be argued that these so-called middle sectors are in fact elements of the new and traditional petty bourgeoisie that either emerged or found fresh forms of articulation within the new development strategy. They are small merchants and small farmers linked to expanding areas of the domestic market (like dairy products and poultry farms) and other small producers who survived or adapted to the new model. The new petty bourgeois elements were mainly linked to the expansion of services (especially services to industry) and the managerial and supervisory tasks that accompanied the process of industrial growth. The labor aristocracy was a fraction of the working class linked to the high-productivity sector of industry. The middle sectors diverged in their relation to the means of production, yet shared a privileged position (in terms of income and access to the market) within capitalist stratification characterized by relatively high income, relatively high consumption standards, stable employment, and an intermediary position between the dominant and the subordinated classes. Since the well-being of these middle sectors was a consequence of industrial expansion under the CI/EP strategy, these sectors became a key element of the social and political support for it. They provided an image of social mobility and progress that "hid" the reality of

Table 3.7 Shares of Employment by Occupations: 1950 and 1960 (percent)

Category	1950	1960	Change
Professionals and technicians	4.8	7.8	3.0
Managers, officials, proprietors	5.9	7.3	1.4
Sales workers	5.2	6.3	1.1
Clerical and kindred workers	4.9	7.8	2.9
Service workers	5.3	7.7	2.4
Domestic service	5.8	3.4	-2.4
Craftsmen and foremen	7.5	11.0	3.5
Operatives and kindred workers	16.4	18.0	1.6
Other laborers except farm	5.6	6.2	0.6
Farmers and farm managers	6.5	3.2	-3.3
Farm laborers and foremen	30.9	19.8	-11.1

Source: U.S. Bureau of the Census, *Census of Population, Puerto Rico, 1960*, Vol. I, Pt. 53, pp. 53–126, Table 52.

the displacement and impoverishment of large sectors of the working classes.

The adaptation of the local bourgeoisie to the expansion of U.S. capital took two directions. First, some of the local sugar bourgeoisie stepped up rum production and entered other activities, like real estate and finance. Some of those linked to rum production had been on the boards of directors of Fomento subsidiaries during the 1940s, and the promotion of Puerto Rican rum exports to the United States became a major activity of Fomento in the 1950s. Members of families linked to the sugar sector entered banking, such as the Roig family through the Roig Bank and the Bird family through Banco de San Juan. Others simply sold their lands for suburban development.[61]

Second, some of the local industrial bourgeoisie thrived on producing for the local market or subcontracting production for the U.S. market. As Table 3.3 showed, there was an increase in the share of the value of shipments of local enterprises to the United States in the areas of paper, manufacturing of electrical and nonelectrical machinery, and other miscellaneous manufactures. In 1958, twenty-four out of ninty-four subcontractors and autonomous manufacturers exporting to the U.S. market were local. Overall, the dividends received by local corporations quadrupled from $4.1 million to $16.3 million between 1948 and 1963. Even though this was a limited participation, it indicates that a fraction of the local industrial bourgeoisie was beginning to integrate itself successfully into the export-oriented manufacturing sector.[62]

The financial fraction of the local bourgeoisie also benefited from the process of industrial expansion. According to Werner Baer, this fraction expanded significantly during the 1950s by financing local economic activities. Furthermore, during this period the integration of Puerto Rican financial institutions into the U.S. federal government's regulatory mechanisms was intensified. In 1950, Puerto Rican banks came under the jurisdiction of the Federal Deposit Insurance Corporation, a federal agency that guaranteed bank deposits. In 1952, at the request of the local colonial government, a depot of the U.S. Treasury was established in Puerto Rico to facilitate the availability and handling of cash on the island. Finally, during the 1950s the Federal Reserve Bank of New York opened an account for Puerto Rican banks to facilitate check clearances and other transactions between Puerto Rican banks and their U.S. correspondents.[63]

The emerging urban industrial working class experienced a noticeable improvement in living standard throughout this period. The average real weekly salary in the manufacturing sector increased from $18 for men and $12 for women in 1952 to $44 and $37 in 1963. This was true also for all wage earners, whose real average weekly wages grew at an annual rate of 8.4 percent during this period.[64] The share of national income that went into salaries increased from 63.3 percent in 1948 to 68.8 percent in 1963. Personal consumption expenditures increased by 190 percent, from $620 million in 1948 to $1,796 million in 1963. Personal expenditures on recreation, education, and travel increased from $58 million in 1948 to $277 million in 1963, 378 percent.[65]

A key factor in improving the living standards of working-class families was the rapid integration of women into the labor force. During this period women entered the work force in significant numbers, especially in assembly manufacturing in apparel, food processing, and electronics, as well as in the services.[66] The average real weekly wages of women between 1952 and 1963 grew at an annual rate of 12 percent. Although women's wages were usually lower than men's, this high rate of growth reflects the fact that women were entering nonagricultural activities where wages were higher. The massive entrance of women into the paid labor force also brought about the increase in two-income working-class households, which was an important factor in the expansion of the middle sectors.

This, however, does not mean that the exploitation of the working class was disappearing or that the rate of exploitation was diminishing in any significant manner. Rather, it means that exploitation assumed new forms. According to a study of Edward N. Wolff, the rate of surplus value for the manufacturing sector in Puerto Rico remained the same over the 1948–1963 period. Thus, the increased consumption of the workers did not mean a decrease in the rate of exploitation. In Wolff's words, "increased consumption of labor absorbed the relative surplus value generated by increased labor productivity."[67]

It is true that workers' consumption increased and that their salaries improved, but, in reality, the share of the product of their labor (surplus value) returned to them as wages diminished. Table 3.8 shows the decreasing percentage of the workers' share (wages) of the product of their labor (value added) in the manufacturing industries between 1949 and 1963. Logically, this means an increase in the rates of exploitation, an increase in the share of surplus value appropriated by capital. Although the share of wages in net

Table 3.8 Wages of Production Workers in Manufacturing as Percentage of Value
Added: 1949-1963 (million dollars)

Year	Wages	Value Added	Wages as % of Value Added
1949	36	93	38.7
1954	59	188	31.3
1958	93	292	31.8
1963	179	621	28.8

Sources: U.S. Bureau of the Census, *Census of Manufactures, Puerto Rico*, 1949, 1954, 1958, 1963.

income increased, that figure excluded the share of income paid to foreign capital. When payments to foreign factors are included, the wage share of net income increased only slightly, from 62.7 percent in 1948 to 63.3 percent in 1963. Conversely, the share of net income paid to external factors grew from 1.1 percent of net income in 1948 to 8.7 percent in 1963.[68]

Clearly, the new economic strategy was producing a contradictory pattern of increased exploitation rates and increased income and living standards for the employed population due to increased productivity. The process of capitalist restructuring entailed a redefinition of the forms of exploitation from that based on the extraction of absolute surplus value, in primary production, to exploitation based on the appropriation of relative surplus value, in manufacturing. This change allowed the improvement of the immediate living conditions of the nondisplaced working class while increasing the rate of surplus value expropriated by the industrial sector. However, the viability of this economic model was based on the exclusion (the absolute impoverishment) of a large sector of the working population from the productive process.

To sum up, it could be said that the adoption of the CI/EP strategy had the following effects on the socioeconomic structure of Puerto Rico:

1. The restructuring of the accumulation process was completed. The axis of accumulation shifted from U.S. capital in agriculture to the small and medium fractions of U.S. capital in manufacturing.
2. The local bourgeoisie adapted to the new economic strategy.
3. The colonial relation was restructured, giving a greater role in running local affairs to the PPD technobureaucracy.
4. The emerging "middle sectors" became the basis of political support for the new political and economic arrangements.
5. A large sector of the working population was excluded from the productive process and expelled from the country through emigration. This diminished the political and economic pressures that might have threatened the viability of the new colonial arrangements.

6.   The immediate economic conditions of the nondisplaced working classes improved, providing further legitimacy to the emerging social order.

The New Developmentalist Discourse: Class Character and Contradictions

The economic model that resulted from the implementation of the CI/EP strategy was proclaimed a success by the technobureaucracy and the imperialist bourgeoisie. According to them, this model had succeeded in moving Puerto Rico in the direction of overcoming poverty and underdevelopment. The U.S. government made Puerto Rico its showcase. The island was presented to the colonial and underdeveloped world as a successful example of a "pacific revolution," living proof of the "virtues" and "benefits" of capitalist development in close cooperation with the imperialist metropolises under new forms of colonial and neocolonial arrangements. Earl Parker Hanson, a consultant to the Puerto Rico Department of State and one of those U.S. cadres involved in the propagandization of the "Puerto Rican model," described his endeavors in this respect in the following manner:

> My earlier book on Puerto Rico, *Transformation: The Story of Modern Puerto Rico*, published in 1955 by Simon and Schuster, told the story of a new society reshaping itself and rising from the anguish of former colonialism. Many such societies are found in the world today, and my intention was to present Puerto Rico as an example of principles and techniques that are important to the entire modern world.
>
> In 1958, after *Transformation* was out of print, Lord John Boyd-Orr wrote to me, urging that a new edition be published soon, as a rebuke and a prod to those many Europeans who seemed unable to shed their long-standing but outmoded imperialistic habits of thought. The United States Information Agency also read similar implications into the book and distributed copies all over the world.[69]

Operation Bootstrap and the commonwealth formula were thought of as "America's answer to Communism."

Puerto Rico became a training and resource center for "technical aid programs," such as the Point Four Program of President Truman, in which technicians and policymakers from "underdeveloped" countries came to the island to learn of this "new model." The 1954/55 annual report of Fomento said that "this activity is of great importance to strengthen the international prestige and relations of the Commonwealth, and to promote good will for the United States of America." Later on, under the Kennedy administration, the government of Puerto Rico also became directly involved in the Alliance for Progress, designed to counterbalance the political influence of the Cuban Revolution. Teodoro Moscoso, the creator of Operation Bootstrap, was appointed head of the alliance.[70]

However, behind the appearance of progress reflected in the nearly 7 percent annual rate of growth in real GDP and the 5 percent in real per-capita income during this period, there were a number of contradictions that were never publicly acknowledged. The high rate of unemployment, the massive migration of displaced workers, the persistence of poverty, the problems of capital formation and excessive vulnerability of the economy to international economic fluctuations, and changes in the interests of the metropolitan classes that controled the dynamic sector of the economy were never part of the picture presented to the world and the local subordinate classes.

The CI/EP development strategy was unable to combine economic growth with the creation of enough jobs to absorb the workers displaced from the agricultural sector and those entering the labor force. Worker displacement became a structural feature of the CI/EP model, resulting in unemployment, poverty, migration, crime, and other such social problems. This contradiction was rooted in the very logic of a capitalist model of accumulation led by the export-processing sector driven by productivity and profit maximization in the context of competition for the U.S. market. This resulted in a limited demand for local labor, which in turn led to the displacement of a mass of workers who became permanently redundant. In the case of peripheral capitalist societies, where the linkages of the dynamic sector are mainly with the productive centers in the core, this displaced sector becomes a marginalized mass of workers that is divided into an industrial reserve army for capital (in the periphery as well as in the metropolis as migrant labor), cheap labor supply for the low-productivity sectors, and a lumpenproletarianized mass permanently displaced from the labor market.[71] Thus, the contradiction between wage labor and capital was twofold in Puerto Rico: the impoverishment and displacement of a large sector of the working classes and the increased rate of exploitation.

A second contradiction was the vulnerability of the political and economic structure of the colony, i.e., the core/periphery contradiction. The economic dynamics of peripheral societies are determined by the needs of the international process of capitalist production and accumulation. The decisions that affect the direction and fate of economic development in the periphery are made by social and political actors in the core with limited input from and leverage of social forces in the peripheral society. A key issue here is the ability of core groups to appropriate a substantial share of the surplus value created in the periphery. The continued transfer of surplus from the periphery to the center without a counterbalancing movement of resources in the opposite way leads to problems of capital accumulation and economic expansion in the long term, unless a constant inflow of capital from the metropolitan center is maintained. In other words, what represents a gain for the peripheral economy in the early stages of the CI/EP strategy may end up as a loss, since foreign capital "takes out" more than it "puts in." This, in turn, creates a tension between the accumulation needs of foreign capital and the needs of the economic sectors not linked to the internationalized sector of the peripheral economy. In the case of Puerto Rico, where the colonial structure was barely altered by the commonwealth formula, this meant limited bargaining power for the local dominant sectors, the technobureaucracy, and the local bourgeoisie vis-à-vis U.S. capital over the direction of the development process. The colonial government could not choose to erect tariff barriers or foreign exchange restrictions to protect local industries, or to impose conditions to foster domestic capital accumulation at the expense of U.S. capital. This vulnerability proved inimical to the CI/EP strategy when, toward the end of the 1950s, the local government confronted its impotence vis-à-vis the federal government to adopt measures to counter wage and transportation cost increases that threatened the continued growth of the colonial economy.

In the early stage of the CI/EP strategy these contradictions were not acute and were easily reconciled in the developmentalist rhetoric of the PPD:

> In view of the limitations imposed by nature on the extension of our land, and in view of the needs of our growing population, it was logical to gear our greater efforts to the employment of the surplus labor from agriculture in industrial production. With the coming to power of the Partido Popular Democrático, effective action was taken on the need for industrialization and it became an effective reality.
>
> The success of the factories and industrial enterprises that have been established lately on the island by private and government initiative are living testimony of the fruitful prospect offered by industrialization to the creative effort of our people if we keep open the line of access to external markets. The free entrance of our products to the great U.S. market, the facilities that exist there to obtain machinery and raw materials and the willingness of Puerto Rican and U.S. capital to invest heavily here [in Puerto Rico] under the recently approved tax exemption law, are essential factors for the industrial development of Puerto Rico.[72]

The direction for the PPD development strategy is presented as imposed by natural and demographic limitations; the adoption of the CI/EP strategy is presented as a function of social and natural necessities rather than of political decisions. Likewise, the colonial relation is now presented as an "essential factor" in industrial development, and the incentives and tax exemptions to private capital are given as an economic imperative to encourage "Puerto Rican and U.S. capital willing to collaborate in this great effort to increase our [Puerto Rico's] production."[73]

Here, we see a shift in the developmentalist discourse of the PPD— before, U.S. capital was "evil absentee capital"; now it is a collaborator in the development enterprise. The interests of the reconstituted power bloc (the small and medium fractions of U.S. capital, the local technobureaucracy, and fractions of the local bourgeoisie) are presented as being in the interest of all of society, as the requisite or necessary conditions for economic progress. The "logic" of the economic policy of the dominant classes is transformed into common sense. If the land is limited and the population is too large, agriculture is insufficient. Therefore, industry must be developed and, since this requires large sums, the help of U.S. capital is needed because without it industrial development would be impossible. In this logic, capital is willing to collaborate and the colonial relation is the key to getting capital for production and a large market for selling the products.

Rhetorically, this syllogism appears impeccable, yet the important thing is to understand how it was articulated at the level of praxis. That is, how the logic of the dominant classes acquired the character of a social truth for all of society, and how the economic policy that articulated the CI/EP strategy made viable the realization of the interests of the dominant classes by legitimizing them not only in the "verbal consciousness" but also in the practical or "implicit consciousness" of the subordinate classes.

It is relatively easy to understand why the beneficiaries of the CI/EP strategy adopted developmentalism as their ideology. For the technobureaucracy and the middle sectors, progress, development, mobility, modernization, and other similar categories of the developmentalist ideology were not merely abstract concepts but concrete ingredients of their quotidian life—a better salary, a new house, a washing machine, etc., were living testimony of progress and modernization. These groups, who constituted the political and social leadership of the country, were the principal bearers of developmentalism. Teachers, journalists, and technicians became the organic intellectuals of the PPD's developmentalism. For them, at the level of praxis, it was "true" that the CI/EP strategy meant progress. The industrial development fostered by U.S. investment meant the realization of their interests and aspirations.

For the local and metropolitan industrialists, developmentalism provided a "transcendental" meaning, a sense of mission to profit-making. Developmentalism represented private capital as a progressive force, as a friend of progress. The odious portrait of the sugar barons of the past (both local and foreign) was now replaced by the picture of "friendly" industrial investors. Developmentalism provided the substance for the basis of the hegemony of the imperialist bourgeoisie. It was the very terrain for the forging of a social consensus that permitted the restructuring of imperialist capitalism in Puerto Rico by preserving the strategic basis for capitalist accumulation.

Yet the question remains how developmentalism condensed the contradictions between wage labor and capital and created a social and political equilibrium that involved the consent of those whom it exploited. It is important here to analyze two key components of the PPD's economic policy: emigration and the continued increase in government services and in the wages of workers.

One of the unprecedented elements of the emigration policy in Puerto Rico was its deliberate character. Beginning with the Chardón Plan in 1934, migration appears as a desirable policy to deal with the problems of poverty and overpopulation.[74] By 1945, the PPD's ideologues formulated a theoretical justification that served as the premise for encouraging migration. According to a report written by one of the members of the PPD's brain trust:

> Every country has something to export. If some have petroleum, others nitrate and others sugar, we [Puerto Rico] are the only country in America that besides sugar, has an incalculable wealth that should be exported and should be used for the benefit of all. We have men, intelligence and working hands.[75]

The PPD established the Employment and Migration Bureau to stimulate and organize migration. The creation of the bureau was mentioned in their 1948 program as one of the measures of social justice implemented by them and as part of the "admirable set of laws passed to protect the worker's rights as a man, a citizen, a worker and creator of wealth."[76] Despite the PPD's claims that its official policy on migration was one of neutrality, in practice the PPD not only stimulated but actually organized the migration of Puerto Rican workers to the United States.

A corollary of the emigration policy was the adoption of population control measures. The promotion of women's migration was an important goal within this policy. The PPD bureaucrats reasoned that "exporting" women to the United States not only would reduce the unemployed population but its potential growth. The PPD government created an experimental program to train low-skilled Puerto Rican women in domestic service to be placed in jobs in the United States. For the women workers who stayed on the island, Fomento-promoted plants provided family planning education as part of their health services. All methods of birth control, especially sterilization, were encouraged.[77]

The migration policy achieved two things at the same time. On the one hand, it was presented as helpful to the workers who were allegedly being displaced by the rapid growth of the population, thus turning attention away from the process of their impoverishment. On the other hand, the emigration policy made the colonial relation appear as beneficial to Puerto Rican workers. Since, as colonials, Puerto Ricans were U.S. citizens, they could enter the United States without restriction. The PPD presented this as a "benefit" that gave Puerto Ricans the chance to look for a better living within the "great American Union" of which they were part.[78]

In reality, the Puerto Rican migrants were employed in the lowest paid jobs and suffered from racial discrimination. However, in immediate terms, the income of the migrants was on the average higher than that of the workers in Puerto Rico. Also, they were able to find jobs in the metropolis, while their chances of employment in Puerto Rico were virtually none. In 1959, the median family income for Puerto Ricans in the United States was $3,811 per year, which was 46 percent more than the average income of Puerto Ricans on the island ($2,603).[79] Although the median family income of Puerto Rican migrants was only two thirds that of white U.S. families, the immediate economic condition of the migrant had most certainly improved in comparison to his previous condition and his immediate point of reference, Puerto Rico.

The second element of the PPD's economic policy that attempted to reconcile the contradiction between wage labor and capital was the increase in government services for the workers, which represented an indirect increase in worker's income, together with the increase in real wages. Following the pattern of the 1940s, by 1962/63 the most important areas of government expenditures were education ($73.1 million, 25.5 percent of all expenditures) and health and public welfare ($49.1 million, 17 percent of all expenditures). In other words, the government dedicated 42.5 percent of its total expenditures in 1962/63 to public services for individuals.[80] Clearly, increased rates of productivity and the reproduction needs of industrial capitalism permitted and necessitated a better development of human resources.

The developmentalist rhetoric of the PPD was based on this immediate "appearance" of improvement (i.e., increased monetary income). The fragmentary character of social relations in quotidian life prevents workers from realizing that they produce more wealth yet receive a declining proportion of it. Their immediate perception is limited to the fact that they have a larger salary and consume more. The social relations that the workers establish "confirm" this perception, making the developmentalist notions of progress, mobility, etc., appear true. So it is the form in which the structure "presents" itself that provides the strength of a material force to the developmentalist discourse. It is the way in which reality appears in fragmentary praxis that makes it possible to present migration policy as a measure of social justice or capitalist industrialization as the project of the "people."[81] It is in the fragmentary praxis of quotidian life that the categories of the ruling classes are generalized and "accepted" (albeit in a contradictory and conflictive manner) by the subordinate classes, where the working classes are "inscribed" in the categories of the dominant ideology (i.e., developmentalism).

At the politicoideological level the core/periphery contradiction was solved through the creation of the commonwealth. The question is, how did this become acceptable to the majority of the Puerto Ricans? That is, how did Puerto Rico become a colony by consent? Better yet, why did the Puerto Rican bourgeoisie or the technobureaucracy not articulate an irreconcilable contradiction with the imperialist bourgeoisie, as happened in many countries of the periphery after World War II?

As a social category, the PPD technobureaucracy was not interested in disputing control over the means of production. On the contrary, it was interested in maintaining the necessary political conditions for the reproduction of a system in which it occupied a position of power. For its part, the local bourgeoisie was too weak to dispute the hegemony of the imperialist bourgeoisie, and fractions of it benefited from the CI/EP strategy and the colonial relation. In this sense, the colonial situation was presented by the PPD not as a contradiction but as a beneficial and necessary ingredient of economic development. Even when this contradiction surfaced, the solution of the technobureaucracy and the local bourgeoisie would move in the direction of restructuring the colonial relation. If, as the PPD argued, U.S. capital and the U.S. market were indispensable for the development of Puerto Rico, independence would only harm the chances of development. For the PPD technocrats, the costs of altering the colonial relation were greater than its benefits. Their only solution was to try to renegotiate the colonial pact.

The fractions of the local bourgeoisie that did not support the PPD supported the Partido Estadista Republicano (PER). While the PER was still dominated by remnants of the old sugar bourgeoisie, it also included an important fraction of the local bourgeoisie represented by Luis A. Ferré, vice president of the party and the major Puerto Rican industrialist. Yet the PER program in the 1950s and early 1960s did not intend to go beyond the colonial relation. The annexation of Puerto Rico as a state would not mean the end of U.S. hegemony in Puerto Rico; the annexationist bourgeoisie wanted "equality" vis-à-vis U.S. capital, not the demise of imperialist capitalism.[82]

For the working classes, aside from their immediate material gains, their involvement in World War II and the Korean War was probably the most intense experience in their ideological praxis. The Puerto Rican workers, as U.S. citizens, went to fight first against fascism and then communism. They participated in the war on the side of "democracy" and "freedom" as U.S. soldiers and participated in and "enjoyed" victory insofar as they were "Americans." For those who remained on the island, the ideological unity fostered by the German and the communist "threats" in the 1940s and 1950s became an important link with the United States. U.S. troops on the island were there now to defend the "people" against foreign enemies. The image of the "Yankee imperialist," embodied by the colonial officials, the sugar mill managers, and the English teachers, was replaced by the "benevolent" Governor Tugwell or a trench partner in the battlefield. Even though this new image was not necessarily devoid of conflicts, it certainly was different. Moreover, this new image was not derived from an advertising campaign; it came from the concrete experiences of daily life, which in turn were reinforced by war propaganda.[83]

There are, of course, other elements that contributed to defusing the metropolis/colony contradiction. One of these was the political concessions made by the metropolis to the technobureaucracy in Law 600. There also was the inadequacy of the PIP in presenting the proindependence project as the project of the "people," something that the PPD had clearly achieved.

The emergence of developmentalism as the dominant ideology in the 1940s and 1950s successfully completed the formation of a new historic bloc; that is, it made possible the restructuring of colonial domination in such a way as to reestablish the correspondence (not the identity) between the economic structure of imperialist capitalism and the ideological and legal-political superstructure. Developmentalism paved the way to colonialism by consent.

The PPD leadership succeeded in developing a discourse that presented the CI/EP development strategy as the only alternative that "made sense." It also succeeded in inscribing the working classes in the categories of the dominant ideology. The changes in the developmentalist rhetoric did not represent a rupture in its logic. The classless, nonantagonistic character of economic development remained the underlying and unifying premise of this ideology. The rest were rhetorical changes that expressed the new correspondence between the praxis of imperialist capitalism and the PPD's discourse. The lived relations of people were explained "adequately" by the new developmentalist discourse. The subordinate classes supported the PPD because the immediate progress and economic improvement that took place was perceived as potentially unlimited in quotidian praxis.

Although the PPD leadership could not bring progress for all, their interests as a social category and their keenness in understanding emerging trends in the international division of labor led them to create a new development model. Their understanding that the Puerto Rican economy was an open economy in regard to the United States and that they could do nothing to change that, short of a break in the colonial relation, coupled with an effective reading of the expansionist interests of U.S. industrial capital after WW II, enabled them to chart a strategy for capitalist growth within the colonial constraints. Moreover, they were shrewd enough to use the very colonial relation to "dispose" of the "excess" labor created by peripheral capitalist development. In the process, they created a model of export-led industrialization that would be propagated by the U.S. government as a blueprint of development for peripheral countries.

Notes

1. Bayrón Toro, *Elecciones y partidos*, pp. 202–205.
2. Anderson, *Party Politics*, pp. 56–59, 100–103; Tugwell, *The Stricken Land*, pp. 664–666; Silén, *Historia de la nación*, pp. 252–253; Wolf, "San José," p. 247.

3. Sáez Corales, "CGT, informe," pp. 118–124. This report was to the Third Congress in 1945.

4. Mattos Cintrón, *La política y lo político*, pp. 113, 122, 199–203, and notes 143–145 and 155–158. See also Silén, *Historia de la nación*, pp. 263–265; and Silén, *Apuntes*, pp. 105–118.

5. Fromm, *César Andreu Iglesias*, pp. 25–26; NACLA, "U.S. Unions in Puerto Rico," pp. 7–14; and García and Quintero Rivera, *Desafío y solidaridad*, Chap. 6.

6. The question of just how many proindependence supporters were within the PPD leadership and how honest they were about it needs further research. The evidence suggests that there was a large element within PPD that paid lip service to the independence cause when it was convenient but who, in practice, were not for independence. See Silén, *Historia de la nación*, pp. 271–272; Anderson, *Party Politics*, pp. 102–103.

7. Partido Independentista Puertorriqueño, "Programa del Partido."

8. Editorial Edil, *Leyes Fundamentales*, pp. 195–199; and Fernós Isern, *Estado Libre Asociado*, pp. 69–80.

9. Piñero, *Mensaje*, pp. 4–5.

10. Muñoz Marín, *Discurso Inaugural* (1949), p. 7.

11. Bayrón Toro, *Elecciones y partidos*, pp. 210–213; Anderson, *Party Politics*, pp. 43–44.

12. Silén, *Historia de la nación*, pp. 285–289; Maldonado Denis, *Puerto Rico*, pp. 190–191, 195–197.

13. The Committee on Civil Liberties formed by the governor in 1958 revealed that immediately after the Nationalist uprising the internal security division of the Puerto Rican police had prepared a list of 4,257 followers and sympathizers of the PN. In 1958, there were up-to-date reports on each of these individuals except for 215 that were pending investigation. (This practice continues today.) Anderson, *Party Politics*, p. 46; Maldonado Denis, *Puerto Rico*, pp. 193–198; and Silén, *Historia de la nación*, pp. 284–289, 308–313.

14. Carr, *A Colonial Experiment*, pp. 76–81; Fernós Isern, *El Estado Libre Asociado*, pp. 99–197.

15. Fernós Isern, *El Estado Libre Asociado*, p. 101.

16. Muñoz Marín, *Mensaje* (1951), p. 8.

17. Fernós Isern, *El Estado Libre Asociado*, pp. 135–136, 168.

18. Emerson, "Puerto Rico and American Policy," p. 10.

19. The idea that the main achievement of the PPD was the forging of a new historic bloc that allowed the continuation and deepening of capitalist imperialism in Puerto Rico was first put forward by Mattos Cintrón, *La política y lo político*, Chap. 6.

20. The last attempt of the authority to apply the law to violators was prevented by an injunction of the U.S. Federal Court against the authority, which prevented action against Luce and Company, a subsidiary of the U.S.-owned Central Aguirre Associates. The authority did not contest the injunction. Mathews, "Agrarian Reform," pp. 117–118; and Edel, "Land Reform," 2, p. 40.

21. Wells, *Modernization*, p. 148.

22. The 1948 PPD program does not even mention the Land Authority or agrarian reform on the section on agriculture. PPD, *Compilación*, pp. 29–30.

23. Before 1947, tax exemption laws had been passed in 1919, 1925, 1930, and 1936, with no visible effects. Santiago Meléndez, *Reforma Fiscal*, p. 64.

24. Ross, *The Long Uphill Path*, pp. 84–95. For an example of the publicity campaign, see the pamphlet, "Industrial Opportunities in Puerto Rico U.S.A." published by the Puerto Rico Development Company (Fomento) between 1946 and 1947. The pamphlet was addressed to "any American businessman seeking a site for a plant or branch on U.S. soil."

25. Law 346, Section 3, in Puerto Rico, *Leyes* (1947), p. 656.

26. O'Connor, *Puerto Rico's Potential*.

27. Puerto Rico, *Leyes* (1948), pp. 482–515.

28. Ross, *The Long Uphill Path*, pp.126–128; Puerto Rico, Compañía de Fomento Industrial de Puerto Rico (CFIPR), *Informe anual, 1950/51*; and Puerto Rico, Administración de Fomento Económico de Puerto Rico (AFE), *Informe anual, 1951/52*. Hereafter, AFE. Fomento's name was changed three times between 1942 and 1950. It was called the Compañía de Fomento de Puerto Rico (CFPR) from 1942 to 1945; the Compañía de Fomento Industrial de Puerto Rico (CFIPR) from 1946 to 1950; and in 1950 it became the Administración de Fomento Económico de Puerto Rico (AFE).

29. Ross, *The Long Uphill Path*, pp. 107–123.

30. Puerto Rico, *Leyes* (1954), pp. 13–57.

31. See AFE, *Informe anual, 1953/54*, pp. iii–iv.

32. See the sections on "Relaciones Públicas" and "Promoción" in AFE, *Informe Anual*, 1950/51 to 1960/61; and Ross, *The Long Uphill Path*, pp. 88–95.

33. AFE, *Informe anual, 1952/53*, p. 97; and Ross, *The Long Uphill Path*, pp. 143–147.

34. Puerto Rico Economic Development Administration, *Locally and Nonlocally*, pp. 139, 143–144. Hereafter, PREDA.

35. Allusions to these themes appear constantly in the official addresses and reports of the PPD government. For the specific context of the phrases quoted here see Muñoz Marín, *Mensaje* (1949 and 1950); and *Discurso inaugural* (1949).

36. The specific character of the changes in the patterns of foreign investment in peripheral countries after WW II depended on the level of development of the productive forces where the investment was made. Thus, for example, foreign investment in Argentina in the postwar period was centered in capital goods industries; in Puerto Rico, in light industries, since there was virtually no infrastructure basis for the efficient development of heavy industries; and in Central America, in agricultural production. The pattern of investment was uneven and varied according to the level of structural development in peripheral countries and the role each country was assigned in the international division of labor. See Peralta Rámos, *Etapas*; and Furtado, *La economía*.

37. PREDA, *Annual Statistical, 1964/65*, pp. 60–61. The definition of the term "local" varies among government agencies. Fomento defines as local industries those where 50 percent or more of its shareholders have been residents of Puerto Rico for at least ten years. The Puerto Rico Planning Board and the U.S. Bureau of the Census define them as those where 50 percent or more of its shareholders have lived in Puerto Rico for at least one year. The figures in Tables 3.1 and 3.2 use the latter definition. See, PREDA, *Locally and Nonlocally*, p. 11.

38. Curet Cuevas, *El desarrollo económico*, pp. 281–282.

39. Calculated from Puerto Rico, Junta de Planificación, *Balanza de pagos, 1942–1961*, pp. 51–52.

40. Junta de Planificación, *Balanza de pagos, 1978*, pp. 63–66.

41. U.S. Bureau of the Census, *Census of Manufactures; 1954*, p. 56.

42. Planning Board, *Economic Report*, p. A-28. In 1954, 69 percent of all consumer goods bought in Puerto Rico were imported (81 percent of all durables and 65 percent of all nondurables). By 1960, 63 percent of all consumer goods bought on the island were imported (72 percent of durables and 61 percent of nondurables). Despite this relative improvement, after almost two decades of industrialization a large share of domestic consumption was still satisfied by imports. See also PREDA, *Locally and Nonlocally*, p. 23.

43. The import coefficients in some of the most industrialized countries of Latin America for 1957 were Argentina, 5.9 percent; Brazil, 6.1 percent; Mexico, 8.2 percent; and Colombia, 8.9 percent. Furtado, *La economía*, p. 110.

44. Planning Board, *Economic Report*, p. A-2.

45. Calculated from sources in Table 3.3.

46. PREDA, *Annual Statistical*, Section II, table 23-b; and AFE, *Apéndice económico, 1965*, Table 6.

47. AFE, *Informe anual, 1952/53*, p. 17.

48. AFE, *Informe anual, 1954/55*, p. 4.

49. AFE, *Informe anual, 1958/59*, p. 13.

50. AFE, *Informe anual, 1956/57*, pp. 11–12; this report mentions eleven industrial plants that were subsidiaries of large U.S. corporations, which were only a minor proportion of industrial establishments.

51. Calculated from Pizer and Cutler, "U.S. Foreign Investments," p. 22.

52. Ibid.

53. See Castells, *La cuestión urbana*, pp. 51–78.

54. See Maldonado Denis, *Emigration Dialectic*, Chap. 1.

55. Friedlander, *Labor Migration*, p. 98; Centro de Estudios Puertorriqueños, *Labor Migration Under Capitalism*, p. 150.

56. Friedlander, *Labor Migration*, pp. 90–95.

57. Planning Board, *Economic Report*, p. A-22.

58. The concept of marginalization should not be taken to imply that this group is simply excess population in a "crowded" country. On the contrary, they are potentially productive workers displaced by the dynamics of peripheral capitalist development. This mass of displaced workers, in time, is split into different fractions. One fraction becomes an industrial reserve army for metropolitan capital, entering the process of internationalization of the labor market as migrant labor. Another fraction becomes an industrial reserve army for the domestic industry. And yet another becomes a permanently marginalized sector that generates subsistence economic activity, which does not affect the levels of production and productivity of the dynamic sector. This is basically a residual economy based on simple commodity production and residual market activities. Penny vendors, family production, etc., are typical activities of this marginalized sector. Aníbal Quijano calls this sector the marginalized pole of the economy and this labor force, the marginalized labor force. The sociological and political implications of this phenomenon are too complex to be disposed of by thinking of it merely in terms of an industrial reserve army. See Quijano, "The Marginalized Pole of the Economy"; Nún, "Superpoblación relativa"; Cardoso, "Comentario."

59. Planning Board, *Economic Report*, p. A-22.

60. Poulantzas, *Classes in Contemporary Capitalism*, Pt. 3.

61. See Cochran, *Puerto Rican Businessman*, pp. 38, 105. On the rum industry see Fomento's annual reports between 1943 and 1960.

62. Junta de Planificación, *Informe económico, 1967*, p. A-25; Baer, *The Puerto Rican Economy*, p. 91.

63. Baer, *The Puerto Rican Economy*, pp. 62–73.

64. Puerto Rico, Departamento del Trabajo y Recursos Humanos, "Series de salario." Hereafter, Departamento del Trabajo.

65. Junta de Planificación, *Informe económico, 1967*, pp. A-5, A-8.

66. Acevedo, "Industrialization and Employment," pp. 234–240.

67. Wolff, "Capitalist Development," pp. 144, 147–148.

68. Junta de Planificación, *Informe económico, 1967*, p. A-5.

69. Hanson reports that his book had been translated into Spanish, Arabic, Burmese, and Hindi. Hanson, *Puerto Rico Land of Wonders*, pp. vi–vii. Another instance of such propagandistic efforts was the translation into Chinese of William H. Stead's book referred to in the introduction.

70. See AFE, *Informe anual, 1954/55*, p. 78; Planning Board, *The Point Four Program* and *Puerto Rico: Training Ground*; Hanson, *Puerto Rico Ally for Progress*; and Muñoz Marín, *Mensaje* (1962), p. 7.

71. See note 58.

72. PPD, *Compilación*, pp. 27–28.

73. Ibid., pp. 28–29.

74. Chardón Report, pp. 4, 6–7.

75. Salvador Tió, "Informe al Señor Rector de la Universidad de Puerto Rico" (1945), as quoted in Nieves Falcón, *El emigrante puertorriqueño*, p. 13.

76. PPD, *Compilación*, pp. 30–31. The 1950/51 Fomento annual report prominently displayed a photograph of three large airplanes being boarded by hundreds of men, with the following caption: "The Department of Industrial Services cooperated closely with the Department of Labor in sending Puerto Rican workers to the farms on the Continent." AFE, *Informe anual, 1950/51*.

77. Ramírez de Arellano and Seipp, *Colonialism, Catholicism, & Contraception*, pp. 76–77, 143.

78. Muñoz Marín, *Mensaje* (1951), p. 6.

79. Wagenheim, *A Survey of Puerto Ricans*, p. 96; Junta de Planificación, *Ingreso y producto, 1978*, p. 9.

80. Junta de Planificación, *Anuario estadístico, 1964*, p. 158.

81. See Muñoz Marín, *Mensaje* (1949), p. 7.

82. Meléndez, *Statehood Movement*, pp. 87–93.

83. There are no studies of the sociological impact of Puerto Rican involvement in these wars. It would be interesting to study the perception of the war expressed in the popular culture of the time (e.g., songs, poems, and other popular expressions). The musical, *La verdadera historia de Pedro Navaja*, provides some fascinating insights into the ideological impact of the wars on Puerto Ricans.

4

Transnational Capital: The Second Stage of the Capital-Importation/ Export-Processing Strategy

One common misconception is that Operation Bootstrap represents an undifferentiated model of export-led industrial development dominated by U.S. capital. Although the key features of the CI/EP model are essentially the same, as a development strategy it implies changing arrangements among the sociopolitical forces behind it; that is, it implies shifting arrangements in the mode of accumulation. The continuation of the CI/EP strategy thus entails changes in the political and social conditions that allow the expanded reproduction of capital (i.e., the continued production and appropriation of surplus value). In this sense, this strategy is a dynamic one, constantly changing through contradictions. Peripheral capitalist development does not imply a fixed relation between the core and the periphery but a constantly changing and dynamic one.

The Politicoeconomic Basis for the Deepening of the CI/EP Strategy

The implementation of the CI/EP strategy was accompanied by a series of political and economic developments that affected negatively the advantages that had attracted U.S. capital to Puerto Rico. According to Fomento's 1958/59 annual report, a number of conditions conspired against the "favorable" industrial climate in Puerto Rico at that time:

1. Rapid increases in minimum wages due to the imposition of higher minimum wage standards by the federal government.
2. Drastic increases in the shipping rates of the U.S. merchant marine, which affected all trade between Puerto Rico and the United States.
3. Problems with the communications system.
4. The undermining of the tax exemption incentive because of the propaganda in favor of statehood for Puerto Rico.

5. The introduction of gang-style violence in the labor movement.
6. The restrictions imposed on oil imports by the U.S. president.
7. The lack of a stock exchange as a means of providing capital funds for investments.
8. The termination of the tax exemption period for many U.S. industries established in the early 1950s and the threat that these industries would close down operations.
9. An investment lag due to the 1958 recession in the United States.[1]

The bases of the CI/EP strategy (cheap labor, low level of unionization, tax exemption, easy access to the U.S. market) were being threatened. To make matters worse, the colonial condition itself restricted what the PPD government could do to solve some of the problems (e.g., the rise in federal minimum wage levels and shipping rates).

Fixing minimum wage levels in Puerto Rico came under the jurisdiction of federal government agencies after the enactment in 1938 of the Fair Labor Standards Act. At first, the application of this part of the New Deal program was welcomed by the PPD as a measure of social justice. Its immediate effect improved the wages of the workers and forced the disappearance of industries, such as home needlework, that paid wages below subsistence levels. In the short run, federal legislation did much to weld popular support for the PPD; in the long run, it became a limitation for the CI/EP strategy.

The U.S. government, and Congress in particular, argued that the minimum wage legislation aimed to improve the standard of living of the Puerto Rican workers. But behind these noble declarations pressures were being brought to bear on Congress by the U.S. trade union movement and sectors of U.S. industry. The trade unions argued that low wages in Puerto Rico were stimulating "runaway shops," particularly in the textile industries, creating unemployment and weakening the bargaining power of the unions in an already weakly unionized sector. The sectors of the North American bourgeoisie that had no investments in Puerto Rico complained that the Puerto Rican producers enjoyed privileges that they did not have and, therefore, presented them with unfair competition. Sensitive to the pressures of their constituents, the U.S. Congress used minimum wage legislation as a means to limit Puerto Rico's competitive advantage.[2]

This did not mean that Congress wanted to eliminate this advantage altogether. On the one hand, the politicostrategic and economic interests of the United States made it necessary to stimulate industrial development in the colony to maintain its stability. On the other hand, the development of Puerto Rico's economy at the expense of other regions and economic interests in the United States had to be avoided. Hence, the application to Puerto Rico of the minimum wage regulations was selective and maintained a wage differential between Puerto Rico and the United States. Between 1950 and 1960, average wages increased in Puerto Rico from 42 to 94 cents, and the average wage in the United States increased from $1.50 to $2.30. The average wage in Puerto Rico in 1960 increased to 41 percent of that of the United States from 28 percent in 1950; yet the absolute wage differential increased from $1.08 in 1950 to $1.36 in 1960.[3]

This intervention by the federal government was partially effective in restraining the proliferation of "runaway shops," but it also undermined the immediate economic interest of the small and medium fractions of the imperialist bourgeoisie investing in Puerto Rico. Two North American economists have argued that this was one of the major causes for the reorientation of the industrial incentives policy to favor the attraction of capital-intensive industries.[4] In any case, the colonial state lacked the power to do anything about wage policy, except plead with the U.S. Congress.

In 1901, Puerto Rico was incorporated into the U.S. tariff system and U.S. shipping laws were applied to the island. Among other things, these laws stipulated that merchandise sent between the United States and Puerto Rico had to be carried exclusively on U.S. ships. In 1957, under the protection of federal laws and regulations, the U.S. companies operating in Puerto Rico declared a rate increase of 28.8 percent. The colonial government could do nothing to prevent or change this. The only government body that had the power to approve or deny this increase was the Federal Maritime Commission.[5]

The other issues that worried Fomento are also illustrative of the fragility of the basis of the CI/EP strategy and the incapacity of the colonial government to do anything to remedy it. In 1959, President Eisenhower issued Presidential Proclamation 3279, which imposed limitations on oil imports from foreign countries. This restriction had negative implications for the recently established oil industry in Puerto Rico and threatened to halt its expansion. Proclamation 3279 was at odds with Fomento plans to develop a petrochemical complex on the island, plans that had been in preparation since the mid-1950s.[6]

Two other pillars of the CI/EP strategy called into question were industrial peace between labor and capital and the effectiveness of tax exemptions. By the end of the 1950s, competition among U.S. trade unions for membership in Puerto Rico had brought about a proliferation of gang-style violence in union elections and bargaining processes. The industrial peace forged by the division of the CGT and the U.S. labor unions was coming to an end. Fomento attributed the failure in the promotion of various enterprises to these violent incidents.[7] Fomento was also worried that with the termination of the tax exemption period for many companies due around 1960 and the expiration of Law 6 in 1963, many foreign companies would close down and take home their accumulated profits. They were so concerned with this possibility that a company was hired to conduct a study on the plans of sixty companies whose exemptions were about to expire. Although the study revealed that the majority of the companies intended to stay, the uncertainty remained.[8]

A series of other problems also questioned the continued viability of CI/EP strategy and worried the PPD leadership in 1960: "technological unemployment" (i.e., unemployment created by new technology); rapid urban growth and its corollaries (crime, housing shortages); the decline of agriculture; the high degree of economic concentration and the low degree of Puerto Rican capital participation in the process of industrialization; the materialist and consumerist attitude of society; and the mixing of religion and politics. The PPD was beginning to realize that the new contradictions generated by their economic strategy could have a negative political impact.[9]

These worries were not unfounded. The pro-statehood forces gained strength after the reorganization of the PR as the Partido Estadista Republicano (PER) in 1952. The PER got only 12.9 percent of the vote in the 1952 election, but in 1956 its share soared to 26.7 percent and grew to 31.9 percent in 1960. For its part, the PPD had obtained 64.9 percent of the vote in the 1952 election, 66.9 percent in 1956, and 57.9 percent in 1960.[10]

The PPD leadership was concerned also with the emergence of a political party backed by the Catholic Church, the Partido Acción Cristiana (PAC), which directed its campaign in 1960 mainly against the PPD. It had the public support of the Archbishop of San Juan and the Bishop of the Diocese of Ponce (both of them North Americans). The PAC got 6.6 percent of the vote in the 1960 election, which accounted in part for the reduction in the PPD vote. However, the PAC did not develop into a major political force and disappeared after the 1964 election.[11]

The PER and the PAC were highly critical of the shortcomings of the CI/EP strategy. The problems of poverty and unemployment were loudly denounced by the opposition. The PER, moreover, was expressing the discontent of a fraction of the industrial bourgeoisie, complaining about the privileges that the PPD granted to foreign capital. The PER was also demanding minimum wages for foreign industries, trying to voice the demand of the working classes.[12]

An additional element in this political juncture that worried the PPD was the impact that the Cuban revolution and the worldwide decolonization process might have on the colonial question in Puerto Rico. Though the electoral base of the PIP decreased sharply between 1952 and 1960, the colonial question was always a source of concern for the PPD. Moreover, in 1956 and 1959 two proindependence groups were created, the Federación de Universitarios Pro Independencia (FUPI) and the Movimiento Pro Independencia (MPI). These groups revived the militancy of the PN and attempted to bring the attention of the international community to the colonial situation of Puerto Rico. Although the proindependence movement did not represent an immediate threat to the PPD or U.S. hegemony in Puerto Rico, the possibility of bringing the Puerto Rican colonial case to the attention of international political bodies was a source of concern.[13]

Aware of the politicoeconomic limitations of their development strategy, the PPD leadership attempted to reform the colonial relation. The PPD-dominated Puerto Rican legislature passed and sent to the U.S. Congress Joint Resolution 2 of 19 March 1959 proposing a number of changes to Law 600. Among other things, the resolution proposed the exemption to Puerto Rico from the applicability of some federal laws; the possibility of Puerto Rico entering into commercial treaties of its own, subject to approval by the U.S. president; and more autonomy on certain judicial and tax matters. This proposal was presented to the U.S. Congress as the Fernos-Murray Bill (the names of the Puerto Rican resident commissioner and the U.S. senator who drafted the Senate version of the bill). Consideration of the bill was continually postponed and Congress never took any action on it.[14]

After failing in their attempt to overcome the constraints of the colonial framework by renegotiating the colonial pact, two factions emerged within the PPD with different views on the solutions to the problems of the CI/EP strategy. On the one hand, the upper echelon of the PPD leadership favored continued negotiations with the U.S. Congress and applying pressure to exact some concessions. The idea put forward by Muñoz was to hold a plebiscite in which Puerto Ricans would decide whether they wanted independence, statehood, or commonwealth, and then use the plebiscite to get Congress to agree to grant reforms to the commonwealth. On the other hand, there was an embryonic faction led by a group of young technocrats who were encouraged by a member of the PPD's hierarchy, Roberto Sánchez Vilella (who was the right arm of Muñoz and the secretary of state of the commonwealth). They advocated a return to the reformist style of the 1940s. According to this line of thought, negotiations should be pursued while at the same time the powers of the colonial state should be used to pursue an alternative strategy. In the view of this group, the PPD should turn away from the unconditionalist attitude it had assumed in regard to U.S. capital and get back on the reformist track toward some kind of state capitalism. For them, the cause of most of the evils in the country was to be found in the takeover of the Puerto Rican economy by U.S. capital.

Though this "neoreformist" faction never became a formal group, the political line between them and the PPD high hierarchy was fairly clearly drawn. Most popular interpretations of the factional division explain it as generational, a conflict between the young and the old within the party.[15] However, a closer look reveals that the generational issue is more one of appearance than substance. The neoreformist criticism of the hierarchy's position stemmed from a serious concern with the course that the country's economy was taking. In retrospect, it could be argued that the young technocrats who formed the core of the neoreformist faction were foreseeing that the CI/EP strategy was approaching the limits of its capacity to grow, and that in order to avoid walking into a dead end and falling from power, the PPD had to go back to its reformist origins.

The criticism levied against the PPD's top leadership was expressed in the works of economist Genaro Baquero and sociologist Luis Nieves Falcón published in the *Revista de Ciencias Sociales* (Journal of Social Sciences) of the University of Puerto Rico. Baquero criticized the "capital importation model" for leading the country into an extreme dependency on foreign capital. He warned that unless something was done to reverse this pattern the country would face a serious problem of capital formation. Nieves Falcón criticized the ideological turn of the PPD from its reformist position to a conservative one.[16] But neither Baquero nor Nieves proposed a radical rupture of the colonial relation. They merely suggested that the PPD should moderate the heavy dependency on foreign capital and assume a more conscientious and progressive position.

Confronted with the possibility of a division within the PPD, Muñoz, who still was the undisputed leader of the party, imposed certain measures that were intended to reach a compromise between the two positions. These were the passage of a new industrial incentive law that continued and deepened the CI/EP strategy; the formulation of a program of social reforms known as "El Propósito de Puerto Rico" (The Purpose of Puerto Rico); the retirement of Muñoz from the governorship and the designation of Roberto Sánchez Vilella to succeed him as the party candidate for governor in the 1964 election; and holding a plebiscite as a means to put pressure on the U.S. Congress to grant some reforms to the commonwealth.

Though these measures did not resolve the conflict, the designation of Sánchez Vilella as Muñoz's successor gave some hope to the neoreformist elements. The 1964 election unified, if only temporarily, the PPD ranks. But behind this unity there were deep divisions that expressed the ideological contradictions generated by the implementation of the CI/EP development strategy.

Charting a New Course

The failure of the technobureaucracy to alter the colonial framework to ensure the continuity of the CI/EP strategy led to the adoption of some internal politicoeconomic measures and to negotiating with the metropolitan government for some special concessions. In doing this, the technobureaucracy actually deepened the structural basis of the CI/EP strategy by offering further incentives to U.S. capital. The key legal changes were the enactment of a new industrial incentive law and the allocation to Puerto Rico of special oil import quotas between 1965 and 1973.

Changes in the Legal Framework

The Puerto Rico Incentive Act of 1963, Law 57 of 13 June 1963, extended tax exemption periods to ten, twelve, and seventeen years, depending on the geographical location of industries. Corporations eligible for tax exemptions could begin their exempt period at any point within the first two years of operation. The exemption period could be doubled if the corporations chose to have only a 50 percent tax exemption instead of 100 percent. If at the end of the tax exemption period the corporation showed a net loss, this could be deducted from its taxable profits for a period of up to five years or until the losses had been offset by the profits, whichever came first. The tax exemption periods originally stipulated in Law 57 were increased three times between 1969 and 1974.[17]

Law 57 was intended to offset the negative impact of the increases in minimum wages and shipping rates on the profitability for foreign capital by offering added tax incentives. This law also intended to attract new industries that were less sensitive to wage changes and could benefit more from the longer exemption periods, especially capital-intensive heavy industries. Some of these heavy industries, such as oil refining and chemical production, had operations in Puerto Rico since the 1950s. Fomento and the PPD leadership were aware that the right kind of incentives could maintain the viability of the CI/EP strategy. However, the immediate intention of the PPD in passing Law 57 was not to attract these industries in particular but to continue attracting U.S. investment in general and to avoid any dislocations in the colonial economy.[18]

This local exemption was complemented by Section 931 of the U.S. Internal Revenue Code of 1954, according to which corporations operating subsidiaries in Puerto Rico could request special status and be designated as possessions corporations. The subsidiaries so designated had to prove that 80 percent of the gross income generated by their operation in the possession came from activities within it. The parent corporation would have to pay income taxes to the federal government on profits repatriated to the United States on a current (yearly) basis, but if the subsidiary accumulated profits throughout its years of operation in the possession and decided to liquidate its assets, all accumulated profits could be repatriated without payment of any federal income taxes. A similar tax provision had been on the books since 1921 but it was not until Section 931 was incorporated into the U.S. Internal Revenue Code (IRC) that subsidiaries of U.S. transnational corporations (TNCs) started to locate in Puerto Rico to take advantage of this provision. A trend of TNCs locating on the island started in the second half of the 1950s and accelerated in the 1960s.[19]

Presidential Proclamation 3663 of 10 December 1965 completed the legal framework for the deepening of the CI/EP model. This proclamation amended Presidential Proclamation 3279 of 1959 by changing the limitations on oil imports for Puerto Rico.[20] Two oil refineries had operated in Puerto

Rico since 1955, and they satisfied the local demand for gasoline and lubricants. About this same time, Fomento had begun to conduct studies on the viability of establishing a petrochemical complex in Puerto Rico. The studies found Puerto Rico a suitable site for certain activities, particularly synthetic fiber manufacturing, fertilizer plants, and intermediate-size oil refineries. The principal competitive advantages of Puerto Rico a location for petrochemical manufacturing were the relatively low cost of labor and tax exemptions. Indeed, most of the development in the petrochemical industry that took place on the island between 1955 and 1965 was along the lines pointed out in these studies.[21]

After Rafael Durand replaced Teodoro Moscoso as the head of Fomento in 1961, this agency began pushing for concessions from the U.S. government that would help to develop the petrochemical complex. Their reasoning was that, in view of the increased costs of labor and shipping and other negative developments for light industry, it was better to attract industries that were less sensitive to these fluctuations and less likely to close down operations due to the high investment entailed. With this in mind, Durand had been lobbying in Washington to revise the oil import quota assigned to Puerto Rico under Proclamation 3279. This lobbying effort was supported by the Phillips Petroleum Corporation which, together with Fomento, had devised a plan to establish a "core plant" in Puerto Rico using imported naphtha as the base for petrochemical processing.[22]

In the United States, in 1965, domestic petroleum and naphtha prices were higher than from Venezuela and the Middle East. Therefore, a plant operating in Puerto Rico using non-U.S. imported petroleum and naphtha and selling its product in the U.S. market would have at least three significant production cost advantages over its competitors operating in the United States: cheap labor, tax exemption, and cheaper raw materials. Being able to buy cheap Venezuelan or Arab oil would more than offset the added cost of shipping the processed product to the United States. Since there were no import duties on oil or naphtha imported under the quota system and no duties to be paid on Puerto Rican products entering the U.S. market, the price differential was definitely a major incentive for the establishment of U.S. petrochemical plants in Puerto Rico.

Proclamation 3663 provided the key incentive for the development of the petrochemical industry in Puerto Rico by allowing the U.S. secretary of the interior to assign special oil and naphtha import quotas to Puerto Rico in order to stimulate economic development on the island. Special quotas were granted for the already existing refineries—the Commonwealth Oil Refining Corporation (CORCO); the Caribbean Refining Co., a subsidiary of Gulf; and the Union Carbide Petrochemical Plant. Special quotas were also granted for two other U.S. companies, Phillips Petroleum and Sun Oil corporations.[23]

The development of U.S. petrochemical operations after 1965 marked the massive entrance of transnational capital into Puerto Rico. The CI/EP strategy took a new turn as the axis of capital accumulation shifted from the small and medium fractions of U.S. capital to the transnational fraction linked to capital-intensive manufacturing industries.

The Redefinition of Priorities

In his 1963 Message to the Legislature, Governor Muñoz Marín urged legislators to pass Law 57 and also urged Fomento to step up its efforts to "attain a reasonable balance between external and Puerto Rican capital investment."[24] His promise to strive for what he termed an "entrepreneurial balance" (*balance empresarial*) between foreign and local capital was a response to the criticisms raised by the neoreformist faction within his party and fractions of the local bourgeoisie affected negatively by the expansion of U.S. capital in production for the internal market. But, as PPD member Jaime Santiago Meléndez pointed out, achieving such an entrepreneurial balance was in contradiction to the very aims of a law designed to attract industries with established markets in the United States to take advantage of the local and federal tax holiday. Local industry could not be promoted within this framework.[25] Nonetheless, the concept of "entrepreneurial balance" became an important addition to developmentalist discourse, an added element of legitimacy, reassuring the "people" that the PPD's economic policies were moving in the "right direction."

The PPD also proclaimed the idea of industrial decentralization as a major objective of the new law. The government argued that establishing different exemption periods by geographical zones would stimulate a balanced growth among the different regions of the country. According to the Fomento technocrats, industrial development had been excessively concentrated in the San Juan metropolitan area and this had stimulated a high level of internal migration there from other areas of the country.[26]

The decentralization objective would be partially fulfilled. What the PPD leadership never really said was that this was the only alternative left open to the CI/EP strategy for the development of the rural areas and other regions of the island. The decentralization policy was the product of the failure to restore agricultural development, but in developmentalist discourse it was presented as the coming of progress to the countryside. The presentation of this deepening of the CI/EP strategy as the realization of the interest of the "people" was completed by the proposal of the social program known as "El Propósito de Puerto Rico." Muñoz's government program for socioeconomic action was the product of a series of cabinet meetings dealing with the problems confronting Puerto Rico at that time. Muñoz presented the program in what was to be his last annual message to the legislature, on 11 February 1964. He argued that the success of the PPD government in increasing the wealth of the country required reflection on how to use it best for the good of all Puerto Ricans. To end extreme poverty once and for all and to provide a sense of purpose to the socioeconomic development of the island, there were six areas that the "people" (i.e., the PPD government) should address: public health, education, housing, a socioeconomic balance between the rural and urban areas, entrepreneurial balance, and the abolition of extreme poverty.[27]

The elaboration and announcement of this program presented the deepening of the CI/EP strategy as the realization of the collective aspirations of the working classes, thus bringing back reminiscences of the PPD's reformist populism. It would also provide political unity and continuity to the PPD after Muñoz's retirement from the governorship later in 1964. As a matter of fact, "El Propósito de Puerto Rico" was adopted as part of the PPD's 1964 electoral program.[28]

Having set the course to follow, and probably believing he had settled the factional divisions within the PPD, Muñoz announced his retirement from the governorship in August 1964. He designated Secretary of State of Puerto Rico Roberto Sánchez Vilella as his successor. Although he had shown sympathy towards the neoreformist faction, there was no reason to believe that Sánchez would change the political course of the PPD significantly.[29] Indeed, throughout the 1964 campaign Sánchez expressed publicly his support of "El Propósito de Puerto Rico" and of the mainstream economic policy of the party. He was emphatic in arguing that his administration would promote greater participation of local capital in industry, but he did not reject the importance of foreign investment and was committed to encouraging it.[30]

By the 1964 election, it was becoming clear to the PPD technobureaucracy that it needed to attract sectors of U.S. capital that were economically stronger than those linked to the light industries that had flourished and declined in Puerto Rico during the first stage of the CI/EP strategy. Sánchez announced that attracting heavy industry would be a priority of his administration.[31] The technobureaucracy agreed on the need for the continuity of export-led industrialization. The source of the divisions within the PPD seems to have come from disagreements on the degree to which local capital should be incorporated into the industrial development process. At no time did any faction question the belief that U.S. capital should play the key role within the PPD's industrial development strategy.

The Impact of the Deepening of the CI/EP Strategy

The coming to Puerto Rico of U.S. transnational capital and its emergence as the dominant force in the process of production inserted the Puerto Rican economy at a new level in a vertically integrated international production chain. The island became an intermediate point in the production process of leading U.S. TNCs in capital-intensive manufacturing. With the concession of special oil import quotas in 1965 and 1968, U.S. petrochemical plants and oil refineries established in Puerto Rico gained privileged access to cheap Venezuelan and Middle Eastern oil while their competitors in the United States were forced to buy more expensive oil. For example, in 1969 a U.S. corporation operating in Puerto Rico paid $2.25 for a barrel of Venezuelan oil, while producers in the United States were forced by the quota to buy oil at $3.50 per barrel.[32]

Like the pattern during 1947–1963, the growth and expansion of leading industries between 1964 and 1976 responded to the interests of U.S. capital. With the exhaustion of the conditions that favored capital accumulation through investment in light industries, the axis of capitalist accumulation shifted to the transnational fraction of U.S. capital in capital-intensive manufacturing. Petroleum refining, petrochemicals, scientific instruments, and electrical equipment became the new leading industries.

Table 4.1 shows the changes experienced in the manufacturing sector between 1963 and 1977. This table gives the ten most important industrial groups according to shares of value added, value of shipments, production workers employed, and wages paid to production workers for the years of the census of manufactures. It indicates the development of the following patterns: (a) an overall decline in the relative importance of apparel; stone, clay, and glass; tobacco; textile mill products; and leather products industries; (b) an increase in the relative importance of the chemical and scientific instruments industries; (c) an increase in the relative importance of the fabricated metals and the petroleum and coal products industries between 1963 and 1972 and a lag in both these industries between 1972 and 1977; and (d) the emergence of the nonelectrical machinery and the miscellaneous rubber and plastic products industries as important areas in the manufacturing sector. Most certainly, the fastest growing industries in Puerto Rico during this period were capital intensive.

There are no statistics on capital stock available for the industries in Puerto Rico. This makes it impossible to calculate the ratio of constant (fixed) to variable (wages) capital. Therefore, the capital intensity of industries can only be estimated by extrapolating to Puerto Rico knowledge about these industries in the United States or by approximate measures, such as the rate of value added per worker or the ratio of wages to value added. But these are measures of labor productivity that may or may not reflect accurately the proportions of variable and constant capital involved in the production process. However, Table 4.1 shows that by 1977 the chemical, nonelectrical machinery, petroleum and coal products, and tobacco industries had higher shares of value added compared to shares of production workers than the other industries. This suggests a high proportion of capital to labor in the process of production, which in time suggests a high organic composition of capital in these industries. This pattern is less accentuated for the scientific instruments and the electrical equipment industries. A U.S. Department of Commerce study provides a somewhat similar classification

Table 4.1 Ten Leading Manufacturing Industries: Census Years 1963–1977 (percentages)

	Share of Total Value Added	Rank	Share Value of Shipments	Rank	Share of Production Workers	Rank	Share of Production Workers' Wages	Rank
				1963				
Food products	30.6	1	37.4	1	18.4	2	19.4	2
Apparel	14.6	2	12.1	2	29.6	1	24.8	1
Electrical machinery	8.1	3	6.1	3	5.9	5	7.6	3
Chemicals	7.4	4	5.5	4	2.0	10	2.7	10
Stone, clay & glass	6.1	5	4.6	5	4.8	7	5.8	4
Tobacco products	3.8	6	4.0	6	6.9	3	5.3	5
Leather products	3.3	7	2.9	9	6.5	4	4.9	7
Textile mill products	3.3	8	3.4	7	5.3	6	5.1	6
Fabricated metals	2.7	9	3.3	8	2.4	9	3.0	9
Furniture & fixtures	2.5	10	1.9	10	3.7	8	3.4	8
				1967				
Food products	25.9	1	29.7	1	14.0	2	15.0	2
Apparel	14.4	2	12.1	2	31.0	1	26.1	1
Chemicals	9.9	3	7.5	3	a	a	3.0	10
Electrical equipment	8.6	4	6.3	4	7.3	4	7.7	3
Stone, clay & glass	5.8	5	4.8	5	4.8	7	6.5	5
Leather products	4.6	6	4.0	6	9.4	3	7.7	4
Tobacco products	4.1	7	3.9	7	6.4	5	5.7	6
Fabricated metals	3.9	8	3.4	9	2.8	9	3.8	8
Textile mill products	3.5	9	3.8	8	5.1	6	5.1	7
Scientific instruments	3.0	10	2.1	10	3.1	8	3.6	9
				1972				
Chemicals	23.5	1	18.5	2	5.5	5	8.0	4
Food products	17.9	2	23.4	1	15.6	2	16.8	2
Apparel	13.2	3	11.2	4	28.1	1	23.3	1
Electrical equipment	8.9	4	6.9	5	10.4	3	8.6	3
Petroleum & coal products	4.8	5	11.3	3	a	a	a	a
Scientific instruments	4.4	6	3.1	9	4.2	7	5.0	6
Fabricated metals	4.1	7	3.8	7	3.5	9	4.4	8
Stone, clay & glass	3.8	8	3.2	8	3.8	8	4.5	7
Textile mill products	3.5	9	4.1	6	5.7	4	5.1	5
Tobacco products	2.4	10	2.7	10	3.3	10	3.2	10
				1977				
Chemicals	36.0	1	27.2	1	8.4	4	11.3	4
Food products	11.9	2	14.4	3	13.7	2	14.1	2
Electrical equipment	9.8	3	7.1	4	10.7	3	17.9	1
Apparel	6.8	4	5.9	5	26.3	1	11.3	3
Scientific instruments	6.3	5	4.0	6	4.8	6	5.3	5
Nonelectrical machinery	3.9	6	3.0	7	a	a	a	a
Rubber & plastics	3.6	7	2.3	8	4.4	9	4.9	6
Petroleum & coal products	3.5	8	21.2	2	a	a	3.7	8
Tobacco products	3.0	9	2.1	10	a	a	a	a
Textile mill products	2.7	10	a	a	4.5	8	3.6	9

Sources: U.S. Bureau of the Census, *Puerto Rico: Census of Manufactures*, 1963, 1967, 1972, and 1977.

aNot among the top ten.

categorizing chemical, petroleum, and electrical and nonelectrical machinery industries as capital intensive.[33]

The Deepening of Foreign Control

Associated with this growth of capital-intensive industry, there was a deepening of U.S. control over industrial production in Puerto Rico. A comparison between the 1963 data in Table 4.1 and Table 3.2 shows that U.S. capital controlled production in six of the ten most important industries that year—apparel, electrical machinery, chemical products, tobacco, leather products, and textiles. Also, foreign firms accounted for a sizeable share of the value added and the value of shipments generated in the food sector.[34] By 1967, the foreign sector clearly controlled at least eight of the ten most important groups, as Table 4.2 illustrates. Overall, census figures show that foreign-owned establishments produced 70.6 percent of the total value added and 68.7 percent of the total value of shipments, generated 72.4 percent of all production employment, and paid 72 percent of all wages to production workers in the manufacturing sector.[35]

The 1972 *Census of Manufactures* did not separate foreign-owned industries from locally owned ones. The 1977 *Census of Manufactures* did, but the information is not useful because 585 of the 1,114 industrial establishments surveyed did not reveal the origin of their ownership.[36] Therefore, to examine the degree of foreign control over the manufacturing sector in Puerto Rico during the 1970s, other information must be used.

According to a U.S. Department of Commerce study, in 1973 foreign stockholders (mainly U.S.) controlled 98 percent or more of the shares of the establishments in the drug, chemical and petrochemical, fabricated metal, and electrical and nonelectrical machinery industries. In the petroleum refining and primary metals industries, foreign stockholders controlled between 89 and 95 percent of the shares, and they controlled 60 percent of the shares in the petroleum products industry.[37] According to the 1972 *Census of Manufactures*, these industries were producing 44 percent of the total value added by industry and 47.7 percent of the total value of shipments.[38] These figures leave out the scientific instruments industry, where there was an overwhelming foreign control, and other areas in which U.S. capital was dominant or controlled a sizeable share of production (i.e., textiles, apparel, and food industries). Overall, in the 1970s U.S. investment accounted for about 75 percent of all investment funds in Puerto Rico.[39]

A study made by the Governor's Committee for the Study of Puerto Rican Finances (known as the "Tobin Committee") calculated that in 1974, of an estimated total of $22 billion in tangible and reproducible assets on the island, only $9.7 billion (44.1 percent) was in the hands of the residents of Puerto Rico. Of the rest, $6.1 billion (27.7 percent of the total) represented direct foreign investments, and $6.2 billion dollars (28.1 percent) represented

Table 4.2 Foreign Industries'Shares of Key Production Indicators in Ten Leading
Manufacturing Industries: 1967 (percentages)

	Share of Total Value Added	Share of Value of Shipments	Share of Production Workers	Share of Production Workers' Wages
Food products	55.9	51.9	46.5	51.3
Apparel	82.7	83.4	82.7	84.5
Chemicals	94.5	91.2	78.9	83.7
Electrical equipment	91.9	91.0	92.2	92.1
Stone, clay & glass	16.1	13.5	22.9	18.4
Leather products	88.2	88.4	87.2	87.8
Tobacco products	94.6	91.2	92.2	94.9
Fabricated metals	54.4	50.0	44.0	51.1
Textile mill products	85.3	91.3	87.6	87.3
Scientific instruments[a]	N/A	N/A	N/A	N/A

Source: U.S. Bureau of the Census, *Puerto Rico: Census of Manufactures, 1967*, p. 100.
[a]Although the census did not disclose data for foreign industries, it did reveal that 27 of the 29 establishments in this industry were owned by foreign companies, which would indicate clear foreign dominance.

the private and public external debt—that is, 55.8 percent of the tangible and reproducible capital stock of the Puerto Rican economy was controlled by foreign capital.[40]

In 1974, 110 of the "Fortune 500" corporations operated 336 subsidiaries on the island; 333 of these had been established under the auspices of Fomento. In that same year, there were 1,720 industrial establishments operating under Fomento's industrial promotion programs; 994 of these were U.S.-owned. Put another way: 57.8 percent of all Fomento-promoted industrial establishments were U.S.-owned and 19.4 percent of the Fomento-promoted establishments were subsidiaries of large U.S. corporations or TNCs. Furthermore, one-third of all U.S.-owned manufacturing establishments in Puerto Rico were subsidiaries of 110 "Fortune 500" corporations.[41]

Other information available on ownership by origin of industrial establishments shows a persistent pattern of U.S. dominance in major industries throughout the 1970s. Table 4.3 summarizes the available data on the ownership of industrial establishments operating under the Fomento program in 1978 for some of the most dynamic industries. Although the table does not provide any information regarding investment and production, it suggests a continued pattern of increasing external control over the most dynamic sectors of the manufacturing industry.

A comparison between Table 4.3 and the 1977 part of Table 4.1 suggests that six of the ten most important industrial groups in 1977 were dominated by U.S.-owned establishments. In many of these groups production was also controlled by a few TNCs. For example, twenty-seven of the fifty-one petrochemical plants operating on the island in 1977 were operated by CORCO and Union Carbide. Both these companies had been

Table 4.3 Ownership by Origin of Selected Industries: 1978

	Establishments	U.S.	%	Other Foreign	%	P.R.	%
Pharmaceuticals	78	70	89.7	5	6.4	3	3.8
Scientific instruments	80	67	83.7	6	7.5	7	8.7
Electrical & electronics	152	127	83.6	5	3.3	20	13.2
Petroleum & petrochemicals[a]	56	46	82.1	5	8.9	6	10.1
Textile mill products	42	33	78.6	1	2.4	8	19.0
Nonelectrical machinery	65	41	63.1	2	3.1	22	33.8
Apparel	386	237	61.4	6	1.6	143	37.0
Fabricated rubber & plastics	65	30	46.2	2	3.1	33	50.7
Food products	170	48	28.2	9	5.3	113	66.5
Total	1094	699	63.8	41	3.7	355	32.4

Sources: PREDA industry profiles, various.
[a]1977

ranked among the five hundred largest companies in the United States in 1977 by *Fortune* magazine. Twenty-two of the thirty-four largest U.S. corporations in 1978 owned sixty-two of the seventy-eight industrial establishments operating in the pharmaceutical industry on the island. In the area of electrical and electronic equipment, three TNCs (Westinghouse, General Electric, and GTE-Sylvania) owned over one-third (58 of the 152) establishments in this industry.[42]

Table 4.4 gives an idea of the importance and the impact of the coming of TNCs to Puerto Rico. It compares the position of Puerto Rico within the distribution of U.S. direct investment, income on investment, and rate of return in Latin America in 1960 and 1976. In terms of direct investment, Puerto Rico moved up from sixth place in 1960 to first in 1976. Undoubtedly, the Cuban revolution and the nationalization of Venezuelan oil had much to do with the increased importance of Puerto Rico. Yet, it may be added, Puerto Rico had one of the highest rates of return in the region since 1960. Puerto Rico experienced the highest percentage of growth in direct investment in the region, 986 percent, and the second highest in income, 1,387 percent. Brazil experienced the highest in the latter, 1,524 percent. Overall, Puerto Rico became the Latin American country with the highest U.S. investment and the primary source of income for U.S. capital in the region.

In global terms, U.S. direct investment in Puerto Rico in 1960 represented 2 percent of U.S. direct investment in the world, but by 1976 Puerto Rico's share was 5 percent. Likewise, in 1960 the income on U.S. direct investment in Puerto Rico represented 3.5 percent of U.S. global income on investment; by 1976, this figure increased to 6.7 percent. In 1976, only Canada, the United Kingdom, and West Germany had more U.S. direct investment than Puerto Rico, and only Canada and West Germany generated more income on investment.[43]

During the second stage of the CI/EP strategy, Puerto Rico became an

Table 4.4 U.S. Direct Investment, Income, and Rate of Return in Latin America: 1960 and 1976 (millions dollars)

Country	Value of Investment	%	Income on Investment	%	Rate of return
		1960			
All Countries	9,038	100 .0	726	100.0	8.0
Venezuela	2,569	28.4	371	51.1	14.4
Cuba	956	10.6	N/A	N/A	N/A
Brazil	953	10.5	45	6.2	4.7
Mexico	795	8.8	65	9.0	8.2
Chile	738	8.2	72	9.9	9.8
Puerto Rico	672	7.4	85	11.7	12.7
Argentina	472	5.2	10	1.4	2.1
Peru	446	4.9	48	6.6	10.8
Colombia	424	4.7	19	2.6	4.5
Panama	405	4.5	16	2.2	3.9
		1976			
All Countries	24,427	100.0	3,171	100.0	13.0
Puerto Rico	7,301	29.9	1,264	39.9	17.3
Brazil	5,416	22.2	731	23.1	13.5
Mexico	2,976	12.2	70	2.2	2.4
Panama	1,961	8.0	226	7.1	11.5
Venezuela	1,506	6.2	262	8.3	17.4
Argentina	1,366	5.6	246	7.8	18.0
Peru	1,364	5.6	46	1.5	3.4
Colombia	654	2.7	79	2.5	12.1
Chile	179	0.7	22	0.7	12.3

Sources: Pizer and Cutler, "United States Assets and Investment Abroad," pp. 22–23; Kozlow, Rutter, and Walker, "U.S. Direct Investment Abroad," pp. 27, 35; Junta de Planificación, *Balanza de pagos, 1978*, Tables IX, XXII.

important center for a fraction of U.S. transnational capital. Petrochemical, pharmaceutical, and electronic TNCs integrated Puerto Rico within their international circuit of production and transformed the island into a major producer of intermediate and finished products for export to the U.S. market. This change displaced the axis of capital accumulation from the small and medium fractions of U.S. capital linked to light industry to the transnational fraction linked to capital-intensive industry.

The conditions for this displacement had been created by the structural contradictions of the CI/EP strategy and by a set of exceptional political circumstances. The expanded local tax exemption, the continued exemption from federal taxes on profits repatriated by U.S. corporations under Section 931 of the IRC, the exceptional oil import quotas, and the greater integration of the Puerto Rican financial structure into the United States combined to make many industrial operations more profitable in Puerto Rico than in the United States. In 1973, the transportation equipment, electrical machinery, printing, chemicals, petroleum refining and petroleum products, textiles, primary metals, and stone, clay, and glass industries operating in Puerto Rico had a rate of profit per share at least twice that of those industries operating in the United States. The lowest average rate of profit per share in these industries was 19.3 percent in the textile industry, compared to 9 percent in the United States. The highest average rate of profit per share for U.S. companies in Puerto Rico was 46.1 percent in the primary metals industry, while in the United States it was 10.1 percent. For the leading industries controlled by transnational capital, the average rates of profit per share for Puerto Rico as compared to the United States were: chemicals, 34.1 percent to 14.8 percent; petroleum refining and petroleum products, 25.3 percent to 11.6 percent; electrical machinery, 26.7 percent to 13.1 percent; and scientific instruments, 23.7 percent to 15.9 percent.[44]

Under the enhanced incentives to capital in this second stage of the CI/EP strategy, Puerto Rico became a profit paradise for U.S. TNCs. North American subsidiaries operating in Puerto Rico under Section 931 of the IRC as possessions corporations developed two practices that were detrimental to the economic growth of the island but lucrative for the companies. The first practice was to accumulate a high level of liquid assets in the form of deposits in U.S. banks. Most of the profit made during the period of tax exemption in Puerto Rico was not reinvested directly; rather, it was deposited in banks or invested in financial assets, like government bonds, that paid high interests. The second practice was to liquidate operations of the subsidiaries at the end of the Puerto Rican tax exemption period and repatriate the accumulated profits without having to pay any federal income taxes. In many instances these liquidations were nothing but a paper transaction in which one subsidiary sold its tangible assets to another subsidiary of the same parent corporation. The report of the Tobin Committee described the typical life cycle of the U.S. subsidiary in Puerto Rico as follows:

> The new firm, today probably a pharmaceutic or an electronic plant, not a textile or apparel one, starts with a cash investment provided by the North American parent company. Since the operation is established because of federal and local tax exemptions, as much as for the cheap labor and other advantages of Puerto Rico, there are substantial profits. The parent company has very powerful reasons to establish in Puerto Rico its most profitable operations. Federal regulations on taxes prevent the profits from returning immediately to the parent company. Therefore, the subsidiary starts to accumulate financial assets. The income from these financial assets is tax exempt if they are invested in a U.S. possession. This explains the popularity of the high interest deposit certificates in Guam. When the tax exemption period in Puerto Rico expires, the subsidiary has accumulated a substantial amount of financial assets as well as some depreciated tangible assets in Puerto Rico. The tangible assets are sold, the subsidiary is liquidated and the profits accumulated by the whole operation are sent back to the parent corporation free of any payment of federal or local taxes. The physical plant remains in Puerto Rico. It will only be used if some firm—maybe another subsidiary of the old parent company—finds it profitable. This, in

time, will depend on whether or not a new tax exemption can be arranged.[45]

The report points out that the typical U.S. subsidiary in Puerto Rico maintained 80 percent of its total assets in a financial form. Aside from the negative impact that this had on economic growth, it also distorted the real nature of what was classified as direct investment in Puerto Rico. The Tobin Report estimated that as much as 50 percent of what was classified as direct investment in Puerto Rico was in reality made up of financial assets. This excess of financial investments in high-interest-yielding deposits also helped to increase significantly the rate of return of the U.S. subsidiaries, which was estimated to be somewhere between 35 and 60 percent.[46]

A curious financial practice mentioned in the report was that of depositing profits in U.S. banks with operations in Guam. Since Guam was also a U.S. colony, it enjoyed the same exemption from federal taxes as Puerto Rico. Puerto Rican subsidiaries of U.S. corporations were therefore able to channel their profits to Guam on a current basis without paying any federal taxes. In time, the funds deposited in Guam by the subsidiaries were channeled through financial intermediaries to investments in the Eurodollar market.[47] In this way, the large financial-industrial consortiums that operated in Puerto Rico established a complex financial network that ultimately enabled the parent company to use the tax-exempt profits made in Puerto Rico in other parts of the world, thus avoiding the restrictions of Section 931 of the IRC.

These financial manipulations were facilitated by the colonial framework that permitted a U.S. subsidiary to deposit profits in the branches of U.S. banks operating in Puerto Rico without any major currency or legal restrictions. It was relatively easy for a subsidiary that, for example, made deposits in a branch of the City Bank in Puerto Rico to transfer funds to City Bank in Guam and from there to the Eurodollar market without technically breaking the IRC restrictions. As long as the financial transaction was made in the U.S. banks operating in the "possessions," the profits of the subsidiaries had not been, technically speaking, repatriated.

The deepening of the CI/EP strategy also meant an increased reliance on external trade by the leading economic sector in Puerto Rico. According to a study made by the Puerto Rican House of Representatives, in 1972 the petrochemical industry in Puerto Rico produced 40 percent of all the paraxelene, 30 percent of all the cyclohexane, 26 percent of all benzene, 24 percent of all propylene, and 12 percent of all vinyl chloride consumed in the United States. Similarly, the electronics industry produced 44 percent of all electrodes used in the United States.[48] In 1972, 53 percent of the total value of the shipments of manufacturing industries went to the United States and only 40 percent went to the domestic market. The oil refining and organic chemical industries exported 42 percent of their production to the United

States, despite the fact that the oil quota was supposed to limit such exports. The pharmaceutical industry exported 76 percent of its production to the United States and the electronic industry 87 percent. By 1977, 59 percent of the total value of the shipments of manufacturing industries in Puerto Rico went to the United States and only 34 percent went to the domestic market.[49]

But these high export figures do not constitute a negative factor in themselves. The problem with the CI/EP strategy is that a large share of the surplus capital produced in Puerto Rico is siphoned off in the form of profits made by the subsidiaries of American TNCs, which requires increased government debt to cover the deficit that this creates. A large share of the product generated in the Puerto Rican economy ended up in the hands of the U.S. firms as profits, dividends, interests, and royalties paid to the parent companies by their Puerto Rican subsidiaries. Figure 4.1 shows the impact of this loss of capital on the relation between the gross domestic product (GDP) and the gross national product (GNP) in Puerto Rico. The GDP measures the value of all goods and services produced in the Puerto Rican economy during a given year. The GNP measures the value of the product that is available for consumption within the local economy. The GDP minus the GNP represents the share of the product of the Puerto Rican economy that was appropriated by the external sector. In 1948, the GNP was $37 million more than the GDP, 6 percent. In 1956 this figure grew to $91 million, 10.4 percent of the GDP. This surplus can be attributed to transfer payments and capital investment coming from external sources into the Puerto Rican economy. Although in 1960 the GNP was $15.5 million less than the GDP, only 1 percent, by 1976 this figure had soared to $1,440.6 million, 16 percent.[50]

Another negative effect of the deepening of the CI/EP strategy was that the reduced linkage of the leading economic sector to the domestic market meant little forward or backward linkages within the economy and a low multiplier effect. In 1976 the U.S. Department of Treasury estimated the income multiplier for Puerto Rico to be 1.3.[51] As the growth in the dynamic sector was not mainly the result of the development of productive forces within Puerto Rico, but rather of the internationalization of capitalist production, there was no basis for self-sustained growth. This disarticulation of the industrial dynamic sector from the rest of the Puerto Rican economy is illustrated in the U.S. Department of Commerce *Economic Study of Puerto Rico*:

> In the production process, most raw material and intermediate goods are shipped to the subsidiary firms by their parent companies or by U.S. distributors through arrangements made by the parent companies. The outputs produced are shipped directly to the mainland companies for distribution, including redistribution to Puerto Rico. In other words, the general practice of many U.S. corporations is to use Puerto Rico as a production point only.[52]

Figure 4.1 The GNP/GDP Gap: 1948–1976

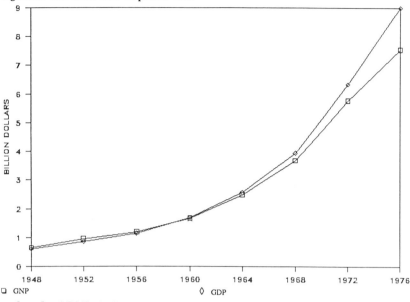

□ GNP   ◊ GDP

Source: Junta de Palnificacion, *Ingreso y Producto, 1978.*

Moreover, throughout both stages of the CI/EP strategy, the Puerto Rican economy maintained a trade deficit that grew from $169 million in 1948 to $1,991 million in 1976.[53] Hence, increased exports did not necessarily translate into income for the local economy that could eventually become accumulated capital. Surplus capital was concentrated in the hands of the transnational bourgeoisie, which decided how to use this capital. The interests of this class were defined in terms of global corporate strategies and might not coincide with the needs of capital formation and accumulation in Puerto Rico.

In order to make up for the negative impact of foreign investment in the rest of the economy, since these companies did not pay taxes, the government had to increase its external debt. By 1976, the Puerto Rican government owed foreign lenders $5,751 million, 532 percent more than it owed in 1965.[54] Although access to dollars was not a problem for the Puerto Rican government, the public sector had to borrow to expand its services and help support the structural imbalances that were accentuated by the CI/EP strategy.

In synthesis, the deepening of the CI/EP strategy between 1963 and 1976 consolidated the role of Puerto Rico as a processing point for U.S. TNCs. The island became a productive backyard for capital-intensive industries; export processing reached a new height; and Puerto Rico became a center of financial maneuvering by TNCs using price transfer mechanisms to evade tax payments and then recirculate profits through a financial labyrinth back to the corporations' international operations. By the mid-1970s, the strategic decisions regarding the direction of the economic development of the island were perhaps more than ever in the hands of the North American imperialist bourgeoisie. The relative autonomy that the colonial technobureaucracy seemed to enjoy in the 1940s and early 1950s was greatly reduced.

The increased vulnerability of the Puerto Rican economy to changes in the interest of the metropolitan classes and in the international economy became evident in 1973, when the favorable conditions that fostered the growth of the petrochemical industry were ended abruptly. The special oil import quota was eliminated by President Richard Nixon. Presidential proclamations 4210 of 17 April 1973 and 4297 of 19 June 1973 replaced the oil import quota by a license fee system. Under the new system, any U.S. producer could import foreign oil as long as it paid the cost of the license fee. Although the license fee system was applied gradually to Puerto Rico, all import advantages disappeared by 1980.[55]

The problems created by ending the import privileges granted to Puerto Rico were made worse by the 1973 Arab oil embargo and the sharp increase in oil prices that followed. The price of a barrel of crude oil imported to Puerto Rico increased from $3.05 in 1972 to $14.06 in 1976. The price of imported naphtha increased from 6 cents per gallon in early 1973 to 37 cents per gallon in 1976. In December 1974, the price for a barrel of crude oil produced in the United States was $7.39, while a barrel of imported crude oil was $12.82.[56] Any hope to cushion the blow dealt to the oil refineries and petrochemical producers in Puerto Rico through political maneuvering or special concessions from the federal government was crushed by the embargo and the price hikes declared by the OPEC countries.

The convergence of the abolition of the oil quota, the embargo, and the price increases drove the most dynamic sector of the Puerto Rican economy into a crisis. The profit rate in the oil refining industry shrank drastically, from 25.8 percent in 1973 to 6.9 percent in 1976. In the chemical industry, it went from 34.1 percent in 1973 to 17.6 percent in 1976. This occurred while the profit rates for these sectors in the United States increased from 11.6 percent in 1973 to 14.4 percent in 1976 for the oil refining industry, and from 14.8 percent in 1973 to 15.5 percent in 1976 for the chemical industry.[57]

Perhaps the most illustrative case of the critical impact of these events was the case of CORCO. This oil refinery, contrary to the other oil and petrochemical companies operating on the island, was not a TNC when it started operations in 1955. Under the exceptional conditions provided by the oil quota, CORCO became the largest corporation in Puerto Rico and ranked among the "Fortune 500" largest companies. However, after the 1973 events, CORCO began having problems; it declared bankruptcy in 1978.[58]

Changes in the Social Structure

During the 1960s and 1970s, fewer workers emigrated to the United States. In the 1960s the average annual emigration rate was 20,400 persons, less than half the rate in the 1950s. Another element that affected the emigration figures was the immigration to Puerto Rico of foreigners, particularly Cuban exiles. Between 1961 and 1970, 105,452 persons immigrated to Puerto Rico from the Virgin Islands and foreign countries. This left a net emigration from the island of 98,985 persons, 9,898 people per year in this period. Between 1971 and 1976, the migratory flow showed a balance of 56,176 people "returning" to Puerto Rico. This process of "return migration" was attributed to the economic crisis that started in the United States in the late 1960s. This does not mean that there were no Puerto Ricans emigrating; rather, it means that as a structural tendency the pattern of migration was reversed. This reverse pattern was further complicated by the continuation of foreign migration into Puerto Rico. Between 1971 and 1976, a total of 121,481 people migrated to Puerto Rico from the Virgin Islands and foreign countries; an estimated 107,342 came from the Dominican Republic.[59]

Table 4.5 shows the tendency of the urban population to grow to the detriment of the rural population. It also shows the drastic reduction in migration occurring during the 1960s. Comparing this to Table 3.6 allows us to observe the continued displacement of the rural population and the fluctuations in migration patterns since the 1940s. While the displacement of rural population to the urban centers continued to be a feature of capitalist development in Puerto Rico, the contradictions and cyclical crises of capitalism were also displacing Puerto Rican migrants from the ranks of the labor force in the metropolis; they were joined by displaced workers from the Dominican Republic.

The change in the emigration pattern combined with the unprecedented immigration of foreigners and the reduced amount of jobs created by the capital-intensive industries was reflected in increases in the rates of unemployment and underemployment. The rate of unemployment grew steadily throughout this period, from 12.8 percent in 1963 to 19.4 percent in 1976. Interestingly, the rate of participation of the adult population in the labor force continued to drop from 44.2 to 41.6 percent in those same years.[60] There were more people unemployed in Puerto Rico than ever and a smaller proportion of the population was economically active. The increase in underemployment was even larger. While in 1967 19.6 percent of the people employed were classified as working thirty-four hours or less a week, by 1977 42.2 percent of all the people employed were in this category.[61]

The "explosion" of unemployment and underemployment prompted the expansion of the informal sector or "marginalized pole of the economy." An army of street vendors set up shop selling anything from homemade cakes and fresh fruits and vegetables to fast food lunches and pillows. Day work in gardening, construction, and similar activities (called *chiripeo*)

Table 4.5 Population Changes: 1960–1970

										Migrants
Population (000)	% Change	Urban (000)	% of Total	% Change	Rural	% of Total	% Change	Migration (000)	% Change	as % of Population
1960 2,349.5	6.3	1,039.3	44.2	16.1	1,310.2	55.8	-0.4	430.5	180.1	18.3
1970 2,712.0	15.4	1,575.5	58.1	51.6	1,136.5	41.9	-13.3	99.0	-77.0	3.7

Sources: U.S. Bureau of the Census, *Census of Population, Puerto Rico*, 1960 and 1970, 2, Pt. 53, pp. 53–59; Maldonado Denis, *Emigration Dialectic*, p. 135.

became commonplace in Puerto Rico. An ominous result of the intensification of the process of displacement of the working classes was the increase in criminal activities, such as drug traffic, clandestine gambling, and theft.[62]

The continued displacement of the working classes not only stimulated the expansion of low-productivity services, it also stimulated the expansion of the public sector to provide services and income to the displaced workers (keeping them at a minimum level of subsistence) and jobs. The U.S. federal government played a major role in this by providing millions of dollars for welfare programs that became the main source of income for the unemployed and a source of employment for the middle sectors and the new petty bourgeoisie. Between 1960 and 1976, transfer payments of the federal government to the residents of Puerto Rico increased from $78.1 million dollars to $1,619.5 million, 1,974 percent. In 1960, most of these transfer payments were benefits to Puerto Rican veterans of the U.S. Armed Forces or Social Security beneficiaries—that is, payments for services rendered or accumulated job benefits. But in 1976, $775.2 million were given to individuals in food stamps and rent subsidies, and almost one-half of all federal transfer payments were for welfare. For fiscal year 1976/77, 50 percent of the population was receiving food stamps.[63] The public sector also became the major source of employment. Between 1964 and 1976, total employment in Puerto Rico increased by 9.8 percent while government employment grew 100 percent. Similarly, in 1964 the government (excluding public corporations) accounted for 12 percent of total employment; in 1976 it accounted for 22 percent.[64]

But the expansion of the tertiary sector in general, and of the public sector in particular, was not exclusively a function of the continued displacement of the working population and the need to prevent the potentially negative political repercussions of this. The expansion of these sectors was a necessary condition for the continuation of the political and social conditions that allowed the reproduction of peripheral capitalism in a wider sense, as a result of the increased technical and bureaucratic needs of capital. This process constituted the basis for the emergence of a new petty bourgeoisie. This class was associated with administrative and bureaucratic, nonproductive, forms of labor.[65]

Table 4.6 shows the growth in the occupational categories linked to these nonproductive forms of labor. The fastest growing categories were clerical workers, professionals and technicians, craftsmen and foremen, and service workers. Of these, only the craftsmen (i.e., skilled workers) are involved directly in productive labor. Although they are not part of the new petty bourgeoisie, they can be categorized as a labor aristocracy that ideologically tends to identify itself as part of the middle sectors. Aside from this group, the other rapidly growing groups were clearly linked to nonproductive forms of labor pertaining to managerial, supervisory, and technical tasks within the productive process or to other nonproductive (bureaucratic or technical) functions.

It is important to note here that one of the categories we might have expected to grow actually decreased, managers and administrators. According to the census, the reduction in this category was mainly due to a decrease in the number of self-employed managers and administrators; that is, small owners who administered their own business. This, then, confirms the expansion of a new petty bourgeoisie and suggests a decline in the traditional petty bourgeoisie. This decline began in the 1950s and became more accentuated with the arrival of transnational capital that brought with it not only large manufacturing industries, but also U.S. department stores, such as Woolworth, Bargain Town, Sears, and J. C. Penney, which displaced many small local businesses. Support for the proindependence movement that, since the 1930s, had established a base of support among this class also decreased.[66]

Table 4.6 also shows that, except for the craftsmen, those categories of workers associated with the production of surplus value remained unchanged. Operatives and laborers remained at around 19 percent of the employed labor force. Including the craftsmen, the occupations associated with direct production outside agriculture increased by only 3.2 percent, from 29.8 to 33 percent of the employed labor force.

Table 4.7 shows that wages of production workers continued to decline. When viewed in conjunction with Table 3.8, it could be said that rates of exploitation in manufacturing continued to increase as Marxist economics would argue.[67]

There was also a slowdown in the growth of real wages for industrial workers. Between 1960 and 1970 real wages increased by 31 percent for men and 46 percent for women. Between 1970 and 1976, however, the real weekly wage of an industrial worker grew 1.3 percent for men and declined 3.3 percent for women. In nominal terms, however, the wages of industrial workers increased 73 percent for men and 93 percent for women between 1960 and 1970; between 1970 and 1976, they grew 55 percent for men and 33 percent for women.[68] A similar reduction in rates of growth took place in the levels of personal consumption of the population; between 1960 and 1970, real personal consumption grew at an average rate of 11 percent

Table 4.6 Shares of Employment by Occupations: 1960 and 1970 (percent)

Category	1960	1970	Change
Professionals and technicians	7.7	11.1	3.4
Managers and administrators	7.6	6.7	−0.9
Sales workers	6.3	6.9	0.6
Clerical and kindred workers	7.6	11.4	3.8
Service workers	7.9	10.2	2.3
Private household workers	3.4	1.5	−1.9
Craftsmen and foremen	11.3	13.9	2.6
Operatives (except transport)	12.1	13.0	0.9
Laborers (except farm)	6.4	6.1	0.3
Transport equipment operatives	5.1	5.0	−0.1
Farmers and farm managers	3.2	1.3	−1.9
Farm laborers and foremen	19.8	5.6	−13.2

Source: U.S. Bureau of the Census, *Census of Population, Puerto Rico, 1970* 2, Pt. 53, pp. 741–755.

Table 4.7 Wages of Production Workers in Manufacturing as Percentage of Value Added: 1963-1977 (million dollars)

Year	Wages	Value Added	Wages a % of Value Added
1963	179	621	28.8
1967	280	1003	27.9
1972	476	1915	24.9
1977	734	4097	17.9

Sources: U.S. Bureau of the Census, *Census of Manufactures, Puerto Rico*, 1963, 1967, 1972, 1977.

annually; between 1970 and 1976, it grew an average of 3.3 percent a year. However, at current prices, personal consumption grew at 17 percent per year between 1960 and 1970 and 16 percent between 1970 and 1976.[69] Thus, the nondisplaced workers experienced an increase in their rates of exploitation and a deterioration in the growth of real wages and consumption during the 1970s. At the same time, their wages and expenditures continued to grow in nominal terms. It could be argued that these increases concealed the relative deterioration of the workers' economic situation. In quotidian praxis, things continued to appear hopeful.

Most of the information about the bourgeoisie in Puerto Rico is scattered and fragmentary. However, according to a study conducted by the consultant firm of Clapp and Mayne, the following were the key characteristics of Puerto Rican industries:

1. Production was principally oriented to the local market. Only 22 percent of the surveyed firms sold their product in the U.S. market, while 99 percent sold their product in Puerto Rico.
2. The principal source of capital for 70 percent of the firms was

owners, associates, or local shareholders; for 25 percent of the firms the principal capital source was local banks.

3. The average employment per firm for all the surveyed firms was 28.2 people; for 53 percent of the sampled firms, employment fluctuated between 1 and 20 employees.

4. Of the surveyed firms, 40 percent had an annual income of $200,000 or less; only 14 percent made $1 million dollars or more per year.

5. For 50 percent of the sample the principal competitor was another local industry; for 14 percent there was no competition; only 22 percent competed with U.S. producers.

6. The areas of operations for 63 percent of the sample were textiles and clothing, machinery and metal, furniture and wood, and food. The rest operated in paper, leather, chemicals, rubber and plastic products, and service industries.

7. Only 16 percent manufactured patented products.

8. Thirty-eight percent of the sample depended on U.S. suppliers for raw materials for their principal product, 28 percent depended on both local and U.S. sources, and 32 percent depended solely on local sources. For their second most important product, 43 percent obtained their raw materials from the United States, 27 percent obtained them from the U.S. and Puerto Rico, and 27 percent solely from Puerto Rico.[70]

This study suggests that the division of labor between local and foreign industry in Puerto Rico continued. The local bourgeoisie remained mainly in production for the local market and, generally, did not compete with U.S. producers; their sources of financing were mainly local and mostly personal. There was, however, a great degree of dependency on the U.S. market for the supplies of raw materials. This industrial fraction of the local bourgeoisie continued to adapt to the dominance of U.S. capital, remaining within the competitive manufacturing sector and assuming a subordinate and complementary role.

But during this period, another fraction of the local bourgeoisie emerged as a consequence of the process of integration of Puerto Rico into the market and financial system of the United States. This process permitted the expansion of and, to a certain degree, the integration of local bourgeois elements into sectors of U.S. transnational capital. This emerging internationalized fraction of the Puerto Rican bourgeoisie is not comparable to those of Brazil and Mexico. This sector was not only small but was greatly assimilated into U.S. capital, and its links with the international economy were mainly articulated through its connections with the U.S.-controlled international financial network. This fraction was clearly connected with the large banking firms and the few large local industrial corporations; some of them were still identified with the families who founded the enterprises, like the Ferré family (Ferré Enterprises), the Serrallés family (rum producers), the Carrión and Roig families (banking), and the González family (chemicals and fertilizers). These corporations thrived under the lead of U.S. TNCs and expanded beyond the local economy.[71]

The Exacerbation of the Politicoideological Contradictions

With the emergence of the new petty bourgeoisie and the embryonic internationalized local bourgeoisie, the political base of support of peripheral capitalism widened. These forces born out of the CI/EP strategy could fulfill the functions of intermediaries as well as, or even better than, the PPD technobureaucracy. This meant the end of the dominance of the technobureaucracy. Their historic role as the "midwife" of the restructuring of imperialist capitalism in Puerto Rico had been fulfilled. Others could direct the process now.

The PPD's ability to continue the task of leading the country on the path of progress was weakened in two ways. First, the persistence of poverty and unemployment, the increase in crime, poor housing, etc., created discontent among the working classes. Second, the limitations of the colonial relation for industrial expansion and the failure of the PPD to renegotiate the colonial pact in 1959 created discontent among sectors of the local bourgeoisie. Issues such as minimum wage, tax exemptions, and uncertainty in the industrial climate due to the unpredictability of changes in federal regulations were major points of contention. The exacerbation of these contradictions were expressed initially in a process of political realignment, the high point of which was the division of the PPD and the PER in 1967, and in the first electoral defeat of the PPD since 1940 in the 1968 election.

The End of the PPD's Hegemony: Political Realignments

Factional conflict was intensified under the governorship of Sánchez Vilella between 1965 and 1968; the neoreformists became openly associated with Governor Sánchez, while the conservative faction became associated with Senate Vice President Luis Negrón Lopez, who now gained the support of Muñoz.[72]

The neoreformist faction, by advocating a return to the reformist policies of the 1940s, intended to preserve the key intermediary role of the technobureaucracy as an autonomous political force (i.e., a social category). According to their views, the role of the party and the PPD government was to mediate the conflicts and contradictions generated by capitalist development. They thought that the PPD should try to conciliate the contradiction between capitalist accumulation and the well-being of the working classes by using the colonial state to intervene in the economy, as it did in the forties.

For its part, the conservative faction, led by founding members of the party and the technobureaucracy linked to the party since the early stages of the CI/EP strategy, argued against any major change in the course of the development strategy, particularly against any attempt to restrict or regulate private capital since this could affect the business climate on the island and endanger the continuity of the CI/EP strategy. Many of the members of this faction had become associated with private business by using their influence in government. This was the case, for example, of Teodoro Moscoso, who went from head of Fomento, to U.S. ambassador in Venezuela, to vice president of CORCO.[73]

Curiously, the principal battles in this factional conflict dealt mainly with the basic aspects of the political orientation, the style of administration, and the public philosophy that the PPD should adopt, rather than with any specific reform project. To a great extent, the conflict emerged in anticipation of possible changes in the political course and leadership of the PPD. On the one hand, the neoreformist faction wanted to lay the basis for the reorientation of the PPD's policies toward social reforms. On the other hand, the conservative faction, partly assimilated to private interests, was trying to prevent any "radical" changes in the political course of the PPD. It can be argued that the factional conflict within the PPD was the result of the ideological contradictions generated by the impact of the CI/EP strategy on the Puerto Rican social structure. The technobureaucracy was divided as to how to resolve the contradiction between being absorbed by capital and disappearing as an autonomous social force or reaffirming itself as an autonomous social force through a revival of state reformism.

Finally, in 1967, Sánchez and the neoreformist faction split from the PPD to form the Partido del Pueblo (PP). This party, like the PPD, favored commonwealth status; hence, it needed to look for its own political space and clearly differentiate itself from the PPD in other directions. The attempt to establish a political identity was directed toward the revival of the populist rhetoric and style that had been lost by the PPD. The PP intended to occupy the political vacuum left in Puerto Rican politics by the PPD's assimilation into corporate interests. Thus, the central issues of the PP's campaign were that the PPD leadership had sold out to corporate power, had forgotten the people, and had become an antidemocratic, self-serving government machine. However, somewhat surprisingly, very little was said about issues like foreign capital's excessive control over the economy, the need to stimulate more local investments, and other questions about the structural problems of the island's economy that had been the object of debate in the past. For the PP, the issues of the 1968 election campaign dealt more with questions of political style than economic development. The PP tried to rearticulate the people/power bloc contradiction in the tradition of the populist reformism of the forties, but it did not put forward a comprehensive reform program.[74]

The neoreformist faction that formed the PP found itself in an ideological trap. To legitimate itself and find its specific political space vis-à-vis the PPD, the PP had to resort to the reformist populist rhetoric of the 1940s, and it had to appeal to the working classes by promising to resolve the problems generated by the CI/EP strategy. Yet, at the same time, to maintain economic growth within the existing colonial relation—to which the PP pledged allegiance—it had to continue to support the CI/EP strategy, which was the very root of the problems that they intended to solve. If the PP was to provide any permanent solution to the problems it denounced, it would have to redefine the political and economic basis of the existing accumulation model, the CI/EP strategy. This was impossible without altering the colonial relation, which the U.S Congress blocked in 1959.

The PPD was not the only party affected by the early signs of political discontent with the colonial status in the mid-1960s, and the PP was not the only attempt by emerging political forces to occupy the political vacuum left by the PPD's incapacity to solve the problems of Puerto Rican society at that time. In 1967, the PER also split, and the Partido Nuevo Progresista (PNP) emerged. The immediate cause for this division was the decision by the dominant faction of the PER leadership not to participate in a plebiscite to be held in 1967 on the colonial status question. The PPD was pushing for a plebiscite, in which the people would choose between the political formulas of independence, commonwealth, or statehood, because if the commonwealth formula won—and they were confident it would—they could use it to pressure the U.S. Congress to grant some of the reforms it had denied them in 1959.

However, the real cause of the division in the PER was over the annexationist political project. The traditional leadership of the PER, who had been linked to sugar production and had survived by diversifying into land speculation, rum production, and other such activities, represented the traditional annexationist position of the wealthy, who wanted statehood as a means of perpetuating their privileged positions. This conservative faction was led by Miguel A. García Méndez, who had been president of the PER since 1952 and was from one of the wealthiest sugar-producing families on the island. The internationalized fraction of the local bourgeoisie and the new petty bourgeoisie represented an emerging political force whose development had been fostered by the CI/EP strategy. This faction was led by Luis Ferré, who had been vice president of the PER since 1952. Although the Ferré family was part of the local bourgeoisie long before the industrialization policies of the PPD began, the growth of Ferré Enterprises accelerated under them.[75]

A series of contradictions had been developing between these two factions on how to articulate an annexationist political project that could compete effectively for political power with the PPD. The traditional sector wanted statehood for Puerto Rico with no substantial alteration of the social structure. For its part, the faction that represented the internationalized bourgeoisie and the new petty bourgeoisie held the view that for statehood to be supported by the majority of Puerto Ricans it had to offer a viable solution to the socioeconomic problems of the island.

Contrary to the PER, identified as the party of the conservative rich, the PNP projected the image of a party committed to social reform for the poor and presented itself as a new reformist alternative in the populist tradition abandoned by the PPD. It launched a massive and well-organized media campaign with slogans promising that things would change (*esto tiene que cambiar*), that they would bring a new life (*la nueva vida*) where the poor would come first (*los humildes serán los primeros*).[76]

The PNP adopted other policies that clearly distinguished it from the PER. For the 1968 election, the PNP declared that the colonial status question was not an issue, that a vote for the PNP was not necessarily a vote for statehood.[77] This shifted the focus of attention from the political issue of annexation to more immediate bread-and-butter issues. By adopting this tactic, the PNP could break the rigid political loyalties associated with the status issue and seek the support of those who wanted social and economic changes without changing the colonial relation. This was what the PPD had done in the 1940s as a transitional measure to renegotiating the colonial pact. The PNP was looking toward a new kind of colonial accommodation, the annexation of Puerto Rico as the fifty-first state.

The PNP posed the question of statehood from a new perspective, which became known as "creole statehood" (*estadidad jíbara*).[78] According to the PNP, Puerto Rico would not have to lose its Hispanic cultural identity or assimilate into the Anglo-Saxon North American culture to become a state. Puerto Ricans would not have to give up Spanish as their main language. Instead, they would only add English to their culture as a vehicle to communicate with their fellow U.S. citizens of the North. Trivial as this may sound, it was a major issue in Puerto Rican politics. The PPD had used the language and culture issues against the PER by instigating fears that statehood would take away the Puerto Rican people's identity—which the proindependence groups reinforced—thus presenting itself vis-à-vis the PER as the alternative that offered the best of two worlds: the economic advantages of a direct link with the United States, combined with the preservation of the "Spanish" cultural identity. The new statehood political project intended to counter this.

The PNP intended to capitalize on the discontent of the working classes, focusing its campaign on better housing for the poor, especially the urban poor in the shanty towns (*arrabales*), better wages, education, public and health services, and more jobs. They also blamed the PPD for the growing drug and crime problems of the island, arguing that the PPD had created a materialistic society that was the cause of these problems.[79] In this context, the PNP cast its political project as the beginning of a "new life" for the Puerto Rican working people. Statehood was but a secondary issue, a goal for the realization of a better society. The immediate issue was to deal with the problems resulting from the PPD's rule, which were threatening the stability of the country.

For their part, the PIP also attempted a renewal of the independence political project. There was a change in its leadership and a new Christian Democratic political platform was adopted, the first in a series of changes that culminated with the adoption of "democratic socialism" as the PIP's political platform in 1972. Historically, the PIP had articulated the nationalist aspirations of the traditional petty bourgeoisie. Now, in the wake of a process of political realignment, it was trying to reach a share of the discontented working classes with a social reformist political program.[80]

This process of political realignment resulted in a victory for the PNP, which won the 1968 election by a narrow margin, receiving 42 percent of the vote to the PPD's 40 percent. The PP received 9.5 percent, the PIP 2.7 percent, and the PER 0.4 percent.[81] The only detailed statistical analysis available of the 1968 election showed that the PNP vote came mainly from the urban sectors. Within these sectors, the vote came from those geographical areas identified in the study as dominated by low, middle-low, and upper social stratas, according to an index combining income employment and education levels.[82] A broader interpretation of these findings would suggest that the electoral support of the PNP came mainly from the marginal sectors, low stratum; the workers not linked to the most dynamic economic sector, low-middle stratum; and elements of the local bourgeoisie and the new petty bourgeoisie, high stratum. If this is a reasonable reading of the empirical evidence, then it can be said that the support for the PNP came from emerging social forces that were the direct product of the socioeconomic processes unleashed by the CI/EP strategy; the PPD had dug its own grave.

Conversely, the same study showed that the support for the PPD came substantially from the rural areas. In the San Juan metropolitan area, the electoral support of the PPD came mainly from the low, middle-low, and middle strata, with little support from the upper strata.[83] Again, interpreting these findings broadly, it could be argued that the PPD still had the support of those who put it in power in 1940 and who, ironically, benefited the least from the CI/EP strategy, the rural population. The PPD also maintained a degree of support among the working population despite a general environment of political discontent. One cannot underestimate also the impact of the PP on the erosion of the electoral base of the PPD. In any case, it is clear that by 1968 the hegemony enjoyed by the PPD was in decline.

From the above arguments it seems reasonable to assert that the main local beneficiaries of the CI/EP strategy (the new petty bourgeoisie and the internationalized fraction of the local bourgeoisie) began to articulate an alternative political project to preserve their privileges as soon as they perceived that the contradictions within the PPD could negatively affect the continuity of the existing order. The leading groups of the PNP believed that the political link to the United States was the cornerstone of their continued socioeconomic prosperity; hence, they favored statehood. Their willingness to accept commonwealth status suggests that their main concern was to preserve the political link with the United States at any cost. Their main fear was the possibility of independence. The fact that statehood would bring the added economic burden of federal income taxes to Puerto Ricans seemed to bother them less than the potential of radical changes in the colonial relation.

A new element in the emerging statehood political project was the support it gained within circles of the North American bourgeoisie. In an article that appeared in the journal of the U.S. Chamber of Commerce, many of the interviewed U.S. businessmen were beginning to think of statehood as a desirable and viable alternative that could be achieved in the foreseeable future. A U.S. executive of one of the world's largest oil companies with operations on the island stated categorically that Puerto Rico should be ready for statehood within ten years. This represented a substantial shift in the thinking of U.S. businessmen on the island who generally had been strong supporters of the commonwealth.[84]

The support for the PNP shown by the discontented working classes, the marginal sectors, and the urban poor is actually evidence of the dominance of the developmentalist ideology of the PPD. The logic of their colonialist posture was now taken to its ultimate expression: annexation to the metropolis. If progress, as the PPD had successfully argued for three decades, was only possible because of the colonial relation, then the continuity of progress must depend on the continuity of the political linkage to the United States. And what greater guarantee of continuity than annexation? In view of the crisis within the PPD, it was "logical" that a sector of the workers immersed in the ideological praxis of developmentalism turned to support the alternative political project that was posed in the very terms of developmentalism.

Two other elements contributed to the increased support of the annexationist political project. One was the influx of Cuban exiles to Puerto Rico in the 1960s, many of whom became very active in launching anti-communist, anti-independence, and pro-U.S. campaigns, thus providing added support to the PNP. The other was the return to the island of Puerto Ricans who had migrated to the United States. Many of these people believed that statehood would automatically bring the standard of living in Puerto Rico to the higher level of the United States.

The PNP's First Turn in Office

Once in power, the PNP continued the same economic strategy centered around the expansion of the petrochemical industry; they made no major changes in development policy. In his second message to the legislature, Governor Ferré reaffirmed the importance of the petrochemical complex and his commitment to continue existing policies, in spite of his often expressed opposition to the tax-exemption policy of the PPD.[85]

The most important changes in economic policy made by the PNP were an increase in government spending and tax reductions. The wages of public school teachers, policemen, and most government employees were increased. A law was passed entitling public employees to a Christmas cash bonus, and tax deductions for individuals were increased. In the long run, this would result in an increase in the government deficit and public debt. In the short run, however, it was the PNP's way of trying to increase its popular base of support. Having come to power with an embryonic political project that articulated the discontent of many social sectors with the shortcomings of the CI/EP strategy, rather than a clear and well-developed alternative, the PNP had to continue with the existing development policy while using the state to deliver on some of its promises.

Despite all of its efforts, the PNP could not hold on to power. Their failure to capitalize on the political opening presented by the leadership crisis in the PPD can be attributed in part to their inability to present statehood as a clearly viable and better alternative. This was not due to intellectual limitations or lack of effort. There was a structural limit to what the PNP could do to veer the country toward statehood. They came to power riding the tide of political and economic discontent with the PPD. Yet, despite all of the contradictions and shortcomings of the CI/EP strategy, the PNP was saddled with this strategy. And, as the PPD had always argued, there was an intimate relation between the industrialization program and commonwealth status. The tax incentives and exceptional oil quotas on which the continued growth of the CI/EP strategy was based would be impossible if Puerto Rico were to become a state. The existing colonial relation embodied in the commonwealth formula was a structural condition of the CI/EP strategy. As long as this strategy remained the cornerstone of the economy, statehood would remain an unattractive alternative to the dominant classes.

It could be argued, thus, that the electoral triumph of the PNP in 1968 was a premature leap forward in the life of the emergent classes who were politically unprepared to provide a clear alternative political project to make statehood appealing to both the dominant and subordinate classes. The leading classes within PNP got caught in a quagmire of trying to use the contradictions of the CI/EP strategy to move the country toward statehood while having to operate within its structure. Until the CI/EP strategy had exhausted its capacity to grow (when intermediate processing activities benefiting from exceptional concessions became unprofitable), the PNP leadership would have problems convincing the majority of the dominant and subordinate classes of the superiority of statehood. The PPD was right, the existing economic model was inextricably tied to the colonial relation.

But it was not only the structural imperatives of the colonial framework that brought the PNP out of power. The exacerbation of politicoideological contradictions in Puerto Rican society continued during the PNP's term in office. Between 1968/69 and 1971/72, there were an average of 87.5 strikes per year involving an average annual total of 17,450 workers. During the last three years of the previous PPD administration, there were an average of 55 strikes per year involving an average total of 9,515 workers.[86] There were also two student riots at the University of Puerto Rico's Río Piedras campus. Both of the riots, in March 1970 and 1971, were related to growing opposition to the Vietnam War and the presence of the Reserve Officers Training Corps (ROTC) on that campus. Some argued that the deeper reasons behind the violence of the protest lay in the polarization between pro- and anti-U.S. forces brought about by the PNP administration.[87]

The increased level of political conflict during the PNP tenure was reflected in part also by the radicalization and the growth in the activism of the proindependence forces. The PIP became a socialist party in 1971, and the MPI became the Partido Socialista Puertorriqueño (PSP) and adopted a Marxist-Leninist platform.[88] Both parties tried to capitalize on the increased labor unrest, developing a working-class political project, and were behind many of the strikes in this period. Although the PNP did try to use this to its advantage, arguing that statehood was the best answer to the "Communist threat," this scare tactic backfired. Many argued that the increased anti-U.S. militancy was a reaction to the PNP's pro-statehood activism.

While the PNP found itself entangled in trying to solve the political and economic problems of the colony, the PPD underwent a significant renovation. They elected a new leader and renewed their program in an attempt to reunite the party. The new leader, Rafael Hernández Colón, was a young lawyer who had "flirted" with the neoreformist faction in its early days. The PPD published a political manifesto known as the "Pronunciamiento de Aguas Buenas," which promised that the party would strive to obtain greater political autonomy for the island to improve economic and political conditions. This new political line met some of the demands of the neoreformist technocrats that had gone to the PP and allowed the return of PP leaders and voters to the PPD.[89]

The PPD thus managed to return to power in 1972. The fact that the short-term stay of the PNP in office had brought forth the structural constraints of statehood and the structural link between commonwealth and the continued expansion of capitalist accumulation under the CI/EP model prompted many to think that the 1968 victory of the PNP was a fluke allowed by the split in the PPD. A comparison of the 1968 and 1972 electoral results would lend credence to this theory. In 1972, the PNP vote went down by 2 percent to 40 percent and the PPD's increased by 6.6 percent to 46.3 percent, while the PP's went from 9.5 to 0.2 percent and the PIP's went up from 2.7 to 4 percent.[90] The evidence seemed clear—the PP vote had "returned" to the PPD. The PPD boasted that now they were in for another four decades. With the crisis of the party behind them, the restoration of the PPD's hegemony appeared to be underway. Yet what the restorationist leaders of the PPD did not understand was that what was taking place was not a shift of votes but a deeper process of political realignment. If the PPD could not deal with the socioeconomic problems and contradictions of the CI/EP strategy effectively, there now was an alternative in the making. The PNP had at least shown that it could run the country as well or as badly as the PPD.

The Collapse of the CI/EP Strategy

The restorationist hopes of the PPD leadership crashed with the structural realities of the vulnerability of the export-led strategy to international economic changes in 1973. The abolition of the oil import quota system and the Arab oil embargo made apparent the key limitation of the CI/EP strategy. The external forces that conditioned the direction of the Puerto Rican economy had taken a series of decisions, as a function of their interests, that ended abruptly the viability of the continued expansion of the intermediate processing petrochemical complex. The Puerto Rican economy had been dealt a crushing blow in the reshuffling of the international division of labor caused by the oil crisis of 1973. The exceptional conditions that gave Puerto Rico a "comparative advantage" in intermediate petrochemical production for the U.S. market disappeared quickly.

Aware of the new realities, the PPD's technobureaucracy attempted to reconnect Puerto Rico to the international circuit of the oil processing industry. They started plans to build a deep-water port on the island as part of a large oil storage, refining, and transshipment complex to supply the U.S. market, mainly the East Coast. The project was to be financed by the government of Puerto Rico and private concerns from the United States, Venezuela, and the Middle East. In the end, the "superport" project, as it became known, was discarded.[91]

The PPD also attempted to attract U.S. capital to other projects, such as a copper mining and processing complex, a car assembly plant, a shipyard, and a steel mill. The first of these projects proposed the commercial exploitation of copper deposits located in the central region of Puerto Rico. Mining contracts had been negotiated in the 1960s with American Metal Climax and Kennecott Corporation. The companies and the government had not been able to reach a final agreement due to the companies' refusal to meet the economic conditions of the government and because of the political opposition of environmentalists and proindependence groups concerned with the environmental and politicoeconomic impact of copper mining activities. After the 1973 oil shock, the PPD tried to revive negotiations with the companies, but no progress was made. The other three projects never went beyond the planning stage.[92]

The 1973 oil crisis and the worldwide recession that accompanied it plunged Puerto Rico into the worst economic crisis it had seen since the 1930s and prompted Fomento strategists to question the viability of restoring economic growth on the basis of export-processing industries.[93] But despite the recognition of the structural nature of the crisis of the CI/EP strategy by some of the more sophisticated technocrats in Fomento, the PPD attributed the crisis to external elements, the oil shock, and the world recession, and tried to deal with it accordingly. The governor appointed two special committees to study the crisis and provide alternatives.

The Committee for the Strategy of Puerto Rico embarked on a comprehensive study of the development strategy to chart a new course. The recommendations of their report, however, ignored the issue raised by Fomento and recommended ways to continue the CI/EP strategy. In the third chapter of the report, which ironically is entitled "New Routes for Industrial Growth," the committee suggests that a successful new strategy should emphasize attracting industries less sensitive to wage increases; promote basic industries, such as petrochemicals, steel, and copper, which provide inputs to existing and new processing activities; and offer new incentives to stimulate the continuation of foreign investment. Other recommendations included the attraction of new light industries, such as precision instruments and electrical machinery, and the creation of a science and technology center to attract these new industries.[94] Additional recommendations in the report were to delay the decline of the still important labor-intensive industries and promote import substitution, agricultural development, and the expansion of services, particularly tourism.

The thrust of the report was the restoration of the export manufacturing sector. Export processing was seen as the fulcrum of the economy and the other sectors were seen as supportive of it. The report was mainly a restatement of the old development strategy, with a new interest in agriculture and production for the local market as palliatives to the current recession. At no point did the report consider a major change in the course of the CI/EP strategy; the categories of developmentalism still confined the analysis of the committee. The "new strategy" was more of the same—new export-processing industries or activities to complement the leading export-processing sector. The lack of vision in this report was such that at one point it implied that the petrochemical industry in Puerto Rico would recover as soon as current oil price distortions became normalized.[95]

The other committee appointed by the governor was the "Tobin Committee," which was to deal with the financial crisis of the colonial state. Curiously, this committee had no Puerto Rican members. Most of the original members came from North American universities, consulting firms, or think tanks, with the exception of Ralph Saul, who was the president of the First Boston Corporation, a major bond agent for the government of Puerto Rico. Although Saul resigned four months after being appointed, this gave credence to the notion that Wall Street holders of government of Puerto Rico bonds had imposed this scrutiny of Puerto Rican finances on the PPD. Indeed, the connection between First Boston Corporation and the government of Puerto Rico was not a figment of anyone's imagination. Gordon K. Lewis described the dealings between the two institutions as follows:

> [T]he economy's largest public corporation, the Water Resources Authority, is controlled by a complex network of North American interests which it would take the genius of a first class accountant to unravel. Its bonds are floated, at interests, in the American market by the First National Boston Corporation; the construction firm of Jackson and Moreland designs and builds its electrical plants, while the firm Burns and Roe act as its technical advisers and consultants; both of these are subsidiaries of United Engineers and Construction Company, a subsidiary of Raytheon, which in turn is the property of the First National Boston Corporation. The Authority, moreover, buys its combustible fuels from CORCO; one of the principal stockholders of CORCO is the First National Bank of Boston; and the latter is the property of the First National Boston Corporation thus bringing the wheel full circle.[96]

Certainly, the main conclusions of the report reflected the class biases of the members of the committee. The report recommended harsh fiscal measures in the period immediately preceding the 1976 elections: a freeze on wages of public sector employees, an increase in personal income taxes, a reduction in public expenditures, and an increase in tax incentives to U.S. investment. All this in spite of repeatedly pointing out that the key problems of the Puerto Rican economy originated in the high degree of dependence on external investment, excessive drainage of capital, and the unstable character of U.S. subsidiaries' operations on the island.[97] The formula proposed by the committee was fairly simple: the working classes would have to pay the cost of stability. No government-appointed committee interested in the reelection of the PPD would have made such recommendations. Clearly, this report was not palatable to the workers; neither would it be for the PPD in an election year.

Finally, aware that in order to restore its political hegemony it needed to secure the politicoeconomic conditions for the renewal of the CI/EP strategy, the PPD once more proposed to the U.S. Congress a revision of Law 600. In December 1975, the PPD's resident commissioner in Washington presented a proposal that was introduced in the U.S. House of Representatives as H.R. 11200. This bill was similar to the Fernos-Murray Bill of 1959. It proposed to exclude Puerto Rico from the application of federal minimum wage laws and to allow the commonwealth government to have control over the immigration of foreigners, jurisdiction over environmental regulations, and to set tariffs on certain foreign goods under special agreements with the consent of the U.S. Congress. The bill asked to provide the governor or the resident commissioner of Puerto Rico with the right to object to nonessential federal legislation, subject to congressional approval for exclusion from such legislation.[98]

As in 1959, the PPD technobureaucracy was trying to renegotiate the colonial pact to enhance the exceptional politicoeconomic conditions upon which the CI/EP strategy was based. To continue the existing process of capital accumulation dominated by U.S. TNCs, some political changes within the colonial relation were needed. Yet, as with the case of the Fernos-Murray Bill, Congress did not act.

The attempts to restore the PPD's hegemony were dealt two fatal blows in 1976. First, the PPD lost the election to the PNP. Second, President Gerald Ford announced publicly his support for statehood for Puerto Rico and introduced a bill in Congress to study its viability.[99] This would initiate a process of revision and restructuring, charting a new direction for both the CI/EP strategy and the existing colonial relation.

By 1976, it was clear that the conditions for continued capital accumulation under the CI/EP strategy were collapsing. The role of Puerto Rico as the backyard of U.S. manufacturing industries was becoming less profitable and, hence, less viable. Yet developmentalism was holding the collapsing structure together. The alternative to the PPD was the PNP, which moved within the confines of colonialism and the categories of developmentalism. The politicoideological bases of imperialist capitalism were not being questioned. The search was on for a new accommodation between the emerging local dominant groups and U.S. capital. One group thought statehood would achieve this; the other proposed more autonomy within the colonial relation. At this juncture the situation was fluid but, as usual, metropolitan interests would lead and the local colonial groups would have to follow.

Notes

1. AFE, *Informe anual, 1958/59*, p. 4.
2. NACLA, "U.S. Unions in Puerto Rico," pp. 10–11. Calero and Herrero, "Statements," pp. 1–6; and Reynolds and Gregory, *Wages, Productivity and Industrialization*, pp. 44–45, 304.
3. U.S. Department of Commerce, *Economic Study*, 2, p. 56. Aside from different general minimum wage levels, there were differential levels of minimum wages among industrial branches in Puerto Rico; Reynolds and Gregory, *Wages, Productivity and Industrialization*, Chap. 2; also AFE, *Informe anual, 1958/59*, pp. 12–13.
4. Reynolds and Gregory, *Wages, Productivity and Industrialization*, p. 83.

5. AFE, *Informe anual, 1958/59*, pp. 10–11; U.S. Department of Commerce, *Economic Study*, 2, pp. 443–447.

6. In 1954, Fomento requested research proposals on the viability of a petrochemical complex on the island from various North American research institutions. There are two of these proposals in the Fomento library (see Illinois Institute of Technology, "Survey;" and Battelle Memorial Institute, "Proposed Research"). Three studies on the viability of developing a petroleum processing complex were published. See Vietorisz, *The Feasibility*; Airov, *The Location*; and Isard, Schooler, and Vietorisz, *Industrial Complex*. For a comprehensive account of the U.S. oil import regulation programs, see Bohi and Russell, *Limiting Oil Imports*.

7. AFE, *Informe anual, 1958/59*, pp. 9–10; García and Quintero Rivera, *Desafío y solidaridad*, pp. 137–138; and NACLA, "U.S. Unions in Puerto Rico," pp. 12–13.

8. Omega Management, Inc., "Intention of Sixty Companies."

9. PPD, *Programa, 1960*, pp. 30–34; García Passalacqua, *La crisis política*, p. 19.

10. Bayrón Toro, *Elecciones y partidos*, p. 349; and Figueroa Díaz, *El movimiento estadista*, pp. 54–55.

11. Bayrón Toro, *Elecciones y partidos*, p. 349; Anderson, *Party Politics*, pp. 42–45, 111–113.

12. Meléndez, *Statehood Movement*, pp. 98–99.

13. Silén, *Historia de la nación*, pp. 365–380; and Mari Bras, *El caso de Puerto Rico*, pp. 10–13.

14. Fernós Isern, *El Estado Libre Asociado*, pp. 416–418.

15. This thesis was initially proposed by García Passalacqua, *La crisis política*, but it was later subscribed to by others. See Velázquez, *Muñoz y Sánchez Vilella*; Lewis, *Notes*, p. 22; and Silén, *Historia de la nación*, pp. 370–371, 407–408.

16. Baquero, "La importación de fondos" and "Magnitud y características"; Nieves Falcón, "El futuro ideológico."

17. Puerto Rico, *Leyes* (1963), pp. 92–134; AFE, *Elementos claves*, p. 24. An amendment in 1969 to Law 57 changed the tax exemption periods to 10, 12, 15, and 17 years, depending on the zone in which the industry was located. Another amendment in 1972 changed the periods to 10, 12, 15, 1, 7, and 25 years. The 25-year exemption was applicable only to the municipalities of Vieques and Culebra (two islands off the east coast of Puerto Rico). In 1974, yet another amendment changed the tax exemption periods to 10, 15, 25, and 30 years.

18. Muñoz Marín, *Mensaje* (1963), p. 3.

19. See p. 79 for the TNCs that initiated this trend. U.S. Department of Commerce, *Economic Study*, 2, pp. 73–77; and U.S. Department of Treasury, *Operation and Effect: First Annual Report*, pp. 9–11.

20. Bohi and Russell, *Limiting Oil Imports*, pp. 66–71, 168–174; Bellah, "The Impact," pp. 68–77.

21. Vietorisz, *The Feasibility*; Airov, *The Location*; Isard, Schooler, and Vietorisz, *Industrial Complex*.

22. *Chemical Week*, 23 July 1966, pp. 29–32; *Chemical Week*, 25 May 1968, pp. 26–27, 31.

23. Bellah, "The Impact," pp. 4, 72; and Bohi and Russell, *Limiting Oil Imports*, p. 170; *Chemical Week*, 20 February 1965, pp. 21–22; *Oil and Gas Journal*, 22 April 1968, p. 116; *Oil and Gas Journal*, 7 July 1969, p. 98; *Chemical Week*, 29 April 1967, pp. 29–31.

140   *Development Strategies as Ideology*

24. Muñoz Marín, *Mensaje* (1963), p.3.
25. Santiago Meléndez, *Reforma fiscal*, p. 124.
26. Durand, "Progreso," pp. 176–178.
27. Muñoz Marín, *Mensaje* (1964), pp. 4–8.
28. Muñoz was directly involved in the preparation of the 1964 program. See Farr, *Personalismo y política*, pp. 57–58, 67; and PPD, *Compilación de Programas*, pp. 92–93.
29. Muñoz's decision to retire was not disclosed until a few hours before its official announcement to the PPD's general assembly on 16 August 1964. See Velázquez, *Muñoz y Sánchez Vilella*, Chap. 2. The most accepted interpretations of Muñoz's retirement argue that it was his intention to complete the process of institutionalization of the party. According to Wells, this was a classic example of Weber's "routinization of charisma." Wells, *Modernization*, pp. 317–319; and Farr, *Personalismo y política*, p. 43.
30. Sánchez Vilella, *Discursos de campaña*, p. 38.
31. Ibid., p. 39.
32. Bellah, "The Impact," p. 81.
33. U.S. Department of Commerce, *Economic Study*, 2, p. 50, Table 2.
34. U.S. Bureau of the Census, *Census of Manufactures, 1963*, p. 155, Table 1.
35. U.S. Bureau of the Census, *Census of Manufactures, 1967*, p. 100, Table 1.
36. U.S. Bureau of the Census, *Census of Manufactures, 1972*, and *1977 Economic Censuses of Outlying Areas, Manufactures*. Data on economic performance of industries by ownership's origin is kept by Fomento and the Planning Board, but it is not published and is only selectively available to the public.
37. U.S. Department of Commerce, *Economic Study*, 2, p. 37.
38. U.S. Bureau of the Census, *Census of Manufactures, 1972*, Table 1, summary statistics.
39. Dietz, *Economic History*, p. 259.
40. Puerto Rico. Comité para el estudio, *Informe al gobernador*, pp. 85–86. Hereafter *Informe Tobin*.
41. Calculated from unpublished data obtained from the Economic Division of Fomento and PREDA, *List of Firms*.
42. PREDA, *The Petroleum Refining Industry, 1977*, p. 5; PREDA, *The Drug and Pharmaceutical Industry*, pp. 2–4, 28–36; PREDA, *The Electrical and Electronic Industry*, pp. 3–4, 21–48.
43. Calculated from the same sources as Table 4.4.
44. U.S. Department of Commerce, *Economic Study*, 2, p. 67, Table 16.
45. *Informe Tobin*, pp. 59–60.
46. Ibid.
47. Ibid., and U.S. Department of Commerce, *Economic Study*, 2, p. 75.
48. Puerto Rico. Cámara de Representantes, *Informe*.
49. U.S. Bureau of the Census, *Census of Manufactures, 1972*, pp. 43–45, and *1977 Economic Censuses of Outlying Areas, Manufactures*, pp. 66–69.
50. Calculated from Junta de Planificación, *Ingreso y producto, 1984*, pp. 6–11. The negative impact of this tendency on the Puerto Rican economy has been pointed out in various studies. See U.S. Department of Commerce, *Economic Study*, 1, pp. 61–62; and Dietz, *Economic History*, pp. 245–246.
51. U.S. Department of the Treasury, *Operation and Effect: First Annual Report*, pp. 52–53; Costas Elena, "I.R.C. Section 936," p. 257.

52. U.S. Department of Commerce, *Economic Study*, 2, pp. 89–90.
53. Junta de Planificación, *Balanza de pagos, 1942–1961* and *1978*, p. 6, and p. 6, respectively.
54. Junta de Planificación, *Informe económico, 1978*, p. A-31.
55. Bohi and Russell, *Limiting Oil Imports*, pp. 230–235.
56. U.S. Department of Commerce, *Economic Study*, 2, pp. 234–237; and Perry, "The United States," p. 75.
57. U.S. Department of Commerce, *Economic Study*, 2, p. 67.
58. U.S. Department of Commerce, *Economic Study*, 2, pp. 229–244.
59. Maldonado Denis, *Emigration Dialectic*, Chap. 7 and Table 6, p. 135; Junta de Planificación, *Anuario estadístico, 1976*, p. 142; and Duany, "De la periferia a la semi-periferia," p. 50. The figures present a disproportionate migration of Dominicans because they come from different sources and the government of Puerto Rico calculates net migration by subtracting total passenger departures from arrivals.
60. Junta de Planificación, *Informe económico, 1967* and *1977*, pp. A-21 and A-26, respectively.
61. Puerto Rico, Departamento del Trabajo, *Empleo y desempleo, 1967, 1977*, pp. 6 and 4, respectively.
62. See Quijano, "The Marginalized Pole of the Economy;" Toro Calder, "Violencia individual en Puerto Rico," pp. 43–58; Vales and Hernández, "Modernización de la violencia," pp. 111–132.
63. Junta de Planificación, *Balanza de pagos, 1978*, pp. 45–46; and *Informe económico, 1977*, pp. 283–284.
64. Junta de Planificación, *Informe económico, 1967* and *1977*, p. A-22 and p. A-27.
65. Poulantzas, *Classes in Contemporary Capitalism*, pp. 251–270.
66. Carrión, "The Petty Bourgeoisie."
67. Mandel, *Marxist Economic Theory*, pp. 153–154.
68. Departamento del Trabajo, "Series de salario."
69. Calculated from the data in Junta de Planificación, *Informe económico, 1979*, p. A-2.
70. Clapp and Mayne, Inc., *Características de la industria puertorriqueña*, pp. vii–xvi.
71. Not only did these enterprises expanded in connection with U.S. TNCs, but many of these families invested in stock of TNCs. There are no studies of this process; this analysis is based on personal observations and information gathered from various sources.
72. García Passalacqua, *La crisis política*, p. 22 and passim.
73. In February 1972 the president of the PIP made public a list of PPD and PNP leaders linked to private businesses, both U.S. and local. A large number of PPD leaders on the list had made their way into business by using their influential position in government. *La Hora*, 8–14 February 1972, p. 2.
74. See the main speeches of the 1968 campaign in Sánchez Vilella, *Que el pueblo decida*.
75. Edgardo Meléndez argues that the group challenging the conservative traditional leadership was led by the middle classes and the local industrial bourgeoisie discontented with the privileges that Operation Bootstrap gave to U.S. capital. Here I attempt to specify the particular fractions within these sectors since, as it was argued, there was a fraction of the local bourgeoisie that thrived under the CI/EP strategy and supported the PPD and the middle class was not a homogeneous group. See Meléndez, *Statehood Movement*, pp.

93–100; Mattos Cintrón, *La política y lo político*, pp. 162–163; and Figueroa Díaz, *El movimiento estadista*, p. 54.

76. Meléndez calls this "the politics of redemption;" *Statehood Movement*, pp. 104–108. See some of the campaign speeches of PNP leader Luis A. Ferré in *El propósito humano*.

77. Ferré, *El propósito humano*, p. 296.

78. Ibid., pp. 304–305.

79. Ibid., pp. 299–300 and passim; PNP, *Programa preliminar*.

80. PIP, *Programa* (1968), p. 4. The petty bourgeois character of the PIP in particular and the independence movement in general is analyzed in Carrión, "The Petty Bourgeoisie," esp. pp. 246ff.

81. Calculated from Bayrón Toro, *Elecciones y partidos*, p. 349.

82. Quintero, *Elecciones de 1968*, pp. 31–45.

83. Ibid., pp. 16, 45–50.

84. *Nation's Business*, 57 (December 1969), p. 54.

85. PNP, *Programa preliminar*, p. 4; Ferré, *El propósito humano*, pp. 181–182.

86. Calculated from data of the Negociado de Conciliación y Arbitraje, Departamento del Trabajo de Puerto Rico.

87. Nieves Falcón, García Rodríguez, and Ojeda Reyes, *Grito y mordaza*, pp. 11–36; Figueroa Díaz, *El movimiento estadista*, p. 112.

88. PIP, "Programa, 1972," in Banco Popular, *Guía para las elecciones*, pp. 47–91; and PSP-MPI, *Declaración general*.

89. PPD, "Programa, 1972," in Banco Popular, *Guía para las elecciones*, p. 37; and Figueroa Díaz, *El movimiento estadista*, p. 112.

90. Calculated from Bayrón Toro, *Elecciones y partidos*, p. 349.

91. PPD Governor Rafael Hernández Colón went to visit King Faisal of Saudi Arabia to sell him on the idea of the superport. The PPD government thought that if the OPEC countries had a stake in the Puerto Rican complex they might be willing to provide oil at lower prices, which would restore the competitiveness to the Puerto Rican-based industries. But nobody endorsed the Puerto Rican plan. *Oil and Gas Journal*, 11 December 1973, p. 6; AFE, *Hacia una política*.

92. Ross, "Island on the Run," p. 365; AFE, *Base preliminar*.

93. PREDA, *Competitive Position*, p. 8.

94. Puerto Rico. Comité Interagencial, *El desarrollo económico*, pp. 27–37.

95. Ibid., pp. 29–30.

96. Lewis, *Notes*, pp. 235–236.

97. *Informe Tobin*, pp. 1–9, 24–26, 59–61, 85–94, and passim.

98. Tansill, "Independence or Statehood?", pp. 95–96.

99. Ibid., p. 96.

5

Crisis and Restructuring: The High-Finance Strategy

If anything should be evident from the Puerto Rican experience it is that peripheral capitalism can be dynamic and generate economic growth. The notion associated with the dependency school that views peripheral capitalism as stagnant is inadequate to explain the dynamics of countries like Puerto Rico and Brazil. The Puerto Rican and other cases of "dependent development," as Fernando Henrique Cardoso and Peter Evans characterize this type of peripheral accumulation, show that the ability to sustain capitalist accumulation in the periphery depends to a large degree on class interests. That is, the possibility of overcoming cyclical crises and other structural constraints of peripheral accumulation is to a large extent a function of the ability of the power bloc to adjust through shifts in development policies and strategies. Structural changes in the international economy, such as technological innovations, changes in consumption patterns and tastes, and new forms of organization in production and marketing, provide the structural constraints of peripheral accumulation. The ability of the dominant sectors to adjust to these constraints determines the possibility of continued accumulation. In this sense, class interests are not fixed. They may be strategic: for instance, the desire to counter a perceived political threat, as was the case of the Cuban revolution, and U.S. prestige in Latin America in the 1960s, which dictated the need to foster economic growth in Puerto Rico. Or they may be immediate economic interests, as was the case of U.S. capital looking for outlets for its surplus in the 1950s. Whatever the case, successful capital accumulation in the periphery results from the ability to adjust to changing structural social, economic, and political conditions. The ability to adjust in turn depends on the capacity of the metropolitan state and dominant classes and of peripheral propertied classes and state bureaucracies to identify their interests and devise development strategies that are acceptable to the different fractions of the peripheral and metropolitan power blocs. These groups, however, must be able to develop an adequate base of popular support (legitimacy) for their development strategy within the peripheral country or else be prepared to sustain it through authoritarian rule. The experience in Puerto Rico from the 1940s to the early 1970s is one of successful adaptation and legitimation.

Crisis and the Need for Restructuring

Capitalism is a system in which crisis is the norm rather than the exception. Cyclical crises serve to "cleanse" the system, displacing "inefficient" producers and allowing the more "efficient" ones to thrive. In an internationally interconnected system this takes place through changes in the global structure that shift comparative advantages in production from one country or region to another. However, the depth of a crisis is determined by its political as well as its economic impact. Contrary to other cyclical crises, the crisis of 1973–1976 affected not only the working classes and inefficient producers but the colonial state and the leading sectors of transnational capital. What happened in Puerto Rico in the early 1970s was more than routine and could not be solved with minor policy adjustments. It was a structural crisis in the existing model of accumulation that used Puerto Rico as an export platform for U.S. manufacturing industries.

By the mid-1970s Puerto Rico had lost its key advantages as a producer of intermediate manufactures for the U.S. market. First, Puerto Rico lost its wage comparative advantage to other neighboring countries. In 1970 the average hourly wage in manufacturing in Puerto Rico was $1.78, compared to $3.37 in the United States. Although the differential between Puerto Rico and the United States increased from $1.36 in 1960 to $1.59 in 1970, the Puerto Rican average was way above that of its international competitors. In 1969 the average wage in export-processing industries, excluding textiles, was 66 cents per hour in Mexico, 23 cents in other Caribbean countries, and 30 cents in Asian countries.[1]

The early 1970s also saw further increases in the cost of maritime transportation. According to a study of the U.S. Department of Commerce, the three principal American shipping companies handling cargo between Puerto Rico and the United States—Transamerican Trailer Transport (TTT), Seatrain Lines, and Sea-Land Service—increased their rates in 1972 by 18 percent per trailerload and 28 percent for less-than-trailerload. In 1973, these companies imposed a 5.2 percent surcharge on cargo to the United States and 17.2 percent on cargo from the United States. And again, in 1974, TTT proposed yet another rate hike of 12.8 percent. The study concluded that "little can be done that would materially lower the rates" and that "relatively high freight rates can be expected to remain a basic feature of Puerto Rican commercial shipping." The situation was such that the PPD government decided to purchase the assets of the three U.S. companies and create a public corporation to run the island's shipping business at reasonable rates. In 1974, the government formed the Puerto Rico Maritime Shipping Authority, known as Navieras de Puerto Rico. Yet, shortly after starting operations, the Navieras increased rates by 15 percent in 1976, 10 percent in 1977, and were contemplating the need for yet another rate hike in 1978. Meanwhile, some of the U.S. companies reestablished operations on a smaller scale through subsidiaries, competing with the Navieras.[2]

The high cost of energy in Puerto Rico was yet another comparative disadvantage. By 1976 the average annual electricity bill for industrial establishments in Puerto Rico was 31 to 120 percent higher than in the United States, with the exception of the mid-Atlantic region. On average the cost of energy to industries in Puerto Rico was between $700 and $3,390 a year higher, depending on consumption volume.[3]

Finally, the exceptional oil import quotas were lifted and the comparative advantage of cheap foreign oil was erased. The key advantage of the leading industry, petrochemicals, was removed by the stroke of the pen when President Nixon enacted a new energy conservation policy.

In the period following the recession, some economic indicators started to show improvement and others presented a negative long-term perspective. For example, while the GDP grew at a rate of nearly 7 percent between 1976 and 1979 in real terms, real fixed investment declined at a rate of 5.6 percent annually during this period. Private investment in machinery and equipment declined at a rate of 1.3 percent annually between 1973 and 1979. Between 1976 and 1979 private investment in machinery and equipment did grow at a rate of 4.9 percent but this was due in part to the purchase by the PPD government of the Puerto Rico Telephone Company from ITT. The investment of the newly formed Puerto Rico Telephone Authority, a public corporation, was included in the accounts of private investment; thus this transaction was not counted as private disinvestment. Unemployment went from 12 percent in 1972 to 19.5 percent in 1976 and back down slightly to 17 percent in 1979. The number of people unemployed went from 101,000 in 1972 to 153,000 in 1979, while the number of people employed remained at 745,000 both these years.[4] Real wages declined by 2.6 percent between 1973 and 1976, the first decline since the begining of Operation Bootstrap. Personal income declined by 1.5 percent in real terms in 1975, again a first since 1947. It went back up by 3.5 percent in 1976 only because of increased transfer payments from the federal government to individuals, which increased from $223 million in 1974, to $600 million in 1975, and to $1,036 in 1976. Most of these payments came as part of the food stamp program, which started in 1975. The federal government disbursed $387.5 million in 1975 and almost double that, $754.9 million, in 1976; the latter figure represented 21.2 percent of the personal income in 1976.[5]

But the forces that pushed the Puerto Rican economy to a crisis were grounded in the international economy. The crisis of accumulation through productive investment was worldwide. Profitability had dropped in those industries that had led the postwar prosperity throughout the world. The production of durable consumer goods, such as cars, home appliances, and the like, was becoming unprofitable in some core countries because of competition, high labor costs, and market saturation.[6] Puerto Rico was no exception to this trend. The aggregate rate of profit had been declining steadily since the 1960s. Yet in some sectors, such as chemicals, electronics, scientific instruments, and machinery processing, profitability declined but remained higher than in the United States.[7] By the mid-1970s, however, the combination of the worldwide crisis of accumulation through investment in productive activities and the specific comparative disadvantages of export manufacturing in Puerto Rico called for a strategy reassessment. The question was how to reinsert the island into the international circuit of production and exchange within the orbit of U.S. capital when there were no productive advantages for export manufacturing.

The Politics of Restructuring

The PPD tried to come up with a solution—the strategy committee, the Tobin Committee, the superport scheme, and proposing changes to the commonwealth (e.g. H.R. 11200). But before it could do anything the PPD was ousted from power. The PPD did manage to stop Congress from repealing Section 931 of the IRC; rather, its benefits were expanded by amending it with Section 936.[8] Yet this tax advantage to U.S. TNCs coincided with the second and largest PNP electoral victory in 1976. Thus it would fall on the PNP to chart the course of economic restructuring.

The Policy Shift: The PNP's Second Chance

The PNP victory in 1976 demonstrated that the PPD loss in 1968 had been more than a fluke and that there was a significant process of political realignment in the country. The social forces created by Operation Bootstrap had found a new political instrument to express their dissatisfaction with the PPD and their aspirations for the continuation of developmentalism.

In 1968 the PNP had come to power unprepared and was caught up in the contradictions of the political and economic structure created by the PPD. The PNP was unable to find a way to redirect the course of the country in the four years they held power. After their loss to the PPD in 1972, however, the PNP revamped its leadership and strategy to expand its electoral support among the urban working classes and the marginal sectors. From this defeat, a new party leader emerged, Carlos Romero Barceló. He had been the biggest PNP winner in the 1972 election when he was reelected mayor of San Juan, the capital and largest city in the country. In 1973 Romero emerged as the foremost leader of the party and was elected its president in 1974.[9] He reaffirmed the populist politics initiated in the 1968 campaign but gave it a new twist. He published a book in 1973, entitled *Statehood is for the Poor*, which became the cornerstone of the new pro-statehood doctrine. According to the new PNP thesis, the poor would benefit more than anyone else from statehood because this would guarantee the extension to Puerto Rico of all benefits and subsidies of the U.S. federal government. Under the commonwealth, argued Romero, Puerto Ricans only received a fraction of the benefits that the U.S. poor received. Moreover, the rich would have to pay the federal taxes required of the new state. Romero went on to attack the rich industrialists as the beneficiaries of tax exemptions under the commonwealth and as the ones who did not want to assume their social responsibility by paying taxes. The PPD was truly the party of the rich, while the PNP was the party of the poor. The slogan "statehood, progress, security" was added to the party logo (a coconut palm tree) for the 1976 campaign.[10]

To the working classes accustomed to the populist demagoguery of the PPD, this argument had a ring of truth. The many Puerto Rican poor who had lived in the United States or had relatives there knew that the federal welfare system was much better than the colonial one. The notion that statehood was for the poor made sense also to the nearly 50 percent of the population receiving food stamps since 1975. The fact that Romero, a new petty bourgeois lawyer, and not Ferré, the old money Republican industrialist, was the central figure in the PNP strengthened the credibility of the new populist rhetoric.

But while the PNP renewed its image for public consumption as the alternative of the poor, in reality it maintained its commitment to preserving the interests of U.S. capital in Puerto Rico. In its 1976 program the PNP promised to continue to stimulate local and external private investment and to search for new incentives without altering the tax exemption program until the effectiveness of other incentives had been proven.[11] That very statement, however, expressed the implicit objective of moving beyond the existing framework of the PPD's CI/EP strategy. The reassurance that no drastic measures would be taken against existing tax exemptions for manufacturing industries was clearly framed in the context of trying alternative incentives to revise and change exemptions.

The PNP program did not state what other incentives it might substitute for tax exemptions, nor did it say if changing that policy would imply a shift in emphasis to other economic sectors and away from export manufacturing. The section of the program on "the development of industry" was divided into two parts. The first one was dedicated to manufacturing and followed the PPD policy of promoting U.S. investment in export manufacturing while emphasizing the need to stimulate local investment, industries producing for the local market, and "high-tech" industries. The second part introduced a new element into the economic development strategy, the promotion of service industries. With the exception of tourism, PPD strategy had never contemplated providing incentives to service industries, much less making this a key target of economic growth. The PNP program keenly pointed out the magnitude and importance of services in job creation and pledged to include service industries in the promotion program of Fomento. Moreover, the PNP proposed the fusion of Fomento and the Department of Commerce into a Department of Economic Development and Commerce with the specific purpose of promoting manufacturing and service industries on an equal footing.[12] This was an unprecedented move. The new petty bourgeoisie at the helm of the PNP was beginning to shape a new economic development policy based on moving the country toward statehood with an economic base outside productive activities.[13]

The PNP leadership that took office in 1977 was better prepared to move beyond the PPD's legacy than their 1968 predecessors. They had learned their lesson. Ideologically, statehood seemed viable; the new social sectors were convinced that "progress" was linked to the continuation of a political and economic relation with the United States. The task at hand for the PNP was to show that statehood was economically feasible, to prove that statehood would not hinder capital accumulation for U.S. transnational capital or local capital. The crisis of the CI/EP strategy provided an ideal setting. The PNP needed to figure out a restructuring of the economic basis of the colony that would restore accumulation within the orbit of U.S. transnational capital but which at the same time would permit a new political arrangement, namely statehood.

As was the case in 1965 with the oil import quotas, the metropolitan government—Congress in this case—provided a special incentive to sustain the profitability of U.S. investment that would become the cornerstone of the restructuring of the colonial economy. In 1976, Section 936 of the IRC, which replaced Section 931, removed the limitation of tax-free profit repatriation only to accumulated profits of subsidiaries upon liquidation. Now U.S. subsidiaries operating under Section 936 (popularly known as 936 corporations) could repatriate profits free of taxes to parent companies on a current basis. Since this was done to curtail investing profits of Puerto Rican subsidiaries in the Eurodollar market through financial intermediaries in Guam and to stimulate investment in Puerto Rico, the colonial government was allowed to impose a 10 percent "tollgate tax" on profits repatriated by 936 corporations in order to prevent a possible sudden loss of financial funds to the Puerto Rican economy. To avoid paying the full tollgate tax, 936 corporations were required to either reinvest profits or deposit them in special certificates eligible for tollgate tax exemption. By depositing profits in special bank certificates and tax-exempt U.S. and Puerto Rican government securities and municipal bonds, the companies could reduce the tollgate tax to 5 percent or less. This reproduced the practice of 931 corporations before 1976 of maintaining a high level of liquid assets, only now these were deposited in banks in Puerto Rico rather than in Guam. By 1977, $1.6

billion of the $5 billion of accumulated profits of possessions corporations were in these special bank certificates. About 50 percent of the bank deposits of 936 profits were kept in Citibank and Chase Manhattan Bank.[14]

True to their vision of a new economic policy that would not focus on export manufacturing, the PNP policymakers enacted the Industrial Incentive Act of 1978 (Law 26). Total tax exemption was replaced with a diminishing tax-exemption scale for eligible manufacturing industries. Law 26 reduced tax exemption to 90 percent of applicable income and property taxes during the first five years of operations and to 75 percent for another five years, up to a total of ten years in highly industrialized areas. In areas classified as intermediate industrial development zones there would be an additional five years of exemption of 65 percent of applicable taxes, and in low industrial development zones there would be another five years of 55 percent tax exemption. For companies established in Vieques and Culebra there would be yet another five-year, 50 percent tax exemption, for a total of twenty-five years.[15]

Radical as this may seem, the ending of total tax holidays was not a drastic measure. Estimated effective tax rates ranged from 2.2 to 4.5 percent for the first five years; 5.5 to 11.25 percent for the next five years; 8.75 to 15.75 percent for the eleventh through fifteenth year; and 9.9 to 20.25 percent for the sixteenth through the twentieth year. Yet creative accounting techniques and other tax deductions tended to keep those rates at the lower end of the scales.[16]

The other new element in Law 26 was the extension of tax exemptions to export-service industries. Services produced for external markets would enjoy a 50 percent tax exemption on income, property, excise, and municipal taxes as well as license fees. The periods of exemption were ten years for high industrial development zones, fifteen years for intermediate and low zones, and twenty for Vieques and Culebra. The services eligible for this exemption would have to be provided for foreign markets, including the United States; 80 percent of the company's employees had to be residents of Puerto Rico and work in excess of twenty hours a week; and 80 percent of the value of services invoiced had to be generated by the Puerto Rican branch. Some of the eligible services listed in the law were international commercial distribution facilities, investment banking, public relations, consulting services, insurance, filmmaking and processing, repair services, laboratory services of various kinds (dental, photographic, optical), and computer services.[17]

Although it would be difficult to argue that Section 936 and Law 26 were part of a master plan of economic restructuring, they constituted the legal framework of a new economic strategy that would emerge as a coherent alternative during the second term of PNP Governor Carlos Romero Barceló. At the time of their enactment, however, these measures were mainly designed to try to do something about the economic crisis. In enacting

Section 936, Congress wanted to curtail the financial practices that siphoned off the profits of 931 corporations from Puerto Rico to the Eurodollar markets and to channel these funds either back to the Puerto Rican economy or to the United States. Law 26, on the other hand, was meant to deal with the deep fiscal crisis of the colonial state, diagnosed by the Tobin Committee, by expanding the tax base of the country; getting companies used to the idea of paying taxes, which had been a key argument against statehood; and promoting the expansion of services toward exports, a sector that not only promised growth but provided an important constituency for the PNP.

By the end of the first term of the Romero administration the PNP articulated a clearer picture of what their economic strategy was aiming at. Since the PNP saw the solution to the crisis as part of the transition toward statehood, their economic strategists geared their policies to achieve this aim. José R. Madera, a Citibank executive who became head of Fomento in 1979, expressed the basic premises and objectives of the PNP industrial development policy in a special issue of the Fomento publication *Puerto Rico, U.S.A.* According to Madera, the Puerto Rican economy was open and had been already integrated into the U.S. economy. Labor-intensive, low-wage industries were leaving the island and could not constitute the basis of any future economic growth. Any economic strategy had to face these facts. The island had become a region within the U.S. economy and therefore must compete with other regions in the United States to attract investment. The future then was to internationalize further the Puerto Rican economy, "to become the gateway through which European companies will penetrate the Latin American market and will, at the same time enable U.S. goods produced both in the Mainland [the United States] and in Puerto Rico to reach the markets of Central and South America." High-tech industries, international trade, and services would be the backbone of such an economy.[18]

Another PNP strategist, Bertram Finn, head of the Governor's Economic Advisory. Council, presented the broader view of the new PNP strategy. Arguing for a transition period of twenty years to achieve statehood, Finn envisaged a diminishing but continued role for export manufacturing. High-tech industries would lead the revamped manufacturing sector. But in the changing Puerto Rican economy, as a region of the U.S. economy, the island would enjoy distinct comparative advantages in tourism, agriculture, international services, and trade. In his view, as in that of Madera, the island would play the role of commercial distribution center (entrepôt) and of regional financial, service, and administrative center for U.S. TNCs in the Caribbean and Latin America. The exploitation of potential oil and copper deposits was also envisaged in the transition to statehood economy.[19]

By the end of the first term of the Romero government, the pieces of the PNP economic strategy were in place. Aside from approving Law 26,

Act Number 16 of 1980 was passed by the PNP-dominated legislature creating an international banking center. Plans for the creation of an international trade center were approved. Mining was renewed as an alternative for economic growth with the revision of copper mining contract proposals and guidelines for potential negotiations and the hiring of the services of a U.S. company to explore for oil deposits in the north coast. Finally, agricultural development was brought back into the agenda with the creation of the Agricultural Promotion and Development Administration.[20]

A much disputed election in 1980 returned Romero Barceló to the colonial governorship but gave control over both chambers of the local legislature to the PPD.[21] In spite of this, the Romero administration continued to pursue the policy of economic restructuring set around Law 26 and Section 936 of the IRC. The proposal of the Romero administration to support President Reagan's Caribbean Basin Initiative (CBI) provided an opportunity for the PNP to further their strategy of integration into the U.S. economy by expanding Puerto Rico's role as a regional intermediary of U.S. TNCs.

The CBI proposed to allow the duty-free import of many manufactured and agricultural products from the Caribbean and Central America to the United States to promote trade, investment, and economic diversification in these regions. It also contemplated providing tax exemption to U.S. investments in these countries.[22] The opening of the U.S. market to manufactures from the Caribbean was perceived by local businessmen as a threat to Puerto Rico's privileged access to that market. Local manufacturers in particular perceived the possibility of being displaced from both the Puerto Rican and U.S. markets by competing products from lower wage countries. The PPD, for its part, saw the CBI as a threat to the CI/EP strategy. Giving free access to the U.S. market to Caribbean Basin manufactures and tax exemptions to U.S. investments in the lower wage countries of the Caribbean and Central America would, for the PPD leaders, put the last nail in the coffin of Operation Bootstrap.[23]

The PNP supported Reagan's initiative while negotiating protective measures for Puerto Rico. Tax exemptions on investments were excluded from the legislation, as were duty-free treatment to tuna imports and other products of importance to Puerto Rico-based producers. Moreover, under Madera, Fomento adopted a plan to establish complementary production projects for manufacturing firms in Puerto Rico and other countries of the Caribbean. The prototype of this plan was developed by the accounting firm of Coopers & Lybrand who, with a grant from the U.S. Agency for International Development, conducted a viability study for what it termed a twin plant program. The plan contemplated the establishment of the labor-intensive segment of the production of electronic and apparel industries in low-wage countries in the Eastern Caribbean and the finishing and packaging processes in Puerto Rico. The allowance of duty-free imports on electronic products under the CBI would make such a venture advantageous in this industry, while the absence of quota restrictions for textile imports from Puerto Rico to the United States would provide an advantage for the apparel industry. An added incentive was, of course, that 936 corporations could realize their profits in Puerto Rico rather than in their Eastern Caribbean subsidiaries using transfer pricing mechanisms. This would enable profit repatriation to the United States free of federal taxes.[24]

The PNP administration also lobbied the IRS and Congress together with 936 corporations to try to minimize the adverse effects of the Tax Equity and Fiscal Responsibility Act of 1982 (TEFRA), which was passed to curtail tax-evasion practices of 936 corporations.[25] This unconditional support of the PNP for the CBI and the privileges of 936 corporations endeared the PNP to the Reagan administration and U.S. TNCs. The new petty bourgeoisie and the internationalized fraction of the local bourgeoisie that constituted the leading groups within the PNP had no quarrel with Reagan's neoliberal policies. It seemed as if, finally, the PNP could break out of the colonial trap of having to rely on incentives to export manufacturing for economic growth. The transformation of Puerto Rico into an international financial, trade, and service center and a coordinating center for twin plants (*maquiladoras*) in the Eastern Caribbean appeared to be a feasible alternative to pull Puerto Rico out of the economic crisis by moving beyond the CI/EP strategy and its political corollary, the commonwealth. If all went well, tax holidays to export-manufacturing industries would not be a necessary condition for economic expansion. Statehood could be achieved by transforming Puerto Rico into a service-led economy where U.S. transnational capital in service and finance would become the leading economic force.

By 1984 it appeared that the PNP had managed to lay the foundation for the consolidation in power of a new ruling coalition integrated by the internationalized fraction of the local bourgeoisie, the local new petty bourgeoisie, the financial fraction of U.S. transnational capital, and the conservative Republicans who supported statehood for Puerto Rico.[26] The internationalization strategy of the PNP, with its emphasis on the service and financial sectors, converged with emerging trends in the international economy. The global trend of declining profitability of productive investments in the 1970s was prompting diversification of corporate investments into new service and financial ventures as companies scrambled to maintain profitability. In the process of redefining the dynamics of global accumulation, financial activities and speculation emerged as the new axis of accumulation.[27] The fact that PNP policy signaled a willingness to move in that direction was music to the ears of U.S. TNCs. The PNP leadership seemed to have come up finally with the right formula to achieve statehood.

The High-Finance Strategy

Unlike the Bahamas, Bermuda, or the Cayman Islands, Puerto Rico is not a place where financial manipulations are made mainly through banks or paper corporations. Most U.S. federal financial regulations and corporate laws apply to Puerto Rico, making it extremly difficult to engage in practices similar to those of foreign tax havens. In order to enjoy the advantage of tax-free profit repatriation, companies have to be engaged in active business on the island. According to Section 936, to enjoy possessions corporation status, and thus enjoy tax exemptions, 80 percent of the gross income of a 936 subsidiary has to originate from sources within the possession with at least 50 percent of this gross income coming from the active conduct of trade or business there. That is, to be able to shelter financial or "passive" income, a company must have the capacity to produce in Puerto Rico for the international market or the ability to transfer to a production subsidiary on the island profits from operations in other parts of the world. Hence, export-processing industries with international financial capacity would become the major beneficiaries of this new incentive. Yet another major beneficiary of this kind of arrangement would be the financial and professional service companies. The large amounts of liquid assets previously channeled to Guam could now stay in banks operating locally. The accountants, lawyers, and other professional services needed to manage these large sums would lead to the expansion of those services.

The use of federal tax exemptions by U.S. TNCs in Puerto Rico to increase global profits was not new. What was new about Section 936 was that companies would have to keep their money in Puerto Rico in order to boost their tax-free global profits. Thus the transition from Section 931 to 936 was relatively easy. As early as 1977 a group of U.S. transnational manufacturing companies declared to have derived over one-fifth of their global income from operations in Puerto Rico. Pepsi Co. declared 21 percent of their global profits on the island; Union Carbide, 25 percent; Digital Equipment, 57 percent; Motorola, 23 percent; G. D. Searle, 150 percent; Abbott Laboratories, 71 percent; Eli Lilly, 22 percent; and Baxter Travenol, 37 percent.[28]

These companies were engaging in three practices initiated under Section 931. First were paper transactions, termed "creative accounting," by which profits were transfered from parent companies and other subsidiaries to the Puerto Rican 936 subsidiary. Second, companies that developed patented products could transfer or sell the patent to a 936 subsidiary, thus transfering to it the royalties on such patents. This was a common practice among pharmaceutical companies and soft drink manufacturers producing patented drugs and syrups. Yet another practice was to establish in Puerto Rico the final production segment of a highly profitable product or line of products. Since the profit margin of finished products sold to final customers was

higher than for intermediate products, there were significant tax savings on
company profits. Often these practices were combined. For example, in the
production of a patented product manufactured to be sold in the U.S. market,
a 936 subsidiary in Puerto Rico could buy components below market price
and sell the final product at a high profit. Royalties on the patent for the
product could be channeled to the 936 subsidiary, thus avoiding payment of
federal taxes; meanwhile, the company had received tax deductions in the
United States for the cost of research and development of the product. The
936 companies also made additional tax-free profits in the form of interest on
special bank deposits or tax-exempt government bonds.[29]

The enactment of Section 936 also accelerated the restructuring of the
Puerto Rican financial system. The 1973–1976 recession led to the
bankruptcy of a number of local banks. Between 1975 and 1977, three
Spanish and one Canadian banks took over four local banks. The process of
taking over or buying out failing local banks continued beyond the recession
with another six local banks being taken over by two Spanish, one Puerto
Rican, and three U.S. banks between 1978 and 1983. By 1983, ten locally
owned banks had disappeared and three Spanish and another three U.S.
international banks had opened operations in Puerto Rico. By 1980, the
Banco de Santander, Banco Central, Banco Occidental (Bilbao Vizcaya),
Continental Illinois Bank, Bank of America, and Bank of Boston had made
their entrance into the rapidly internationalizing Puerto Rican commercial
banking sector.[30]

Brokerage houses also proliferated in the local financial scene. Until
1976, only a handful of these houses operated on the island; Merrill Lynch,
Payne Webber, Prudential Bache, Citibank, and Chase Manhattan Bank had
limited operations. After 1976, E. F. Hutton, Kidder Peabody, Drexel
Burnham, Dean Witter Reynolds, and First Boston Corp. opened local
offices, while the existing ones expanded operations.[31]

Although neither the federal nor the colonial government would admit
it, Section 936 made Puerto Rico a major tax haven for manufacturing
TNCs within the legal and financial system of the United States—an
exceptional situation that the IRS called a "tax loophole." Not that U.S.
companies had not used the island as a tax haven before. There had been
disputes between the colonial government and the U.S. Department of the
Treasury on U.S. companies' tax avoidance practices since 1959.[32] But
Puerto Rico was not the kind of tax haven where money was warehoused or
laundered by engaging in dubious legal practices, according to the views of
the IRS; now companies could legally repatriate profits to the United States
and not pay taxes, which was not always possible in other tax havens. To be
able to shelter financial or "passive" income, however, TNCs needed to have
a productive infrastructure. Export-processing manufacturing had returned
through the back door, so to speak, into the new emerging economic
strategy. The financial income of export manufacturing 936 corporations

became the fuel of the whole system. Billions of dollars in global profits were transferred to or declared in export manufacturing operations in Puerto Rico through a highly complex and sophisticated international financial network.

Much to the chagrin of the PNP, the emerging economic structure came to rest yet again on another exceptional concession of the metropolis to the colony. The hopes of transcending not only the CI/EP strategy but the commonwealth crashed with the realities of the colonial polity and economy. The PNP had managed to steer a new course away from the CI/EP strategy, but the high-finance strategy that they designed led back to the "advantages" (for U.S. TNCs) of the colonial relation.

Consolidating the High-Finance Strategy: The Resurgence of the PPD

The defeat of the PNP in the 1984 elections had as much to do with the dire economic situation brought about by the recession of 1980-1982 as it did with the corruption and political abuses of the Romero administration. In 1981 a Senate investigation revealed PNP involvement in a plot to entrap and assassinate two proindependence youths who allegedly tried to blow up a communications tower on Cerro Maravilla, a mountain in the southern town of Villalba, on 25 July 1978 (the eightieth anniversary of the U.S. invasion of Puerto Rico and the twenty-sixth anniversary of the establishment of the commonwealth). Later, a federal government investigation uncovered a high incidence of government corruption that reached the upper echelons of the Romero administration.[33]

Aside from alienating large sectors of the population with an autocratic, repressive, and corrupt political style, the PNP did not manage to pull the island out of its economic crisis. Unemployment went from 20 percent in 1977 to 22 percent in 1984. The number of people employed during the eight years of Romero's governorship grew by only eight thousand. The average annual growth rate was 0.9 percent for the GNP and 0.6 percent for per-capita income.[34] These political and economic developments led to internal opposition to Romero and, ultimately, to the division of the PNP. A faction of the PNP, led by the mayor of San Juan, Hernán Padilla, split from the party and created the Partido de Renovación Puertorriqueña (PRP). Contrary to the PNP under Romero, the PRP deemphasized the importance of statehood and concentrated its campaign on political reconciliation and economic renovation.[35]

The main beneficiary of the PNP debacle was the PPD. As the opposition party, it criticized PNP policies of economic restructuring, opposed the reduction in industrial tax exemptions of Law 26, and opposed the CBI/twin plant proposal. But once in power the turn of events would make the PPD realize that the PNP policies were congruent with the interests of transnational capital and the metropolitan state; that not to follow them would mean economic and political suicide; and that the high-finance strategy had only worked to reaffirm the viability and desirability of the commonwealth for U.S. capital.

In January 1984, the Committee for the Economic Development of Puerto Rico, Inc., a nonpartisan group of local entrepreneurs, made public a report on the economic crisis. The committee objected to the extension to Puerto Rico in 1977 of the federal minimum wage across the board and proposed a number of measures to reduce ("rationalize") taxes and lower energy and transportation costs. But their recommendations to revitalize the economic development program were a de facto endorsement of the PNP's development policies.[36] Curiously, among the members of the committee were Teodoro Moscoso, the architect of the CI/EP strategy, as well as other prominent local businessmen identified with the PPD and the PNP. This could be interpreted as an indication that a consensus was developing among the local bourgeoisie on the desirability of the high-finance strategy.

But what turned the PPD around in favor of the high-finance strategy was the threat of the Reagan administration to repeal Section 936 as part of the tax reform proposal of 1984. The threat to eliminate Section 936 finally made it clear to PPD strategists that the island had no competitive advantage other than federal tax exemption on repatriated profits. Any attempt to restore the CI/EP strategy would be futile and the only hope of restoring the dynamism of the manufacturing sector was by utilizing the financial advantage provided by the metropolis. The only way to go was forward with the process of restructuring, where finance and manufacturing were indissolubly brought together. The island was a tax haven and the only thing to do was to make the most of it.

Following on the heels of the PNP strategists and prompted by the 936 corporations, PPD Governor Rafael Hernández Colón announced in his inaugural speech plans to channel 936 funds into twin plant investments in CBI beneficiary countries. With the support of 936 corporations and the Puerto Rico Manufacturers Association—which had opposed the CBI twin plant proposals before—PPD government officials marched to Washington to defend Section 936.[37]

Critics and supporters of the CBI alike had expressed concern that this program could fail to promote economic development in the Caribbean and Central America since it lacked incentives to investment. The twin plant program was a clever way to try to promote investment. Twin plants, or outsourcing in neighboring countries, was not new; many U.S. corporations with operations in Puerto Rico had been doing it before the Coopers & Lybrand proposal.[38]

After intensive lobbying and debate on the specifics of the proposal, the PPD administration made a commitment to Congress to guarantee $100 million of new private direct investment annually in CBI countries from 936 funds, provided that Section 936 was retained intact in the new tax reform act. Moreover, when the proposal was submitted on a memorandum of agreement to the representatives of the Reagan administration, eighteen 936 companies had committed to invest $66 million in CBI countries if Section 936 was retained.[39] The PPD CBI/936 proposal was endorsed from the beginning by the prime ministers of Jamaica, Grenada, and Dominica; the Puerto Rico U.S.A. Foundation (PRUSA), the lobbying arm of the 936 corporations; the Puerto Rico Chamber of Commerce; and the Puerto Rico Manufacturers Association.[40]

The Tax Reform Act of 1986 retained Section 936 with minor modifications to permit the implementation of the CBI/936 program, later named by Fomento the Caribbean Development Program. The basis of the high-finance strategy had not only been preserved but enhanced. Now not only could 936 corporations and the financial intermediaries that handled 936 funds profit from tax-free financial investments in Puerto Rico, they could also finance the expansion of productive operations in the Caribbean and Central America with low-interest capital from their own tax-free financial deposits. The companies stood to benefit in at least five ways. First, they could borrow from their own deposits at discount rates, which in turn increased the attractiveness of deposits that reduced the tollgate tax. Second, establishing operations in the Caribbean meant the ability to operate the labor-intensive segment of production in low-wage countries that offered local tax holidays. Third, imports and reimports of manufactured products to Puerto Rico were free of duty if the product was eligible for such treatment under the CBI, which was almost always to be the case. Fourth, profits realized in the final stages of processing and marketing of 936 subsidiaries were, again, tax exempt. And, finally, the newly made profits could be placed in tax-exempt bonds and certificates of deposit to gain credits against the tollgate tax, while previous deposits matured and could be repatriated paying a negligible tollgate tax. The CBI/936 program made the Caribbean Basin a huge tax- and duty-free export-processing zone and financial center, allowing the legal tax-free repatriation of profits to the United States.

The PPD also revised the 1978 Industrial Incentive Act and expanded tax breaks for both manufacturing and export services. The Puerto Rico Tax Incentives Act (Law 8) was approved on 24 January 1987. The replacement of the traditional title of industrial incentive for that of tax incentive suggests an awareness that tax avoidance was the key to Puerto Rico's attractiveness to transnational capital. The most important change from Law 26 was to establish a uniform tax exemption of 90 percent for periods of ten, fifteen, twenty, and twenty-five years, depending on location. The 90 percent exemption was also applied to service industries that before had been granted a lower exemption.[41]

These actions helped the PPD technobureaucracy to rekindle its role as the main ally of U.S. capital. The PPD managed to rearticulate a coalition between U.S. financial capital, the local commercial and industrial bourgeoisie, and the local financial sector around the high-finance strategy. The PNP could not do this partly because statehood clearly implied the end of the colonial economic "privileges" on which that strategy rests. This is a case where the rhetoric of the PNP on the advantages of equal treatment for the poor under statehood clashed with the real advantages to capital of the status quo. After the political dust settled, the PPD emerged as the winner in the battle of the high-finance strategy.

Peripheral Postindustrialization

The shift in development strategy has meant a change in the industrial structure of the country; segments of the high-tech manufacturing industries have emerged as the leading component of industry. However, calling this a high-tech stage of the CI/EP strategy would be misleading. What is happening is not simply the replacement of capital-intensive heavy industries by knowledge-intensive ones. Puerto Rico is moving toward a structure where postindustrial manufacturing, service, and financial activities are becoming dominant. The axis of accumulation is shifting from transnational export-processing manufacture to transnational financial industries, where manufacturing plays a secondary, although not unimportant, role. Yet, since Puerto Rico was never an advanced industrial society, its postindustrial structure cannot be the same as that of advanced capitalist countries. The determinants of the movement beyond peripheral industrialization and its social consequences are quite different from those in the United States or Europe. More accurately, Puerto Rico is moving along the path that John Jacobsen calls peripheral postindustrialization.[42]

Although Jacobsen did not provide a definition of this concept, he uses it to characterize the current shift in the development strategy in Ireland along a similar path as Puerto Rico, suggesting the basis for a definition. Peripheral postindustrialization refers to a type of peripheral capitalist development in which segments of high-tech and knowledge-intensive industries (postindustrial industries) lead the process of growth. Typically, these industries would be subsidiaries of transnational companies looking for particular and often exceptional advantages in the production of goods and services for the international market. These companies seek to establish activities in politically stable and relatively low-operations-cost countries with a fairly advanced transportation and communications infrastructure, a highly skilled labor force, an existing industrial export base, privileged access to major core markets (the European Community, the United States) and potentially easy access to developing new markets (Eastern Europe, the Caribbean), a sophisticated financial system with access to prime financial markets (Eurodollar, 936 funds), and considerable tax advantages. Aside from

Ireland and Puerto Rico, societies such as Hong Kong and Singapore may fit this description.

Key to the label of peripheral postindustrialization is that the decisionmaking process and the technology-producing, research-and-development segment of these postindustrial industries remain in the core countries where the companies are based. Moreover, the machinery, capital, and basic components used in these industries continue to be mainly imported. In the case of nonmanufacturing industries, the services generated by these companies are mainly geared toward international clients and only marginally toward the local economy. Transnational services follow on the heels of their clients. Although they may be operating in Puerto Rico, Ireland, or Hong Kong, their logic, strategy, and organization are internationally based and oriented. Postindustrial peripheral economies thus serve as halfway houses between high-cost, highly regulated advanced capitalist countries and very low-cost but infrastructurally inadequate and politically unstable peripheral countries. They allow transnational corporations to shuffle products and profits globally and circumvent "disadvantageous" regulations (tax, wage, environmental, health) enforced in advanced societies.

The Emerging Economic Structure

The high-finance strategy was supposed to stimulate the growth of export manufacturing and services with the major involvement of segments of high-tech industries, business and professional services, and finance. A quick look at some macroeconomic indicators suggests some success in orienting the process of economic restructuring in this direction. Figure 5.1 shows that within the context of a noticeably reduced rate of real growth, the financial and manufacturing sectors led economic growth. The government, which had been the leading sector in the previous stage (1964–1976), hardly contributed to GDP growth in the later stage; services and transportation followed. In terms of employment, financial activities and services grew faster than the other economic sectors, as Figure 5.2 shows. The government, which led employment growth in the previous stage, retrenched but played a bigger role than manufacturing. Overall, the picture that emerges during this stage of economic restructuring is one where manufacturing provides the larger share of GDP while services and finance are catching up with the government as the major providers of jobs, as shown in Figures 5.3 and 5.4.

The growth of the manufacturing sector was led by the subsidiaries of high-tech industries. Table 5.1 shows the increasing role of these industries between 1977 and 1982 in manufacturing income (value of shipments), employment, and establishments. High-tech subsidiaries increased their share of industrial income from 21.1 to 46.2 percent and their share of employment from 18.2 to 31.7 percent in the first five years after the enactment of

Figure 5.1 Average Growth Rates of Real GNP

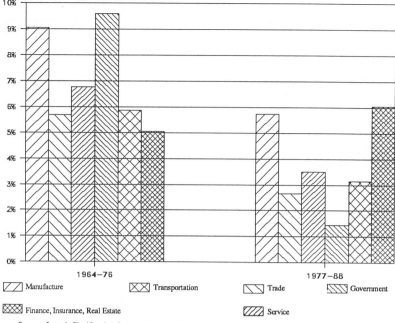

Manufacture Transportation Trade Government

Finance, Insurance, Real Estate Service

Sources: Junta de Planificacion, *Ingreso y Producto, 1984* and *Informe Economico, 1988.*

Figure 5.2 Average Growth Rates of Employment

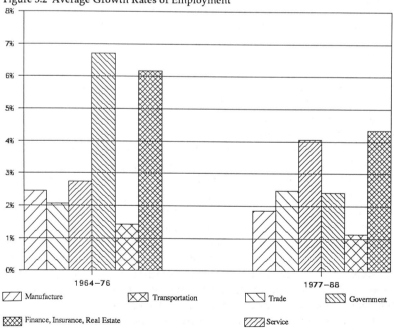

Manufacture Transportation Trade Government

Finance, Insurance, Real Estate Service

Source: Departamento del Trabajo, "Series de empleo."

Section 936. But in spite of this, manufacturing experienced a loss of 3,767 jobs, 2.6 percent. (By 1988, however, manufacturing employment went up by 17,655 jobs to 157,022. The high-tech segment of industry [chemicals, electronics, and instruments] contributed about 6,000 new jobs while food processing provided another 5,000.)[43]

The growth of segments of high-tech industries can be directly attributed to the enactment of Section 936. Indeed, as Table 5.2 demonstrates, pharmaceutical, electronics, and scientific instruments industries combined held 54.5 percent of all the assets of 936 corporations in 1983. High-tech industries are seeking the advantages of Puerto Rico as a peripheral postindustrial location: an existing, well-developed physical infrastructure; free access to the U.S. market; easy access to the Caribbean and Latin American markets; lower wages relative to the United States; relatively highly skilled labor force, partially bilingual (English- and Spanish-speaking); and, more importantly, unique tax advantages that allow for financial manipulations on a global scale. Section 936 is also stimulating growth in other industries responsible for new jobs creation, such as food processing, financial services, and transportation.

On the side of the service sector some of the industries targeted by Law 26 did not fare as well as desired. Table 5.3 shows the performance of some services designated by Law 26 as eligible for tax exemption. Between 1977 and 1982, income in all services surveyed by the census grew by 39 percent. Of the eligible services listed, only photofinishing laboratories, computer and data processing, and legal services grew more than the industry average. Some services that would have been expected to grow with the proliferation of high-tech manufacturing subsidiaries, such as consulting and engineering services, grew substantially less than the industry average. In terms of employment, however, the business and professional services as a whole fared better than the rest of the industry, with the exception of commercial photography, and engineering, architectural, and surveying services. The fact that employment grew more than income may suggest a trend of subcontracting local service companies by transnational companies serving their clients in Puerto Rico and, hence, a slow development of the export service sector. There is very little detailed data available on services, especially export services, but a recent study by a Fomento consultant suggests that export services are only begining to develop on the island.[44]

Commercial banking has been the main beneficiary of the economic restructuring process. The assets of commercial banks grew by 83 percent from $10 billion in 1978 to $18.3 billion in 1988. However, their net income grew by 1,245 percent (from $23.8 million to $320.1 million) during the same period.[45] A study made for the Puerto Rico Bankers Association attributes this impressive growth to the creation of 936 funds.[46] Indeed, 936 deposits in commercial banks have grown steadily from around $1.6 billion dollars in 1977 to $6.5 billion in 1988.

Figure 5.3 Shares of GDP by Sector: 1977–1988

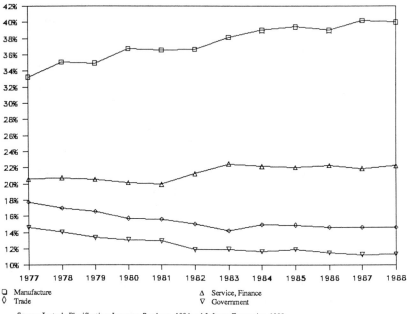

Manufacture ☐   △ Service, Finance
Trade ◇   ▽ Government

Source: Junta de Planification, *Ingreso y Producto, 1984* and *Informe Economico, 1988.*

Figure 5.4 Shares of Employment by Sector: 1977–1988

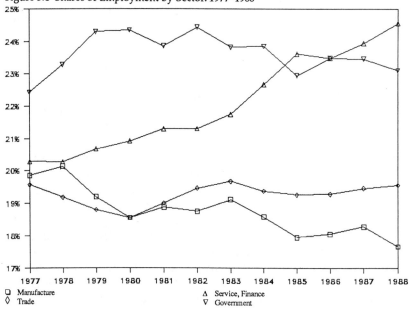

Manufacture ☐   △ Service, Finance
Trade ◇   ▽ Government

Source: Departamento del Trabajo, "Series de empleo."

Table 5.1 Growth of Selected High-Tech Industries

Industry	Value of Shipments 1977 (000)	1982 (000)	Change %	Employment 1977	1982	Change %	Establishments 1977	1982
Drugs	1,348,813	4,235,108	214.0	8,963	13,137	46.6	64	76
Office & computing machines	N/A	795,794	N/A	3,077	5,130	66.7	5	15
Electronic distribution equipment	170,828	451,830	164.5	4,384	5,387	22.9	31	41
Electrical industrial apparatus	167,143	249,695	49.4	2,283	2,408	5.5	13	17
Electronic components	121,415	649,130	434.6	3,380	7,988	136.3	20	49
Scientific instruments	4,351	68,426	1,472.6	131	366	179.4	6	8
Measuring & controlling devices	69,448	133,974	92.9	1,233	1,744	41.4	20	20
Medical instruments	229,125	654,656	185.7	2,616	8,024	206.7	21	37
High-tech industries	2,111,123	7,238,613	242.9	26,067	44,184	69.5	180	263
All other industries	7,912,842	8,437,741	6.6	117,067	95,183	−18.7	1,165	1,062
Total manufacturing industries	10,023,965	15,676,354	56.4	143,134	139,367	−2.6	1,345	1,325
High-tech as % of total	21.1	46.2		18.2	31.7		13.4	19.8

Sources: U.S. Bureau of the Census, *1977 Economic Censuses of Outlying Areas, Manufactures*, pp. 4-13–4-65; *1982 Economic Censuses of Outlying Areas, Manufactures*, pp. 4-12–4-65; Note: Establishments with ten employees or more only.

Table 5.2 Assets of Leading 936 Industries: 1983 (thousand dollars)

Industry	Corporations	Assets	% of total
Pharmaceuticals	62	7,386,638	33.3
Electronics	134	3,668,945	16.5
Finance, ins. & real estate	23	3,620,076	16.3
Food and kindred products	25	1,484,123	6.7
Instruments	42	1,047,066	4.7
Transportation, comm. & util.	5	946,914	4.3
Subtotal	291	18,153,762	81.8
Total	625	22,204,669	100.0

Source: U.S. Department of the Treasury, *Operation and Effect; Sixth Report*, Table 4.1.

But within commercial banking, the main beneficiaries of the 936 funds bonanza have been U.S. banks, which have held a better than 50 percent share of these funds since 1979. Table 5.4 shows the distribution of 936 funds deposited in commercial banks in 1979 and 1984. With the entrance to Puerto Rico of the Bank of Boston, Continental Illinois Bank, and Bank of America between 1978 and 1983, the share of 936 funds held by U.S. banks increased from 55.1 to 67.7 percent. At first glance it would seem that this growth was mainly at the expense of Canadian banks. The reduction in these banks' share, however, is a reflection of the shift of their activities to locally owned subsidiaries, such as the Scotiabank, formerly Banco Mercantil, and the Banco de San Juan, acquired in 1980 by the Royal Bank of Canada. The main net losers have been Puerto Rican-owned banks whose share of these

Table 5.3 Growth of Selected Business and Professional Services

Industry	Income 1977 (000)	1982 (000)	Change %	Employment 1977	1982	Change %	Establishments 1977	1982
Advertising	91,669	112,121	22.3	1,133	1,213	7.1	93	77
Commercial photography, arts, & graphics	2,945	1,997	-32.2	118	55	-53.4	25	10
Computer & data processing	12,160	22,658	86.3	388	640	64.9	37	49
Management, consulting, and public relations	28,619	32,731	14.4	936	2,493	166.3	91	64
Photofinishing laboratories	2,663	7,422	178.7	141	199	41.1	14	6
Legal services	70,535	101,140	43.4	2,242	2,311	3.1	952	831
Engineering, architectural, and surveying services	49,706	59,573	19.9	1,762	1,419	-19.5	268	238
Subtotal (I)	258,297	337,642	30.7	6,720	8,330	24.0	1,480	1,275
Total services (II)	859,590	1,197,807	39.3	41,704	38,364	-8.0	4,981	3,917
% of total (I/II)	30.0	28.2		16.1	21.7		29.7	32.6

Sources: U.S. Bureau of the Census, *1977 Economic Censuses of Outlying Areas, Retail, Wholesale and Services*, pp., 1-42–1-43; and *1982 Economic Censuses of Outlying Areas, Retail, Wholesale and Services*, pp. 1-33–1-35.

Table 5.4 Distribution of 936 Deposits in Commercial Banks

Category	Amount (million)	Share %	Amount (million)	Share %
	1979		*1984*	
Locally registered	886	31.0	1,489	26.8
Puerto Rican	549	19.2	903	16.3
Foreign	228	8.0	586	10.6
Others	109	3.8	—	—
Foreign	1,976	69.0	4,065	73.2
United States	1,576	55.1	3,762	67.7
Canadian	400	14.0	303	5.5
Total	2,862	100.0	5,553	100.0

Sources: U.S. Department of the Treasury, *Operation and Effect; Third Report*, p. 92; *El Nuevo Día*, 3 February 1985, p.5.

funds dropped in spite of the fact that the Puerto Rican and foreign shares of the small locally registered banks classified as others in 1979 were included in the 1984 figures.

Other important beneficiaries of 936 funds were federal savings and loan associations. The crisis that these institutions suffered in the United States was solved in Puerto Rico by channeling 936 funds to them through repurchase agreements set up by brokerage houses. This also benefited brokerage activities, which gained access to 936 funds in addition to their regular corporate and individual accounts. By 1987 there were some $15 billion of 936 funds invested in Puerto Rico—commercial banks held $9.3

billion of these, federal savings and loan held $3.1 billion, and brokerage houses $2.5 billion.[47]

Clearly, Section 936 has provided the basis for restructuring the Puerto Rican economy. The emerging trend is one of internationalization of sectors that previously were dominated or substantially controlled by local capital. The restructuring of ownership in commercial banking is the best example of the deepening internationalization in areas beyond manufacturing. This trend seems to be emerging in advertising as well. Of the two top-ranked firms, the largest one, Badillo/Saatchi & Saatchi, was bought by the British firm Saatchi & Saatchi from a local firm, Badillo Compton. The second one, Martí, Flores, Prieto, also a local firm, is now a partner of J. Walter Thompson, an independent division of Hill & Knowlton. Other North American firms were established in the early days of Operation Bootstrap, such as Young & Rubicam and McCann-Erickson. But there is a distinct tendency of local firms to join in partnership with transnational ones to serve new clients. In the field of accounting, ten of the top fifteen firms are transnationals; some of the most well-known include Arthur Andersen, Arthur Young, Coopers & Lybrand, and Peat, Marwick, Main & Co. Brokerage houses, as was discussed earlier, are following a similar path, while in real estate joint partnerships or local subcontracting are emerging as common practices. Tourism is an area where TNCs have always had a controlling interest; the trend now is for European and Japanese TNCs to invest in this sector.[48]

It would be misleading, however, to argue that the local sectors are being simply displaced from the emerging dynamic sectors of the economy. As in the past, there is both displacement and accommodation within the restructuring. This process has brought about a reshuffling of the leading groups in Puerto Rico. Bankers are leading the expansion of the internationalized fraction of the local bourgeoisie. Of the banks with most assets in Puerto Rico in 1988, the Puerto Rican-owned Banco Popular and Banco de Ponce were ranked first and third, respectively. Citibank and Chase Manhattan Bank were ranked second and fourth; although if measured in terms of global assets both banks rank below all U.S., Canadian, and Spanish banks operating on the island. The two local banks recently proposed a merger that would make them the largest local company and would increase their international competitiveness.[49] Further, eight of the eleven locally owned public companies on the island are banks, where only eight of the top hundred businesses are public companies. Indeed, Puerto Rican bankers have become the leading local group of the high-finance economy.[50]

But bankers are not the only local beneficiaries of the high-finance strategy. Many of the top executives in the service industries operating locally, as well as subsidiaries of 936 manufacturing corporations, are Puerto Ricans, a great number of whom have been trained in U.S. universities and have the advantage of being bilingual.

Other beneficiaries of the high-finance strategy are British and Japanese transnationals. Before 1976 there were only two large British firms with significant operations in Puerto Rico, Dutch Shell and Smith Kline, Beecham. Eight British transnationals came to Puerto Rico after 1976—two chemical manufacturers (Imperial Chemicals and BOC Group), three insurance companies, and an advertising, a transportation, and a retail company. Four large Japanese firms were in Puerto Rico before 1976—two electronics companies owned by Matsuhita; one apparel manufacturer, Carlin; and a tuna packing company, Neptune, owned by Mitsui. After 1976 nine new firms were established, including subsidiaries of Mitsubishi, tuna canning and auto distribution; Toyota and Sony, service and distribution of automobiles and electronic equipment; and two pharmaceutical companies, Rotho and Fujisawa.[51]

The high-finance strategy anchored in Section 936 of the IRC and promoted by Fomento has propelled Puerto Rico into a highly prominent position within the global circuit of U.S. capital. Table 5.5 ranks U.S. investment in Puerto Rico and other countries of the world. Puerto Rico topped West Germany in total U.S. investment, with only Canada and the United Kingdom having a larger share. Yet, Puerto Rico became the largest single source of income for U.S. capital, having passed Canada, the United Kingdom, and West Germany, who were above it in 1976.[52] The fact that Puerto Rico's gross domestic product at current prices in 1986 was $21.3 billion, compared with $366.8 billion (U.S.) for Canada and $558.1 for the United Kingdom, raises many questions about the nature of U.S. investment in Puerto Rico. How can a country with an economic output that is only 5.8 percent that of Canada and 3.8 percent that of Great Britain generate more income to U.S. transnationals than each of these countries?[53] Puerto Rico is one of the largest tax havens in the world. This means that the definition of what is considered direct investment and the income on that investment in Puerto Rico must be revised. An increasing share of what is counted as production in Puerto Rican manufacturing industries is in fact passive income from tranferred profits and financial investments. National accounts must be reevaluated to understand the full implications of such a structure. Thus, the ever-expanding gap between the GNP and the GDP, which in 1988 reached $7.2 billion, 28 percent of the GDP, may be reflecting global financial flows rather than local production patterns. GNP and GDP figures may not mean much in assessing the performance of the Puerto Rican economy. The emerging economic structure of the island is that of unique tax haven for U.S. TNCs. This is a finance-led economy where transnational manufacturing, banking, and financial services are closely intertwined in a highly complex and secretive business network. The passage of a more liberal international banking law in August 1989, amending the 1980 law, will no doubt accelerate this process. If Section 936 remains unchanged, the island will become a major international financial and service center in the 1990s.[54]

Table 5.5 Global U.S. Direct Investment, Income, and Rate of Return, Leading
Countries: 1986 (millions dollars)

Country	Value of Investment	%	Income on Investment	%	Rate of Return
All countries[a]	284,631	100.0	42,563	100.0	15.0
Canada	50,178	17.6	5,180	12.2	10.3
United Kingdom	34,990	12.3	3,067	7.2	8.8
Puerto Rico[b]	24,741	8.7	5,866	13.8	23.7
Germany	20,344	7.2	4,625	10.9	22.7
Switzerland	17,458	6.1	2,495	5.9	14.3
Bermuda	14,595	5.1	1,795	4.2	12.3
Netherlands	11,874	4.2	3,300	7.8	27.8
Japan	11,333	4.0	3,258	7.7	28.7
France	9,471	3.3	2,177	5.1	23.0
Brazil	9,135	3.2	723	1.7	7.9

Sources: "U.S. Direct Investment Position Abroad," pp. 65, 80; Junta de Planificación,
unpublished statistics.
[a]Total plus Puerto Rico, which is not counted as foreign investments in U.S. national
accounts.
[b]The total for Puerto Rico may be slightly overestimated due to aggregation of other sources
of external investment and income. This is estimated, however, at no more than 10 percent,
which would not change the position that Puerto Rico occupies in this global ranking.

The Emerging Social Structure

It might be assumed that some of the social contradictions associated with
peripheral capitalism, such as high unemployment and marginality, are on
the way to being solved or at least subsiding as a result of the apparent
success of the high-finance strategy. But this is not the case. Although the
number of jobs increased from 678,000 in 1976 to a record high of 873,000
in 1988, and the rate of unemployment dropped from 19.4 to 15.9 percent,
the number of unemployed people remained at about 165,000 (see Table 5.6).
This is in spite of the fact that (1) emigration averaged 25,600 persons a year
between 1977 and 1988, the highest rate since the first stage of Operation
Bootstrap (1948–1963), when it averaged 32,600 per year; and (2) the natural
rate of population growth declined from 1.9 percent annually in the 1970s to
1.3 percent in the 1980s, indicating a success in the birth control and
sterilization campaign unleashed on working women since the 1950s.[55]
    The pattern of immigration of foreigners, especially from the Dominican
Republic, and the "return" migration of Puerto Ricans continued during this
period. Dominicans entered Puerto Rico at a rate of 21,034 a year between
1977 and 1986, compared to an annual rate of 12,961 between 1963 and
1976. These figures do not include, however, undocumented migrants whose
numbers have increased throughout the 1980s. Thus while many of the
Puerto Rican unemployed move to low-paying jobs in the United States,
Dominicans mainly displaced from the rural areas come to Puerto Rico to

Table 5.6 Employment and Unemployment: 1976–1988 (thousands)

	1976	1980	1984	1988
Adult population	2,020	2,094	2,261	2,316
Labor force	841	907	952	1,039
Participation rate %	41.6	43.3	42.0	44.9
Employed	678	753	743	873
Unemployed	163	154	209	165
Unemployment rate %	19.4	17.0	22.0	15.9

Source: Junta de Planificación, *Informe económico, 1988*, p. A-33.

occupy low-paying service jobs. This process has been described by some as population substitution; but more accurately it should be called worker substitution, as the majority of those involved are low-paid laborers. Dominican workers join the ranks of the poor in Puerto Rico while Puerto Ricans join them in the United States. Although an important number of Puerto Rican migrants to the United States are skilled workers and professionals, the majority are still semiskilled and unskilled laborers who, together with a majority of poor Puerto Ricans in the United States, have become the poorer of the minority groups in the metropolis.[56]

The income situation is worse. Real average weekly wages dropped to under $55 after the 1972 high of over $60 (Figure 5.5). Although there was a recovery from the decline after 1975, real wages leveled off below the 1972 mark during the 1980s. Thus, the 1980 census registered 62.4 percent of the Puerto Rican population at below poverty level. In 1988, 43.5 percent of the population were eligible for the Nutrition Assistance Program, the newest version of the food stamp program. Federal government transfers to individuals continue to play a crucial role in preventing a further drop in living standards. In 1988 these represented 21.9 percent of personal income, the same level as the recession year 1976. The situation was such that, notwithstanding the fiscal retrenchment policies of the Reagan administration, federal transfers to individuals grew at an annual rate of 5.7 percent between 1980 and 1988, higher than the 2.9 percent growth in current wages during that period.[57]

While under the CI/EP strategy the tendency was to increase exploitation while increasing real wages, the emerging pattern is different. Table 5.7 shows a declining tendency of wages as a share of product, sales, and receipts in manufacturing, retail and wholesale trade, and services. Although these are not directly comparable measures of exploitation, they do suggest an increasing rate of exploitation of labor in manufacturing and nonmanufacturing activities. This trend, coupled with the decline in real wages, indicates that in Puerto Rico, as in some service-led economies, the shift toward service employment is accompanied by a reduction in wages. Service jobs are not necessarily well-paid jobs.

Indeed, the service and financial sectors led job creation during this

Figure 5.5 Real Average Weekly Wages: 1952–1988

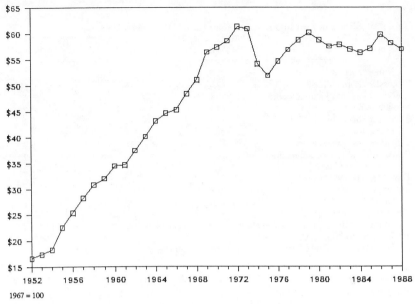

1967 = 100

Source: Departamento del Trabajo, "Series de salario."

Table 5.7 Wages as Percentage of Value Added in Manufacturing, Sales in Trade, and Receipts in Services: 1977-1982

Sector	1977	1982	Change
Manufacture[a]	17.9	12.2	–5.7
Services	31.8	28.4	–3.4
Retail trade	9.7	8.8	–0.9
Wholesale trade	5.9	5.2	–0.7

Sources: U.S. Bureau of the Census, *1982 Economic Censuses of Outlying Areas Manufactures, Retail, Wholesale and Services.*
[a]Production workers.

period. Table 5.8 shows changes in the shares of employment by occupation between 1976 and 1988. Nonproductive or nonmanual categories grew far more than productive ones, from 47.1 percent of all occupations to 52.3 percent. Productive ones declined from 40.6 to 34.4 percent of all occupations. Among nonproductive activities professionals and related occupations grew the most. This category, however, includes many occupations that used to be classified as semiprofessional and that are not well paid, such as nurse and lab technician, as well as low-paying professions, such as teacher, counselor, and librarian.

Summarizing the socioeconomic situation in Puerto Rico, a 1989 study ordered by the U.S. Congress remarked that "chronic high poverty rates persist in Puerto Rico despite an improving economy."[58] Declining living

Table 5.8 Shares of Employment by Major Occupation: 1976–1988

Category	1976	1988	Change
Nonproductive			
Professionals and related	12.1	16.7	4.6
Clerical, sales, and kindred workers	20.6	22.0	1.4
Service workers	14.4	13.7	−0.7
Total nonproductive	47.1	52.3	5.2
Productive			
Craftsmen and foremen	11.9	12.8	0.9
Operatives and related occupations	18.9	15.7	−3.2
Laborers (except farm)	6.1	3.9	−2.2
Farm laborers and foremen	3.7	2.1	−1.6
Total productive	40.6	34.4	−6.2
Others[a]	12.1	13.2	1.1

Sources: Departamento del Trabajo, "Empleo y desempleo en Puerto Rico, 1975-1976, 1987–1988," Tables 8 and 7.
[a]Includes a majority of small owners under the categories of proprietors and farmers.

standards and unemployment have continued to fuel a substantial growth in the marginal or underground economy, comprised of both legal and illegal activities. The size of such an economic sector is hard to determine but, based on estimates for the United States, a Fomento official estimated it to be over 15 percent of the GNP. In Puerto Rico, contrary to most popular images, the underground economy is not limited to street vendors and household workers; it includes a sizeable share of professional services whose income is not declared to the treasury and whose practice is based in the home, as well as growing informal trade and financial activity ("shark loans") in offices and business throughout the country.[59] Thus the informal economy has extended beyond the realm of the poor into the middle classes.

Criminal activities are a big part of the underground economy and have become particularly violent. Although the total crime rate in Puerto Rico is higher than only seven states in the United States, the violent crime rate is higher than that of forty-three states.[60] Armed robberies of banks, retail stores, and other business with cash transactions are reported in large numbers by the daily press, as are the many cases of drug-related violence.

The emerging trend is one of an increasingly impoverished mass vis-à-vis local groups connected to the international economy. Bankers, lawyers, executives, stock brokers, hotel operators, public relations and professional consultants, and politicians are enjoying the benefits of the high-finance strategy while productive and nonproductive wage earners see their standard of living continuing to deteriorate. As in other countries, the expansion of services in Puerto Rico has meant more but lower paying jobs. If anything, the contradictions of the CI/EP strategy are being exacerbated. Puerto Rico's path to the postindustrial era is only deepening socioeconomic divisions.

Puerto Rico as a Model of Peripheral Postindustrialization

One key ideological construction of the PPD around the high-finance strategy is that the incentives that make the island a tax haven are bringing about a new stage of development based on high-tech industries. The proof presented by Fomento analysts is that the leading manufacturing sectors are pharmaceuticals, electronics, and instruments. Indeed, the evidence shows a proliferation of high-tech subsidiaries since 1976. However, there are some questions about whether the growth of these industries can be described as high-tech development in Puerto Rico: What segment of high-tech industry is established in Puerto Rico? Is research and development (R&D) being performed on a significant scale? What kind of productive structure do these industries have and are they fully mechanized—do they use robots and sophisticated computers in production? Do these industries produce some of the sophisticated tools they use in production in Puerto Rico? Are local firms adopting these technologies and entering into competition with U.S. TNCs, as in Asia?

In 1984, Fometo consultant Theodore Lane argued that the existing structure of industrial incentives stimulated the location of the production segment of high-tech industries but provided no significant incentive for transfering R & D operations to the island. According to Lane, there was no clear policy for promoting R&D; although higher education institutions had some capacity to engage in R&D, they were mainly teaching institutions; there was no body above party politics to provide continuity to any R & D program; and the tax exemption structure did not encourage the development of new products.[61] Another dimension not mentioned by Lane is that the politics of transnational corporations may hinder the establishment or transfer of R&D activities from the core to the periphery.

The PPD government has just begun to address some of these issues with the hope of attracting R&D activities and creating a high-tech postindustrial complex. The PPD governor appointed within its Economic Advisory Council a Council on Science and Technology and created in 1988 two public corporations to encourage and coordinate technological development, the Corporation for Technological Transformation (CTT) and the Corporation for Technological Development of Tropical Resources (TROPICO). Furthermore, in January 1989, the Governor's Economic Advisory Council published an outline of the new development strategy that would take Puerto Rico into the twenty-first century. The scenario envisaged in the report is one led by clusters of "industrial excellence" integrated by high-tech manufacturing and service industries. These will become the leading sectors of the new postindustrial economy.[62]

Whether this strategy to turn Puerto Rico into a high-tech complex materializes or not is still to be seen. The experience of the petrochemical complex in the late 1960s shows that the long-term goals of the colonial government and the globally based interests of U.S. transnational capital and the metropolitan state may not always coincide. Changing global conditions may derail the best laid plans. As was the case with petrochemicals before, pharmaceutical, electronic, and instrument corporations are lending some support to the government plans. However, their efforts have been centered on lobbying for the retention of Section 936 rather than on the proposal to develop Puerto Rico into an international center of high-tech production and R&D. They know that the main reason they come to Puerto Rico is tax avoidance.

For as long as Section 936 remains in the U.S. IRC, Puerto Rico will remain a choice location for the production segment of high-tech industries. High-tech industries in Puerto Rico will continue to produce intermediate components and final products of high profitability that permit U.S. TNCs to avoid paying federal taxes on global profits. High-tech imported machines will be used in production, supervision, and quality control to meet the specifications and requirements of the U.S. Food and Drug Administration in pharmaceuticals and to make internationally competitive electronic products, while R&D and decisionmaking remain in the headquarters in the United States. As was the case with the petrochemical industries, Puerto Rico continues to be a link in an international process of production controlled by U.S. TNCs.

Whether high-tech TNCs would transfer to or develop R&D facilities in Puerto Rico to any significant degree and allow a relatively autonomous development of high-tech industries depends on a number of factors that are not present in Puerto Rico now. Aside from the tax and policy issues raised by Lane, one crucial factor is the lack of a high-tech academic/industrial complex. The recent actions of the government to fund the creation of such a complex in Puerto Rico represent a first step in formulating a consistent policy for R&D development. Yet a policy is not enough if it is not adequately funded. This would imply committing to spend about 1 percent of the GDP in R&D, as do other industrializing countries, such as Ireland and South Korea. This would have meant spending $256 million in R&D in 1988, which is nowhere near the funding levels of TROPICO and the CTT, which were assigned a combined total of $5 million.[63] Another disincentive could be the high cost and unreliable supply of electricity.

An alternative way to promote high-tech development is through the local private sector by stimulating local producers to appropriate advanced technologies through joint ventures with TNCs, as was the case of Asian producers. Bringing sophisticated machines and computers to Puerto Rico and training local individuals to run them is not by itself technological transfer. Appropriation of advanced technologies and their utilization to compete internationally is what characterizes technological transfer in a meaningful sense. This has not happened in Puerto Rico to any significant degree. The success stories about Asian subcontractors developing and marketing products under their own brand names in direct competition with their contractors do not abound in Puerto Rico. Historically, Puerto Rican manufacturers have adopted a subordinate role vis-à-vis U.S. companies and are reluctant to enter into a competition in which neither the government nor financial institutions will support them against their competitors. The colonial government, unlike Asian governments, cannot adopt protectionist measures, subsidize exports through foreign exchange manipulations, or adopt low-wage policies outside of the limits of U.S. minimum wage laws.

If there is any lesson to be learned from the Puerto Rican experience, it is that countries with small open economies can negotiate some economic conditions and advantages with TNCs and metropolitan states. But as long as such countries want to remain connected to the leading sectors of the international economy, their governments would have to follow the economic lead of TNCs and core states. Governments of small countries may increase their leverage and bargaining power vis-à-vis TNCs and metropolitan states by making them compete with each other for the locational and resource advantages of their countries, although they must remember that there are many peripheral states competing for investment. In the case of Puerto Rico, as a U.S. colony (a "possession"), the leverage to bargain with U.S. TNCs and the metropolitan state seems more limited than that of independent nations. Commonwealth bureaucrats can promote, coordinate, and even design innovative schemes (such as *maquiladoras*), but TNCs and the metropolitan state have a greater say in deciding the direction of the colonial economy. The success of the high-finance strategy and the peripheral postindustrialization model in Puerto Rico depends then on the fate of Section 936—hence on the decisions of the U.S. Congress.

Yet the process is not as unilateral as it may seem since these decisions are not taken in a vacuum but are the product of the process of class struggle. The fate of the high-finance strategy depends then on the accommodation that would be reached among conflicting local and metropolitan leading political and economic groups. This may seem a precarious and uncertain future, and indeed it is. But the key lesson to be learned from the Puerto Rican experience is that constant conflict and changes are part and parcel of capitalist development, which in the periphery means adjusting to global changes and shifting economic and political alliances to achieve a type of growth that will not benefit all of the population. There is no fixed formula; structural economic constraints impose some limitations on development strategy alternatives. It is the level of class conflict, nonetheless, that determines which development strategy is chosen and who are the main beneficiaries.

New Political Conflicts and the Future

The transition from the CI/EP strategy to the high-finance strategy has produced not only a restructured economy but also a restructured political system. The hegemony of the PPD has been replaced by a bipartisan political structure.[64] The implications of this are far reaching. Party loyalties have been weakened, as has state control over the institutions of civil society. Although the state continues to be a large instrument of patronage, the frequent government changes have made it a less reliable instrument for party clienteles. This has diminished the power of the state and political parties to establish and maintain stable clienteles. Party disaffiliation has led to the proliferation of nonpartisan and nongovernmental organizations (NGOs) as a means of social expression in every aspect of sociopolitical life.

Institutions that used to be controlled by the government or a party have increased their autonomy and power. This is the case, for example, of the Olympic Committee of Puerto Rico, which sent a representation to the Moscow Olympiads in 1980 in spite of the U.S. boycott and opposition from the colonial government. On a smaller scale, feminist, environmentalist, community development, and other groups have proliferated outside of party and government influence. Although this is far from people's empowerment, it certainly points to a strengthening of the colonial civil society. This does not mean that the process of autonomous participation of popular groups is rid of clientelistic overtones. In some instances these groups play on partisan rivalries or contradictions between colonial and metropolitan policies. The latter is true of sectors of the environmentalist movement, where federal government regulations are used to create opposition to the PPD, which wants to "liberalize" federal restrictions that hinder businesses. Some groups play these contradictions to obtain funds and political leverage, which may translate into autonomous power bases vis-à-vis or within government and party structures. In any case, the clear dominance of political parties and the colonial state over civil society has been greatly diminished.

In spite of these changes, the axis of the local political structure and conflict continues to be the colonial status question. To a large extent the economic future of the country is closely tied to the nature of its political relation with the United States. Commonwealth, independence, and statehood assume new constraints for development options. The debate on development strategies is related to the status question as much as the status question is related to development strategies. The transition-to-statehood strategy of the PNP was derailed by the advantages to U.S. TNCs of Section 936, which are only possible under commonwealth. Moreover, the unattractiveness of independence to large sectors of the population is grounded to some degree in the crucial role that federal transfers have played since the 1930s in the income of many poor families. So, the future of the high-finance strategy is indisolubly tied to the future of the colonial relation and of Section 936.

After the PPD seemed to have consolidated its power and the direction of the high-finance strategy with two consecutive electoral victories in 1984 and 1988 and the creation of the CBI/936 program, the Bush administration put forth a proposal to hold a plebiscite to allow Puerto Ricans to decide their political status and exercise their right to self-determination. Many reasons have been given for the timing of this decision. One is that with the restructuring of the world political order and the declaration by the United Nations to work for ending colonialism by the year 2000, the U.S. government wants to avoid any accusations of colonialism in Puerto Rico. Another plausible explanation is that, as a Republican, President Bush supports statehood for Puerto Rico because of its strategic importance to the United States and, like many Puerto Rican statehooders, saw the need to press for statehood before the diminished popularity of the PNP erodes further. Finally, some have argued that at a time of fiscal crisis Puerto Rico represents a drain on federal resources both in transfer payments and lost revenue from the profits of 936 corporations and, therefore, changes in the political relation are needed to curtail the high costs of maintaining a colony.

Clearly, none of these arguments by itself tells the whole story. Combined, they do present a strong case for the metropolitan interest in renegotiating the colonial relation. The emerging libertarian aspirations of peoples throughout the world make colonialism obsolete; combined with the high cost of the colony and the need to secure a strategic outpost in the Caribbean at a time when geographic spheres of influence are being redefined, this makes a compelling case for the conservative Republicans running the metropolitan state to push for statehood. But whatever good reasons the Bush administration may have found to renegotiate the colonial relation at this time, the effect in the colony has been to exacerbate political conflict and threaten the continuation of the high-finance strategy.

The Plebiscite

The proposal for the plebiscite originated in the White House and, only after some arm twisting, PPD Governor Hernández Colón acquiesced to take President Bush's proposal. He announced in his inaugural address in January 1989 the government's support for the plebiscite and was later joined by PNP and PIP leaders. In April three bills were introduced in the U.S. Senate providing alternative ways to define the three main political formulas— commonwealth, independence, and statehood. Bill S. 712 became the one that local party leaders agreed provided the best basis for the definition of each status formula. Hearings on the bill were held in June and July by the Senate Committee on Energy and Natural Resources, which oversees Puerto Rico. A committee report on S.712 was filed in September 1989 and the bill moved to another committee.

Many issues were debated regarding language, citizenship, territorial waters rights, and so forth. The issue of Section 936 became a major bone of contention. Statehooders asked for a transition period of twenty-five years in which Section 936 privileges would be phased out and federal benefits increased; the committe recommended a three-year transition period. Section

936 tax exemptions would be phased out between 1994 and 1997 at a diminishing rate of 20 percent a year. Moreover, the committee estimated that statehood would be the formula that would increase federal spending the most as full benefits are extended to the island. Collections on 936 corporations taxes would offset to some degree the added expenditures.[65]

Commonwealthers asked for enhanced local powers in determining applicability of federal legislation and parity with states on programs such as the Nutrition Assistance Program, Medicaid, and Supplemental Security Income. The permanence of Section 936 was assumed, as this is a matter that can be revised or legislated by Congress at any time. The committee report provided for a mechanism to appeal the applicability of federal legislation and rules to Puerto Rico and the provision of federal aid in a bloc grant that would be revenue neutral. Commonwealth was estimated to imply no increased expenditures to the federal government, other than possible periodic adjustments in the bloc grants.[66]

Proindependence leaders asked for a twenty-five-year period to phase out Section 936; a twenty-year period receiving federal aid in the form of bloc grants in amounts equivalent to federal transfers at the time of independence; foreign trade privileges; and a guarantee that federal pensions and other such social benefits would be continued or a replacement be coordinated. The committee report rejected the twenty-five-year transition period and suggested that tax concessions be replaced by a foreign tax credit, which may be similar to Section 936 credits during an undetermined transition period. Federal bloc grants would be granted for nine years after the proclamation of independence and aid should be negotiated thereafter as with other foreign countries. Pensions are guaranteed and other social programs would be coordinated by task forces. Independence, as would be expected, was the less costly to the federal government as an ever-increasing share of the fiscal responsibilities of the country would be assumed by the new nation's government.[67]

Clearly, the elimination of Section 936 within a short period of time makes statehood and independence unattractive to TNCs and their local allies. The flip side of that coin is that increased federal transfers make statehood very attractive to the poor majority of the country. Commonwealth is at a distinct advantage with capital, while statehood appeals to the poor, as Carlos Romero Barceló argued over a decade ago. Independence is an unknown quantity and many of the specifics of this formula are left to be negotiated in the future, if it gets a majority vote.

The debate on the plebiscite has brought forth some underlying divisions within the power bloc and between it and the subordinate classes. On the side of the power bloc there is a faction of the PNP that favors immediate statehood regardless of the cost. Another faction views the plebiscite as a threat to the business climate on the island and would prefer a transition to statehood over a long period, with gradual reduction of federal tax privileges and eligibility for federal funds.

The first faction is led by Carlos Romero Barceló. Following the logic of Romero's arguments in *Statehood is for the Poor*, this group believes that the gains in federal funding outweigh the loss of 936 corporations. They believe that this is an opportunity they cannot miss. The PPD/936 corporations coalition is strengthening and the three elections of the 1980s show the PNP constantly loosing ground to the PPD.[68] Indeed, the committee's recommendation of equal treatment for a Puerto Rican state within a short period of time makes this a very attractive alternative for the working poor and the unemployed. Polls show a majority of the electorate favoring statehood, which suggest that people who may not vote for the PNP seem willing to vote for statehood on a plebiscite, in which government officials are not elected. This faction could be characterized as a populist coalition led by the new petty bourgeoisie with a base of support among sectors of the population benefiting from federal transfers and some middle-class elements that see in statehood the only stable way to maintain the economic ties to the United States that ensure the "progress" of Puerto Rico.

The other faction within the PNP is the one more closely linked to the internationalized bourgeoisie. This faction does not have a clear leader. Very few PNP leaders would want to admit publicly that statehood has a potentially negative effect on the high-finance strategy. Instead, those who believe this present themselves as the voices of moderation and reason, insisting on the twenty-five year transition period or eschewing the plebiscite altogether. A powerful PNP figure who has bitterly criticized the plebiscite is Manuel Casiano, former head of Fomento under Ferré and owner and editor of *Caribbean Business*. After praising Fomento's success in attracting foreign investment in an editorial in his paper, Casiano warned that "foreign investment in the island is bound to start drying up, as has local [U.S.] investment, if the plebiscite talks continue to dominate Puerto Rico's government agenda."[69] As a loyal PNP member he blames the PPD government for endorsing the Bush administration's plebiscite proposal, but his criticism is a tacit acknowledgment that business does not want statehood and with it the end of Section 936 privileges. In fact, in a feature article in June 1989, it was reported that 73 percent of 270 businessmen surveyed by *Caribbean Business* disapproved of the plebiscite. Again the article was phrased as an attack on the PPD government's endorsement of the plebiscite, ignoring the role of the PNP leadership in it.[70] In spite of Casiano's and his staff's ability to conceal the division inside PNP over the plebiscite, there is no denying that many leaders of that party have come to realize that the rhetoric of equality of benefits for the poor under statehood runs counter to the interests of the internationalized fraction of the local bourgeoisie that supports the PNP.

The internationalized fraction of the local bourgeoisie linked to the PNP, U.S. TNCs, and the PPD find themselves trapped in the logic of developmentalism made dominant by the PPD. The growth of popular support for statehood is to a large degree a function of the developmentalist logic that successfully related continued economic growth to political association with the United States. The pro-statehood rhetoric is grounded in this part of the developmentalist ideology. If association with the United States is the guarantee of Puerto Rico's progress, make it permanent through statehood. During the crisis in the early 1970s, this logic made sense not only to the working poor and the unemployed but to fractions of U.S. capital and the local bourgeoisie. However, the kind of development stimulated by Section 936 has led these groups to reevaluate their earlier position on the desirability of statehood. Yet they find themselves caught in their own political rhetoric about the bankruptcy of commonwealth and statehood as the only dignified and economically superior alternative.

On the PPD side, the dominant position is to support some reforms on the applicability of federal regulations and laws and enhance federal transfers along the lines of earlier proposals. This position has been mildly challenged by a a minority of "autonomists" within the party. These reformists, like the young technocrats in the 1960s, are urging the party leadership to redefine commonwealth and move toward really greater autonomy in the form of an "Associated Republic." This formula would be similar to that granted to the Marshall Islands in 1985. In theory, this formula would provide a greater measure of self-rule (eliminating the applicability of federal statutes), allow for autonomous conduct of foreign relations, and leave matters of defense and national security in the hands of the U.S. government.[71] These "closet independence supporters," as PNP leaders call them, have no substantial popular support and, like the moderate faction of the PNP, are unwilling to confront directly the top leadership of their party. In any case, the proposals of this faction would not threaten the preservation of Section 936.

The proindependence sector remains a minority with very remote chances of winning the plebiscite. Decades of government repression and harassment and the massive federal welfare apparatus have effectively undermined popular support for this alternative. Although in the past two years government intolerance of proindependence supporters seems to have subsided and Congress provided $500 thousand to the PIP to cover part of the costs of participating in drafting the plebiscite legislation, this cannot erase years of persecution and anti-independence propaganda that have developed deep-rooted fears about this alternative among the population. Moreover, the proindependence forces do not have consensus on whether or not to participate in the plebiscite. While the PIP has decided to participate, other smaller groups are still evaluating or boycotting the process. The proindependence vote has stayed around the 5 percent mark since 1976 and is not expected to change substantially in the plebiscite.

Within the metropolitan power bloc there is a division on the status question between groups who support national security interests and TNCs. Traditionally, security-minded Republicans have favored statehood. President

Bush publicly declared his "personal preference" for statehood in announcing his intention to introduce the plebiscite legislation in his first State of the Union address. Illustrative of the position of national security agencies in regard to Puerto Rico was the statement of Acting Deputy Assistant Secretary of Defense Brigadier General M. J. Byron, in the hearings on the plebiscite bill held by the Senate Committee on Energy and Natural Resources. He stated plainly that statehood was "the least troublesome" option for the Department of Defense and independence "would have the most significant implications for DOD."[72]

For their part, 936 corporations are reported to be lobbying frantically behind the scenes using PRUSA as their front to block the plebiscite or make its result nonbinding. Publicly, nonetheless, 936 corporations appear to be above the fray. As the plebiscite is intended to be an exercise in self-determination for the Puerto Ricans it would be an embarrassment to the companies if they appeared to be meddling in the process. But Puerto Rican executives of transnationals are less shy in making their position publicly known. Miguel Ferrer, general manager of Payne Webber in Puerto Rico, sent a paper to Congress supporting commonwealth. Although he claims the paper presented his personal views, not those of the company, logically many local executives of 936 corporations and financial institutions would want to support the status that preserves Section 936—commonwealth.[73]

The divisions within the power bloc around the status issue are compounded by other elements, such as the fact that Puerto Rico is a Hispanic nation where Spanish is the main language. Foreign policy considerations also play a key role as the annexation of Puerto Rico as the fifty-first state may not sit well with Latin American nationalists who would see this as a further act of U.S. imperialism against Latin America—a perception that, on the heels of the invasion of Panama, is bound to gain currency in the region.

The plebiscite project is still under consideration by the U.S. House and various committees there and in the Senate. The tug-of-war that has ensued may simply kill the project, as it did in the past, produce a nonbinding result, or throw Puerto Rico into an unchartered path. Whatever the outcome, the strategic importance of Puerto Rico for the United States has dictated a postwar policy of subsidizing a higher living standard for the island in comparison to the rest of Latin America and the Caribbean. This seems unlikely to change. Living standards may continue to deteriorate but will be maintained above that of neighboring countries to preserve the island's role as a U.S. showcase and to maintain independence as an unattractive alternative. Puerto Rico may remain a colony with periodically changing federal incentives to U.S. investments; it may become a "beggar state," with a higher rate of federal subsidies than any other state of the Union; or it may be declared a federal enterprise zone, such as the Bronx, to maintain tax advantages under statehood. The decision of the Bush administration seems to have raised graver problems than it intended to solve. Developmentalism has made statehood a popular alternative, but TNCs see this formula as a threat to their interests. Security interests advocate statehood but fiscal calculations make it the most costly alternative. The costs and the benefits of statehood do not seem clear for the metropolitan administration and the statehooders who are caught in the contradiction between their political discourse and their economic interests. The PPD and 936 corporations, on the contrary, favor an alternative that reconciles their economic and political interests. The outcome, however, will not be a purely rational one but the result of the accommodations around the emerging contradictions between the different groups and their favored alternative. The foreseeable impasse will probably extend the lease of the commonwealth.

Notes

1. Castillo Rivas, *Acumulación de capital*, pp. 144–145; U.S. Department of Commerce, *Economic Study*, 2, p. 56.

2. U.S. Department of Commerce, *Economic Study*, 1, p. 34, and 2, pp. 445–449.

3. Comité para el Desarrollo Económico de Puerto Rico, "Un estudio, parte I," pp. 52–53, and annex 26–28.

4. Investment figures are from Junta de Planificación, *Ingreso y producto, 1984*, pp. 28–29; employment figures are from Puerto Rico, Departamento del Trabajo y Recursos Humanos, "Series de empleo y desempleo."

5. Junta de Planificación, *Informe económico, 1979*, pp. A-1, A-19, A-20.

6. See Beaud, *A History*, pp. 194–200; Kolko, *Restructuring*, Chap. 1; and Mandel, *La crisis*, Chap. 25.

7. Meléndez, "Crisis económica," p. 197; U.S. Department of Commerce, *Economic Study*, 2, pp. 66–67.

8. U.S. Department of the Treasury, *Operation and Effect, First Annual Report*, p. 1.

9. Meléndez, *Statehood Movement*, pp. 136–137.

10. Romero Barceló, *Statehood is for the Poor*; PNP, *Programa, 1976*.

11. PNP, *Programa, 1976*, pp. 14–15.

12. Ibid., pp. 15–20.

13. Meléndez points out that the core of the first Romero administration came from banking and finance, which accounted for the preference for these sectors; *Statehood Movement*, p. 158.

14. U.S. Department of Treasury, *Operation and Effect; First Annual Report*, pp. 64–65; and U.S. Department of Commerce, *Economic Study*, 2, p. 563.

15. PREDA, *Industrial Incentive Act, 1978*, pp. 2, 20–25, Section 3 (a), (b), (c), (d).

16. U.S. Department of the Treasury, *Operation and Effect; Sixth Report*, pp. 14–15.

17. PREDA, *Industrial Incentive Act, 1978*, pp. 17–19, 41, Sections 2(o), 2(q), and 3(o). Tax exemptions of export services were later increased to 75 percent.

18. Madera, "The Economic Development Administration."
19. Finn, "Economic Implications of Statehood," pp. 184–191.
20. Puerto Rico, Banco Gubernamental de Fomento, "La creación de un centro financiero;" Quiñones, "International Trade Center," pp. 17–18, 33; "Report from the Treasury; International Banking Center," *Puerto Rico Business Review* 8, January–February 1983, p. 16; PNP, *Propuesta de programa, 1981–1984*, pp. 64, 73–75.
21. Bayrón Toro, *Elecciones y partidos*, pp. 288–291.
22. For a more detailed discussion of the CBI see Pantojas-García, "The U.S. Caribbean Basin Initiative."
23. The PPD's opposition to the CBI was registered in a Joint Resolution of the House of Representatives sent to the U.S. Senate. "Resolution of the House of Puerto Rican Representatives," in U.S. Senate, Committee on Foreign Relations, *Caribbean Basin Initiative*, pp. 96–110. A year later, the presidents of the Puerto Rico Manufacturers Association and the Puerto Rico Chamber of Commerce registered their opposition to the CBI in the House of Representatives. U.S. House of Representatives, House Ways and Means Committee, *Caribbean Basin Economic Recovery Act*, pp. 184–192, 254–256.
24. Coopers & Lybrand, "Twin Plants for Puerto Rico;" Stewart, "Puerto Rico," p. B-3; and Stewart, "The Twin Plant Concept," p. 2. Stewart was the director of the Office of Economic Research of Fomento.
25. Madera, *The Impact of the Possessions Corporation*, p. i; and U.S. Department of the Treasury, *Operation and Effect; Fourth Report*, Chap. 2.
26. Traditionally, Democrats have supported commonwealth or paid lip service to the right of Puerto Rico to political self-determination. In sharp contrast to the 1976 declaration of support for statehood by President Ford, President Carter declared support for the right to self-determination in 1978.
27. Kolko, *Restructuring*, Chap. 3.
28. Buttles, "Trouble in Tax Paradise?," p. 9.
29. Ibid., pp. 9, 25–27; *Business Week*, 22 May 1978, pp. 154, 156; Horowitz, "Puerto Rico's Pharmaceutical Fix," pp. 22–36; and U.S. Department of Treasury, *Operation and Effect; Fourth Report*, pp. 15–21.
30. Junta de Planificación, *Informe económico, 1983*, pp. XV-17–XV-18.
31. *Caribbean Business*, 17 September 1987, p. 1.
32. U.S. Department of the Treasury, *Operation and Effect; First Annual Report*, p. 19.
33. See Suárez, *Requiem on Cerro Maravilla*; Nelson, *Murder Under Two Flags*; Carr, A Colonial Experiment, pp. 372–377; and Meléndez, *Statehood Movement*, pp. 167–169.
34. Calculated from Junta de Planificación, *Informe económico, 1988*, pp. A-1, A-4, A-33.
35. Meléndez, *Statehood Movement*, pp. 169–173.
36. Comité para el Desarrollo Económico de Puerto Rico, "Un estudio, parte II," pp. 22–49.
37. *Caribbean Business*, 9 January 1985, p.1; *The Journal of Commerce*, 25 March 1985, p. 3A.
38. Latortue, "Puerto Rico in the CBI," pp. 13–14, 23–24.
39. González, "Is Puerto Rico Fulfilling Its CBI Commitment?," p. 2.
40. See U.S. House of Representatives, *Comprehensive Tax Reform*.
41. For a full comparison of Law 26 and Law 8, see Coopers & Lybrand, "Summary, Tax Incentives Act."
42. Jacobsen, "Peripheral 'Postindustrialization.' "
43. Departamento del Trabajo, *Censo de industrias, 1988*, Table 2.

44. Lane, "Export Services," pp. 19–21. The only reliable detailed statistics for services are those of the census taken every five years. The figures for 1987 are not out yet.

45. Junta de Planificación, *Informe económico, 1979 and 1988*, pp. 131 and 133, and Chap. 6, pp. 2 and 6, respectively.

46. Estudios Técnicos, et al., *The Impact*, pp. 2, 37, and passim.

47. Robert R. Nathan Associates, Inc., *Section 936*, pp. 46–48.

48. Caribbean Business, *The Book of Lists*, pp. 49–57, 64; *Caribbean Business*, 26 October 1989, p. 40; *Caribbean Business*, 30 November 1989, pp. 1–2.

49. *Caribbean Business*, 25 May 1989, pp. 40–41, and 26 October 1989, p. 2.

50. *Caribbean Business*, 4 May 1989, pp. 44–45.

51. *Caribbean Business*, 31 August 1989, p. 2, and 14 December 1989, p. 4.

52. See sources for Table 4.4

53. Calculated from Junta de Planificación, *Informe económico, 1988*, p. A-1; World Bank, *World Tables, 1988–1989*, pp.172–175, 596–599.

54. *Caribbean Business*, 8 June 1989, pp.1–2, and 31 August 1989, p. 10.

55. Calculated from Junta de Planificación, *Informe económico, 1983, 1988*, pp. XIII-3 and A-23, and pp. XI-3 and A-33, respectively. Figures for 1948 to 1963 from sources in Table 3.6. Ramírez de Arellano Seipp, *Colonialism, Catholicism & Contraception*, p. 175.

56. See Duany, "De la periferia a la semi-periferia"; Bonilla and Campos, "Evolving Patterns"; and Nelson and Tienda, "The Structuring of Hispanic Ethnicity."

57. United States General Accounting Office, *Puerto Rico, Update*, p. 22; Junta de Planificación, *Informe económico, 1988*, pp. A-1, A-19; and Departamento del Trabajo, "Series de salario."

58. United States General Accounting Office, *Puerto Rico, Update*, p. 22.

59. Stewart, "Notes on the Underground Economy," p. 23; and *Claridad*, 20–27 October 1988, pp. 12, 29.

60. United States General Accounting Office, *Puerto Rico, Update*, p.21.

61. Lane, "The Effects of Institutional Change," pp. 63–66.

62. See Boyson, "Governor Announces"; Morera, "TROPICO"; and Consejo Asesor Económico del Gobernador, *Estrategia para el desarrollo*.

63. See Boyson, "Governor Announces," p. 6; and Stewart, "Puerto Rico's Options," p. 13.

64. Anderson, "The Party System."

65. U.S. Senate, Committee on Energy and National Resources, *Political Status*, pp. 288–377, and *Status Referendum Act*, pp. 34–39, 54.

66. U.S. Senate, Committee on Energy and Natural Resources, *Political Status*, pp. 190–254, and *Status Referendum Act*, pp. 48–54.

67. U.S. Senate, Committee on Energy and National Resources, *Political Status*, pp. 273–284, and *Status Referendum Act*, pp. 39–48, 54.

68. Bayrón Toro, *Elecciones y partidos*, p. 349.

69. *Caribbean Business*, 31 August 1989, p. 34.

70. *Caribbean Business* 22 June 1989, p. 1.

71. Rodríguez Orellana, "In Contemplation of Micronesia."

72. U.S. Senate, Committee on Energy and National Resources, *Political Status*, pp. 134–144.

73. *El Nuevo Día*, 1 December 1989, p. 20.

Bibliography

Acevedo, Luz del Alba. "American Colonialism and the Emergence of Puerto Rican Nationalism during the Decade of the Thirties." Master's thesis, University of Liverpool, 1978.

————. "Industrialization and Employment; Changes in the Patterns of Women's Work in Puerto Rico." *World Development* 18 (February 1990): 231—255.

Airov, Joseph. *The Location of the Synthetic-Fiber Industry: A Case Study in Regional Analysis*. Massachusetts and New York: Technology Press and John Wiley & Sons, 1959.

Alavi, Hamza. "The State in Post-colonial Societies: Pakistan and Bangladesh." *New Left Review* 74 (July–August 1972): 59–81.

———— "State and Class Under Peripheral Capitalism." In Alavi, Hamza, and Shanin, Teodor. *Introduction to the Sociology of 'Developing Societies.'* New York: Monthly Review, 1982, pp. 289–307.

Althusser, Louis. *Lenin and Philosophy*. London: New Left Books, 1971.

————. *For Marx*. London: New Left Books, 1977.

Anderson, Robert W. *Party Politics in Puerto Rico*. Stanford: Stanford University Press, 1965.

————. "The Party System: Change or Stagnation." In Heine, *Time for Decision*, pp. 3–25.

Baer, Werner. *The Puerto Rican Economy and United States Economic Fluctuations*. Río Piedras: University of Puerto Rico Social Science Research Center, 1960.

Balassa, Bela, et al. *Development Strategies in Semi-industrial Economies*. Baltimore: Johns Hopkins University Press, 1982.

Banco Popular de Puerto Rico. *Guía para las elecciones, 1972*. San Juan: Banco Popular de Puerto Rico, 1972.

Baquero, Genaro. "La importación de fondos externos y la capacidad absorbente de nuestra economía." *Revista de Ciencias Sociales* 7 (March–June 1963): 79–92.

————. "Magnitud y características de la inversión exterior en Puerto Rico." *Revista de Ciencias Sociales* 8 (March 1974): 5–13.

Batelle Memorial Institute. "Proposed Research Program on Investigation of the Economic Possibilities for a Petroleum Chemical Complex in Puerto Rico to the Economic Development Administration." Columbus, Ohio, 9 July 1954.

Bayrón Toro, Fernando. *Elecciones y partidos políticos en Puerto Rico.* Mayagüez: Editorial Isla, 1989.

Beaud, Michael. *A History of Capitalism.* New York: Monthly Review, 1983.

Bellah, Robert N. "The Impact of the Oil Import Program on the Economy of Puerto Rico." Master's thesis, George Washington University, 1970.

Bhagwati, Jagdish. "Rethinking Trade Strategies." In Lewis and Kallab, *Development Strategies Reconsidered*, pp. 91–104.

Bird, Esteban. *Report on the Sugar Industry in Relation to the Social and Economic System of Puerto Rico.* San Juan: Senado de Puerto Rico, 1941.

Bohi, Douglas R., and Russell, Milton. *Limiting Oil Imports; An Economic History and Analysis.* Baltimore: John Hopkins University, 1978.

Bonilla, Frank, and Campos, Ricardo. "Evolving Patterns of Puerto Rican Migration." In Steven E. Sanderson, ed. *The Americas in the New International Division of Labor.* New York: Holmes & Meier, 1985, pp.177–202.

Boyson, Sandor. "Governor Announces Measures to Promote Island's Scientific & Technological Progress." *Puerto Rico Business Review* 13 (August 1988): 6.

———. "Mobilizing Science and Technology Resources in Puerto Rico." *Puerto Rico Business Review* 13 (April 1988): 4–8.

Brown, Wenzell. *Dynamite on our Doorstep: Puerto Rican Paradox.* New York: Greenberg Publishers, 1945.

Business Week, New York, McGraw Hill.

Buttles, John S., II. "Trouble in Tax Paradise? The IRS Probes Corporate Operations in Puerto Rico." *Baron's*, 9 October 1978, p. 9.

Calero, Aristalco, and Herrero, José A. "Statement of Profs. Aristalco Calero and José A. Herrero." United States–Puerto Rico Commission on the Status of Puerto Rico. *Hearings*, 3 vols. Washington, D.C.: Government Printing Office, 1966, 3: 1–16.

Cardoso, Fernando H. "As contradiçoes do desenvolvimento asociado." *Estudos CEBRAP* 8 (April–June 1974): 41–76.

———."Comentario sobre los conceptos de sobrepoblación relativa y marginalidad." *Revista Latinoamericana de Ciencias Sociales* (June–December 1971).

Cardoso, Fernando H., and Faletto, Enzo. *Dependencia y desarrollo en América Latina.* México: Siglo Veintiuno, 1974.

Caribbean Business, San Juan, Casiano Communications.

Caribbean Business. *The Book of Lists. 1989.* San Juan: Caribbean Business, 1989.

Carr, Raymond. *Puerto Rico: A Colonial Experiment.* New York: Vintage, 1984.

Carrión, Juan M. "The Petty Bourgeoisie and the Struggle for Independence in Puerto Rico." In López, *The Puerto Ricans*, pp. 233–256.

Castells, Manuel. *La cuestión urbana.* México: Siglo Veintiuno, 1978.

Castillo Rivas, Donald. *Acumulación de capital y empresas transnacionales.* México: Siglo Veintiuno, 1980.

Centro de Estudios Puertorriqueños. History Task Force. *Labor Migration Under Capitalism; The Puerto Rican Experience.* New York: Monthly Review Press, 1979.

Cestero, Belén H. *Balance of External Payments of Puerto Rico; Fiscal Years 1941–42 to 1947–48.* San Juan: Office of the Governor, 1950.

Chemical Week, New York, McGraw Hill.

Clapp and Mayne, Inc. *Informe sobre el estudio de las características de la industria puertorriqueña y sus dueños.* 1978.

Claridad, San Juan, Editorial Claridad.

Cochran, Thomas C. *The Puerto Rican Businessman.* Philadelphia: University of Pennsylvania Press, 1959.

Comité para el Desarrollo Económico de Puerto Rico, Inc. "Un estudio del 'subcomité para el desarrollo económico de Puerto Rico'; parte I, diagnóstico de la crisis económica de Puerto Rico." San Juan, January 1984.

————. "Un estudio del 'subcomité para el desarrollo económico de Puerto Rico'; parte II, recomendaciones sobre política económica." San Juan, January 1984.

Connerton, Paul, ed. *Critical Sociology.* Middlesex: Penguin, 1976.

Coopers & Lybrand. "Twin Plants for Puerto Rico and the Eastern Caribbean: Estimated Manufacturing Costs," 16 March 1983.

————. "Summary, Tax Incentives Act of Puerto Rico." *Tax Topics Advisory.* n.d.

Corretjer, Juan A. *Albizu Campos y las huelgas de los años treinta.* Guaynabo, 1969.

————. *El líder de la desesperación.* Guaynabo, 1972.

————. *La lucha por la independencia de Puerto Rico.* Guaynabo, 1974.

Costas Elena, Luis P. "I.R.C. Section 936 and Fomento Income Tax Exemptions in Puerto Rico (part III)." *Revista del Colegio de Abogados de Puerto Rico* 41 (May 1980): 225–277.

Curet Cuevas, Eliezer. *El desarrollo económico de Puerto Rico: 1940 a 1972.* Hato Rey: Management Aid Center, 1976.

Dietz, James. *Economic History of Puerto Rico.* Princeton: Princeton University Press, 1986.

————. "Maquiladoras in the Caribbean: Puerto Rico, the Dominican Republic and the Twin Plant Program." Paper presented to the 15th International Congress of the Latin American Studies Association, December 1989.

Diffie, Bailey W., and Diffie, Justine W. *Porto Rico: A Broken Pledge.* New York: Vanguard, 1931.

Duany, Jorge. "De la periferia a la semi-periferia: impacto de la inmigración dominicana en Santurce." *Punto 7 Review* 2 (Fall 1989): 26–64.

Durand, Rafael. "Progreso, problemas y perspectivas del desarrollo industrial en Puerto Rico." In Navas Dávila, *Cambio y desarrollo,* pp. 171–189.

Edel, Matthew O. "Land Reform in Puerto Rico: 1940–1959." *Caribbean Studies* 1 (October 1962): 26–60; 2 (January 1963): 28–50.

Editorial Edil. *Puerto Rico, leyes fundamentales.* Río Piedras: Editorial Edil, 1973.

Emerson, Rupert. "Puerto Rico and American Policy Toward Dependent Areas." *The Annals of the American Academy of Political Science* 285 (January 1953): 9–15.

Estudios Técnicos, Inc., Wharton Econometric Forecasting Associates, and Touche-Ross and Co. *The Impact of Section 936 on Puerto Rico's Economy and Banking System.* San Juan: Puerto Rico Bankers Association, January 1989.

Evans, Peter. *Dependent Development.* Princeton: Princeton University Press, 1979.

Evers, Tilman. *El estado capitalista en la periferia.* México: Siglo Veintiuno, 1979.

Farr, Kenneth. *Personalismo y política de partidos: la institucionalización del Partido Popular Democrático de Puerto Rico.* Hato Rey: Inter-American University Press, 1975.

Femia, Joseph. "Hegemony and Consciousness in the Thought of Antonio Gramsci." *Political Studies* 23 (March 1975): 29–48.

Fernós Isern, Antonio. *El Estado Libre Asociado de Puerto Rico: antecedentes, creación y desarrollo hasta la época presente.* Río Piedras: Editorial Universitaria, 1974.

Ferré, Luis A. *El propósito humano.* San Juan: Ediciones Nuevas de Puerto Rico, 1972.

Figueroa Díaz, Wilfredo. *El movimiento estadista en Puerto Rico: pasado, presente y futuro.* Río Piedras: Editorial Cultural, 1979.

Finn, Bertram. "The Economic Implications of Statehood." In Heine, *Time for Decision*, pp. 183–210.

Friedlander, Stanley L. *Labor Migration and Economic Growth: A Case Study of Puerto Rico.* Massachusetts: The M.I.T. Press, 1965.

Fromm, Georg. *César Andreu Iglesias; aproximación a su vida y obras.* Río Piedras: Ediciones Huracán, 1977.

———. "La historia ficción de Benjamín Torres (V); la huelga de 1934, una interpretación marxista (1)." *Claridad*, Suplemento En Rojo (24–30 June 1977): 6–7.

———. "La historia ficción de Benjamín Torres (VI); la huelga de 1934, una interpretación marxista (2)." *Claridad*, Suplemento En Rojo (1–7 July 1977): 4–5.

Furtado, Celso. *La economía latinoamericana desde la conquista ibérica hasta la revolución cubana.* México: Siglo Veintiuno, 1969.

García, Gervasio, and Quintero Rivera, Angel G. *Desafío y solidaridad; breve historia del movimiento obrero puertorriqueño.* Río Piedras: Ediciones Huracán, 1982.

García López, José, and Meza, Liliana. "Profile of High-Tech Industries in Puerto Rico." *Puerto Rico Business Review* 13 (August 1988): 7–10.

García Passalacqua, Juan M. *La crisis política en Puerto Rico (1962–1966).* Río Piedras: Editorial Edil, 1970.

Gautier Mayoral, Carmen, and Nazario Trabal, Néstor, eds. *Puerto Rico en los 1990.* Río Piedras: Universidad de Puerto Rico Centro de Investigaciones Sociales, 1988.

Gayer, Arthur D.; Homan, Paul T.; and Jones, Earle K. *The Sugar Economy of Puerto Rico.* New York: Columbia University Press, 1938.

Gold, Thomas B. *State and Society in the Taiwan Miracle.* New York: Sharpe, 1986.

González, Emilio. "Class Struggle and Politics in Puerto Rico During the Decade of the 40's: The Rise of P.P.D." *Two Thirds* 2 (1979): 46–57.

González, José R. "Is Puerto Rico Fulfilling its CBI Commitment?" Unpublished position paper, 3 February 1988, p. 2.

Goodsell, Charles T. *Administration of a Revolution.* Cambridge, Mass.: Harvard University Press, 1965.

Gramsci, Antonio. *Selections from the Prison Notebooks.* Edited and translated by Quintin Hoare and Geoffrey Nowell Smith. London: Lawrence and Wishart, 1971.

Hall, Stuart. "Nicos Poulantzas: State, Power, Socialism." *New Left Review* 119 (January–February 1980): 60–69.

Hamilton, Nora. *The Limits of State Autonomy.* Princeton: Princeton University Press, 1982.

Hanson, Earl P. *Puerto Rico Land of Wonders*. New York: Alfred A. Knopf, 1960.

————. *Puerto Rico Ally for Progress*. New Jersey: Van Nostrand, 1962.

Heine, Jorge, ed. *Time for Decision: The United States and Puerto Rico*. Landham, Md.: North-South Publishing Co. 1983.

Henfrey, Colin. "Dependency, Modes of Production and the Class Analysis of Latin America." *Latin American Perspectives* (Summer and Fall 1981): 17–54.

Herrero, José A. "La mitología del azúcar: un ensayo en historia económica de Puerto Rico, 1900–1979." *Cuadernos 5*, CEREP, 1971.

Hindess, Barry. "The Concept of Class in Marxist Theory and Marxist Politics." In Jon Bloomfield, ed. *Class Hegemony and Party*. London: Lawrence and Wishart, 1977, pp. 95–107.

Hirschman, Albert O. "A Dissenter's Confession: 'The Strategy of Economic Development' Revisited." In Meier and Seers, *Pioneers in Development*, pp. 87–111.

Horowitz, Paul. "Puerto Rico's Pharmaceutical Fix." NACLA 15 (March–April 1981): 22–36.

Ianni, Octavio. *La formación del estado populista en América Latina*. México: Era, 1975.

Illinois Institute of Technology. "Survey of Potential Petrochemical Industry in Puerto Rico." Proposal no. 54–701 I for the Economic Development Administration (9 July 1954).

Isard, Walter; Schooler, Eugene W.; and Vietorisz, Thomas. *Industrial Complex Analysis and Regional Development; A Case Study of Refinery-Petrochemical-Synthetic-Fiber Complexes and Puerto Rico*. Cambridge: The M.I.T. Press, 1964.

Jacobsen, John K. "Peripheral 'Postindustrialization': Ideology, High Technology and Dependent Development." In James A. Caporaso, ed. *A Changing International Division of Labor*. Boulder: Lynne Rienner, 1986, pp. 91–122.

Jaguaribe, Helio. "Dependencia y autonomía en América Latina." In Helio Jaguaribe, et al. *La Dependencia político-económica de América Latina*. México: Siglo Veintiuno, 1970.

Journal of Commerce, The, New York, Journal of Commerce Inc.

Kesselman, Ricardo. *Las estrategias de desarrollo como ideologías*. Buenos Aires: Siglo Veintiuno, 1973.

Kolko, Joyce. *Restructuring the World Economy*. New York: Pantheon, 1988.

Kozlow, Ralph; Rutter, John; and Walker, Patricia. "U.S. Direct Investment Abroad in 1977." *Survey of Current Business* 58 (August 1978): 16–36.

Laclau, Ernesto. *Politics and Ideology in Marxist Theory*. London: New Left Books, 1977.

La Hora, San Juan.

Lane, Theodore. "The Effects of Institutional, Technological and Market Change on the Demand for Labor in Puerto Rico." San Juan: PREDA, June 1984.

————. "Services, Export Services, and Development," Discussion paper for the Economic Development Administration of Puerto Rico, 21 April 1987.

Larrain, Jorge. *The Concept of Ideology*. Athens, Georgia: University of Georgia Press, 1979.

Latortue, Paul. "Puerto Rico in the CBI." Paper presented at the Conference, The Lomé Convention and the CBI, St. Augustine, Trinidad, 10–14 December 1985, pp. 13–14, 23–24.

188 *Development Strategies as Ideology*

LeRiverend, Julio. *Historia economica de Cuba*. Barcelona: Ediciones Ariel, 1972.

Lewis, Gordon K. *Notes on the Puerto Rican Revolution*. New York: Monthly Review Press, 1974.

Lewis, John P. "Development Promotion: A Time for Regrouping." In Lewis and Kallab, *Development Strategies*, pp. 3–46.

Lewis, John P., and Kallab, Valeriana, eds. *Development Strategies Reconsidered*. New Brunswick: Transaction, 1986.

Limoeiro Cardoso, Miriam. *La ideología dominante*. México: Siglo Veintiuno, 1975.

López, Adalberto, ed. *The Puerto Ricans: Their History Culture and Society*. Cambridge: Schenkman, 1980.

Lukács, Gregory. *History and Class Consciousness*. Merlin: London, 1971.

Madera, José R. "The Economic Development Administration of Puerto Rico; The Present and the Future." *Puerto Rico U.S.A.* 20, no. 4 (1980).

———. *The Impact of the Possessions Corporation*. San Juan: Economic Development Administration [1983].

Magdoff, Harry. *Imperialism: From the Colonial Age to the Present*. New York: Monthly Review, 1975.

Maldonado Denis, Manuel. *Puerto Rico: A Socio-historic Interpretation*. New York: Vintage, 1972.

———. *The Emigration Dialectic: Puerto Rico and the USA*. New York: International Publishers, 1980.

Mandel, Ernest. *La crisis*. México: Era, 1980.

———. *Late Capitalism*. London: New Left Books, 1975.

———. *Marxist Economic Theory*. London: Merlin, 1974.

Mari Bras, Juan. *El caso de Puerto Rico en las Naciones Unidas*. La Habana: Asociación Cubana de Naciones Unidas, 1975.

Marini, Ruy Mauro. *Dialéctica de la dependencia*. México: Ediciones ERA, 1973.

Marx, Karl. "Preface to a Contribution to the Critique of Political Economy," in Karl Marx and Frederick Engels, *Selected Works; in One Volume*. New York: International Publishers, 1968.

Mathews, Thomas. "Agrarian Reform in Cuba and Puerto Rico." *Revista de Ciencias Sociales* 4 (March 1960): 107–123.

———. *Puerto Rican Politics and the New Deal*. Gainesville: University of Florida Press, 1960.

Mattos Cintrón, Wilfredo. *La política y lo político en Puerto Rico*. México: Ediciones ERA, 1980.

Meier, Gerald M., ed. *Pioneers in Development; Second Series*. New York: Oxford University Press, 1987.

Meier, Gerald M., and Seers, Dudley, eds. *Pioneers in Development*. New York: Oxford University Press, 1984.

Meléndez, Edgardo. *Puerto Rico's Statehood Movement*. New York: Greenwood Press, 1988.

Meléndez, Edwin. "Crisis económica y estrategia de desarrollo en Puerto Rico." In Gautier Mayoral and Nazario Trabal, *Puerto Rico*, pp. 160–219.

Milibrand, Ralph. *The State in Capitalist Society*. New York: Basic Books, 1969.

Morera, Luis C. "TROPICO: Investing in Agro-Biotechnology for Local Economic Development." *Puerto Rico Business Review* 14 (June–July 1989): 12–15.

Muñoz Marín, Luis. *Discurso inaugural.* San Juan: Administración General de Suministros, 1949.

————. *Mensaje de Luis Muñoz Marín, Gobernador de Puerto Rico, a la asamblea legislativa.* San Juan: Government of Puerto Rico, yearly 1949 to 1964.

Myint, Hla. "The Neoclassical Resurgence in Development Economics: Its Strengths and Limitations." In Meier, *Pioneers in Development,* pp. 107–136.

NACLA. "U.S. Unions in Puerto Rico." *NACLA's Latin America and Empire Report* 10 (May–June 1976): 7–14.

Nation's Business, Washington, D.C., Chamber of Commerce of the United States.

Navas Dávila, Gerardo, ed. *Cambio y desarrollo en Puerto Rico: la transformación ideológica del Partido Popular Democrático.* Río Piedras: Editorial Universitaria, 1980.

————. *La dialéctica del desarrollo nacional: el caso de Puerto Rico.* Río Piedras, Editorial Universitaria, 1978.

————. "Surgimiento y transformación del Partido Popular Democrático." In Navas Dávila, *Cambio y desarrollo,* pp. 17–34.

Nelson, Anne. *Murder Under Two Flags: The U.S., Puerto Rico, and the Cerro Maravilla Cover-up.* New York: Ticknor & Fields, 1986.

Nelson, Candace, and Tienda, Marta. "The Structuring of Hispanic Ethnicity: Historical and Contemporary Perspectives." *Ethnic and Racial Studies* 8 (January 1985): 49–74.

Nieves Falcón, Luis. *El emigrante puertorriqueño.* Río Piedras: Editorial Edil, 1975.

————. "El futuro ideológico del Partido Popular Democrático." *Revista de Ciencias Sociales* 9 (September 1965): 237–261.

Nieves Falcón, Luis; García Rodríguez, Pablo; and Ojeda Reyes, Félix, *Puerto Rico, grito y mordaza.* Río Piedras: Librería Internacional, 1971.

Nuevo Día El, San Juan, El Día Inc.

Nún, José. "Super población relativa, ejército industrial de reserva y masa marginal." *Revista Latinoamericana de Sociología* 5 (1969).

O'Connor, Donald J. *Puerto Rico's Potential as a Site for Textile, Apparel and Other Industries.* Washington, D.C.: Office of Puerto Rico, 1948.

Oil and Gas Journal, Tulsa, Oklahoma, The Petroleum Publishing Company.

Omega Management, Inc. "Intention of Sixty Companies in Puerto Rico with Expiring Tax Privilege: A Report to the Economic Development Administration." 15 May 1962.

Pagán, Bolivar. *Historia de los partidos políticos puertorriqueños.* 2 vols. San Juan: Librería Campos, 1959.

Pantojas-García, Emilio. "The U.S. Caribbean Basin Initiative and the Puerto Rican Experience: Some Parallels and Lessons." *Latin American Perspectives* 47 (Fall 1985): 105–128.

Partido Independentista Puertorriqueño (PIP). "Programa del Partido Independentista Puertorriqueño." *El Mundo,* 10 November 1946.

————. Programa político, económico y social. San Juan: PIP, 1968.

————. "Programa, 1972." In Banco Popular de Puerto Rico, *Guía para las elecciones,* pp. 47–91.

Partido Nuevo Progresista (PNP). *Programa preliminar.* San Juan: Novalice Printing Press, 1967.

————. *El programa de gobierno del Partido Nuevo Progresista.* San Juan, 1976.

————. *Propuesta de programa de gobierno, 1981–1984.* San Juan, 1980.

Partido Popular Democrático (PPD). *Compilación de Programas, 1940–1964.* San Juan: PPD, 1964.

————. *Programa; lo que nos enorgullece y lo que nos preocupa, 1960.* San Juan: PPD, 1960.

Partido Socialista Puertorriqueño-Movimiento Pro Independencia (PSP-MPI). *Declaración General de la asamblea constituyente.* San Juan: Ediciones Puerto Rico, 1972.

Peeler, John A. *Latin American Democracies: Colombia Costa Rica and Venezuela.* Chapel Hill: University of North Carolina Press, 1985.

Peralta Rámos, Mónica. *Etapas de acumulación y alianzas de clases en Argentina (1930–1970).* Buenos Aires: Siglo Veintiuno, 1972.

Perloff, Harvey S. *Puerto Rico's Economic Future: A Study in Planned Development.* Chicago: University of Chicago Press, 1950.

Perry, George L. "The United States." In Edward Fried and Charles H. Schultze, eds. *Higher Oil Prices and the World Economy.* Washington, D.C.: Brookings Institution, 1975, pp. 71–104.

Piñero, Jesús T. *Mensaje de Jesús T. Piñero, Gobernador de Puerto Rico a la decimosexta asamblea legislativa en su cuarta legislatura ordinaria.* San Juan: Administración General de Suministros, 1948.

Pizer, Samuel, and Cutler, Frederick. "United States Assets and Investment Abroad." *Survey of Current Business* 41 (August 1961): 20–26.

————. "U.S. Foreign Investment." *Survey of Current Business* 40 (August 1960): 12–24.

Poulantzas, Nicos. *Classes in Contemporary Capitalism.* London: New Left Books, 1975.

————. *Political Power and Social Classes.* London: Verso, 1978.

Prebisch, Raul. "The System and the Social Structure of Latin America." In Irving L. Horowitz, et al., *Latin American Radicalism.* New York: Vintage, 1969, pp. 29–52.

Puerto Rico. Administración de Fomento Económico. *Apéndice económico al informe anual, 1965.* San Juan: Administración de Fomento Económico, 1966.

————. *Base preliminar para el plan de operaciones de 1974/75.* San Juan: Administración de Fomento Económico, 1973.

————. *Elementos claves para el desarrollo de una estrategia de desarrollo.* San Juan: Administración de Fomento Económico, 1974.

————. *Hacia una política de desarrollo industrial para la década del 70: el papel clave del proyecto petrolífero básico.* San Juan: Administración de Fomento Económico, 1973.

————. *Informe Anual al Gobernador.* San Juan: Administración de Fomento Económico, yearly 1950/51 to 1960/61.

Puerto Rico. Banco Gubernamental de Fomento. "La creación de un centro financiero para Puerto Rico." San Juan, 1978.

Puerto Rico Business Review, San Juan, Banco Gubernamental de Fomento.

Puerto Rico. Cámara de Representantes. Comisión de Recursos Naturales. *Informe sobre el establecimiento de un puerto de hondo calado.* San Juan, 1974.

Puerto Rico. Comité Interagencial de la Estrategia de Puerto Rico. *El desarrollo económico de Puerto Rico, una estrategia para la próxima década.* Río Piedras: Editorial Universitaria, 1976,

Puerto Rico. Comité para el Estudio de las Finanzas de Puerto Rico. *Informe al gobernador del Comité para el Estudio de las Finanzas de Puerto Rico* (Informe Tobin). Río Piedras: Editorial Universitaria, 1976.

Puerto Rico. Compañía de Fomento de Puerto Rico. *Informe anual; 1944.* San Juan: Compañía de Fomento de Puerto Rico, 1945.

Puerto Rico. Compañía de Fomento Industrial de Puerto Rico. *Informe anual; 1950/51.* San Juan: Compañía de Fomento Industrial de Puerto Rico, 1951.

Puerto Rico. Consejo Asesor Económico del Gobernador. *Estrategia para el desarrollo económico de Puerto Rico: hacia la segunda transformación económica.* January 1989.

Puerto Rico. Departamento del Trabajo. *Empleo y desempleo en Puerto Rico.* San Juan, June 1967.

———. *Empleo y desempleo en Puerto Rico.* San Juan, January 1977.

Puerto Rico. Departamento del Trabajo y Recursos Humanos. *Censo de industrias manufactureras de Puerto Rico.* San Juan: Departamento del Trabajo, March 1988.

———. *Empleo y desempleo en Puerto Rico.* San Juan, 1986.

———. *Empleo y desempleo en Puerto Rico.* San Juan, 1988.

———. "Series de empleo y desempleo," mimeo, various years.

———. "Series de salario promedio, natural years," mimeo, n.d.

Puerto Rico Development Company. *Annual Reports, 1943–1945.* San Juan: Puerto Rico Development Company, annual.

———. "Industrial Opportunities in Puerto Rico, U.S.A.," [1947].

Puerto Rico. Economic Development Administration. *Annual Statistical Report of EDA Manufacturing Plants, 1964/65.* San Juan: Economic Development Administration, 1965.

———. *Competitive Position of Manufacturing Industries.* San Juan: Economic Development Administration, 1975.

———. *The Drug and Pharmaceutical Industry in Puerto Rico.* San Juan: Economic Development Administration, 1980.

———. *The Electrical and Electronic Industry in Puerto Rico.* San Juan: Economic Development Administration, 1979.

———. *Industrial Incentive Act, 1978.* San Juan: Economic Development Administration, 1979.

———. *List of Firms Among the 500 Largest U.S. Industrial Corporations with Operations in Puerto Rico.* San Juan: Economic Development Administration, 1974.

———. *Locally and Nonlocally Owned Enterprises in Puerto Rico.* San Juan: Economic Development Administration, 1963.

———. *The Petroleum Refining, Petrochemical and Allied Products Industry in Puerto Rico.* San Juan: Economic Development Administration, 1977.

Puerto Rico. Governor. *Forty-Third Annual Report of the Governor of Puerto Rico, 1943.* San Juan: Government of Puerto Rico, 1943.

———. *Forty-Fifth Annual Report of the Governor of Puerto Rico, 1945.* San Juan: Government of Puerto Rico, 1945.

Puerto Rico. Junta de Planificación. *Anuario estadístico, Puerto Rico, 1964.* San Juan: Junta de Planificación, 1965.

———. *Anuario estadístico, Puerto Rico, 1976.* San Juan: Junta de Planificación, 1977.

———. *Balanza de pagos, 1942–1961.* San Juan: Junta de planificación, 1963.

———. *Balanza de pagos, 1978.* San Juan: Junta de Planificación, 1979.

————. *Informe económico al gobernador.* San Juan: Junta de Planificación, yearly 1950–1988.

————. *Ingreso y producto, 1978.* San Juan: Junta de Planificación, 1978.

————. *Ingreso y producto, 1984.* San Juan: Junta de Planificación, 1985.

————. *Serie histórica del empleo, de desempleo y grupo trabajador en Puerto Rico, 1981.* San Juan: Junta de Planificación, 1981.

Puerto Rico. *Leyes de Puerto Rico,* San Juan, Government of Puerto Rico.

Puerto Rico Planning Board. *Economic Report to the Governor, 1966.* San Juan: Planning Board, 1966.

————. *The Point Four Program.* San Juan, 1950.

————. *Puerto Rico: Training Ground for Technical Cooperation.* San Juan, n.d.

Puerto Rico Planning Board. Economic Division. Economic *Development of Puerto Rico, 1940–1950; 1951–1960.* San Juan: Puerto Rico Planning Board, 1951.

Puerto Rico Planning, Urbanizing and Zoning Board. *A Development Plan for Puerto Rico.* Santurce: Office of Information for Puerto Rico, 1944.

Puerto Rico Policy Commission. *Report of the Puerto Rico Policy Commission* (Chardón Report). San Juan, 1934.

Quijano, Anibal. "The Marginalized Pole of the Economy and the Marginalized Labour Force." *Economy and Society* 3 (November 1974): 393–428.

Quiñones, Sandra. "A Look at the Puerto Rico International Trade Center." *Puerto Rico Business Review* 6 (October 1981): 17–18, 33.

Quintero, Marcia. *Elecciones de 1968 en Puerto Rico: análisis estadístico por grupos socio-económicos.* San Juan: Centro de Estudios de la Realidad Puertorriqueña, 1972.

Quintero Rivera, Angel G. "Background to the Emergence of Imperialist Capitalism in Puerto Rico." In López, *The Puerto Ricans,* pp. 97–127.

————. "La base social de la transformación ideológica del Partido Popular en la década del '40." In Navas Dávila, *Cambio y desarrollo,* pp. 35–119.

————. "El desarrollo de las clases sociales y los conflictos políticos en Puerto Rico." *Revista de Ciencias Sociales* 18 (March–June 1974): 145–199.

————. "The Development of Social Classes and Political Conflicts in Puerto Rico." In López, *The Puerto Ricans,* pp. 213–231.

————. *Patricios y plebeyos: burgueses, hacendados, artesanos y obreros.* Río Piedras: Ediciones Huracán, 1988.

————. "The Socio-Political Background to the Emergence of the 'Puerto Rican Model' as a Strategy for Development." In Susan Craig, ed. *Contemporary Caribbean: A Sociological Reader.* Maracas, Trinidad and Tobago: Susan Craig, 1982, vol. 2, pp. 9–57.

Ramírez de Arellano, Annette B., and Seipp, Conrad. *Colonialism, Catholicism & Contraception.* Chapel Hill: The University of North Carolina Press, 1983.

Reynolds, Lloyd G., and Gregory, Peter. *Wages, Productivity and Industrialization in Puerto Rico.* Homewood, Ill.: Richard D. Irwin, 1965.

Robert R. Nathan Associates, Inc. *Section 936 and Economic Development in Puerto Rico.* Washington, D.C.: Puerto Rico U.S.A. Foundation, 1987.

Rodríguez, Octavio. *La teoría del subdesarrollo de la CEPAL.* México: Siglo Ventiuno, 1980.

Rodríguez Orellana, Manuel. "In Contemplation of Micronesia: The Prospects for the Decolonization of Puerto Rico Under International Law." Mimeo, n.d.

Romero Barceló, Carlos. *Statehood Is for the Poor.* San Juan, 1978. (First published in Spanish in 1973.)

Ross, David F. *The Long Uphill Path.* Río Piedras: Editorial Edil, 1969.

———. "Island on the Run" (unpublished manuscript), 1977.

Sáez Corales, Juan. "CGT, informe del secretario general." In Angel G. Quintero Rivera, *Lucha Obrera en Puerto Rico.* Río Piedras: CEREP, n.d., pp. 118–124.

Sánchez Vilella, Roberto. *Discursos de campaña.* San Juan: Comité de Amigos de Sánchez Vilella, 1964.

———. *Que el pueblo decida.* San Juan, 1968.

Santiago Meléndez, Jaime. *Reforma fiscal en Puerto Rico, 1940–1971.* San Juan: Editorial Cordillera, 1974.

Silén, Juan A. *Apuntes para una historia del movimiento obrero puertorriqueño.* Río Piedras: Editorial Cultural, 1978.

———. *Historia de la nación puertorriqueña.* Río Piedras: Editorial Edil, 1973.

Skocpol, Theda. "Bringing the State Back In: Strategies of Analysis in Current Research." In Peter Evans, Dietrich Rueschemeyer, and Theda Skocpol, eds. *Bringing the State Back In.* New York: Cambridge University Press, 1986, pp. 3–37.

———. "Emerging Agendas and Recurrent Strategies in Historical Sociology." In Theda Skocpol, ed. *Vision and Method in Historical Sociology.* New York: Cambridge University Press, 1984, pp. 356–391.

Smith, Dudley. *Puerto Rico's Income.* Washington, D.C., 1943.

Stead, William H. *Fomento: The Economic Development of Puerto Rico.* Washington, D.C.: National Planning Association, 1958.

Stewart, John. "Notes on the Underground Economy of Puerto Rico." *Puerto Rico Business Review* 9 (April 1984):19–30.

———. "Puerto Rico's Options in the Development of Science and Technology." *Puerto Rico Business Review* 13 (April 1988): 10–14.

———. "Puerto Rico Shouldn't Be Fearful of Twin Plant Concept." *The San Juan Star*, 28 August 1983, B-3.

———. "The Twin Plant Concept in the Caribbean Basin." *Puerto Rico Business Review* 9 (January–February 1984): 2.

Suárez, Manny. *Requiem on Cerro Maravilla: The Police Murders in Puerto Rico and the U.S. Government Coverup.* Maplewood, N.J.: Waterfront Press, 1987.

Sunkel, Osvaldo, and Paz, Pedro. *El subdesarrollo latinoamericano y la teoría del desarrollo.* México: Siglo Veintiuno, 1980.

Tansill, William. "Puerto Rico: Independence or Statehood? A Survey of Historical, Political and Socio-economic Factors With Pro and Con Arguments." *Revista del Colegio de Abogados de Puerto Rico* 41 (February 1980): 79–100.

Thomas, Clyve. *The Rise of the Authoritarian State in Peripheral Societies.* New York: Monthly Review, 1984.

Toro Calder, Jaime. "Violencia individual en Puerto Rico." *Revista de Ciencias Sociales* 18 (September–December 1974): 43–58.

Torres, Benjamín. *El proceso judicial contra Pedro Albizu Campos.* San Juan: Editorial Jelofe, 1974.

Tugwell, Rexford G. *The Stricken Land.* New York: Doubleday, 1947.

"U.S. Direct Investment Position Abroad: Detailed Position and Balance of Payment Flows." *Survey of Current Business* 67 (August 1987).

United States. Bureau of the Census. *Census of Manufactures, Puerto Rico, 1949.* Washington, D.C.: Government Printing Office, 1949.

————. *Puerto Rico Census of Manufactures: 1954.* Washington, D.C.: Government Printing Office, 1956.

————. *Puerto Rico Census of Manufactures: 1958.* Washington, D.C.: Government Printing Office, 1960.

————. *Census of Manufactures: 1963, Puerto Rico.* Washington, D.C.: Government Printing Office, 1965.

————. *Census of Manufactures: 1967, Puerto Rico.* Washington, D.C.: Government Printing Office, 1970.

————. *Census of Manufactures, Puerto Rico, 1972.* Washington, D.C.: Government Printing Office, 1974.

————. *Census of Population, Puerto Rico, 1960.* Vol. 1, Part 53, Washington, D.C.: Government Printing Office, 1963.

————. *Census of Population, Puerto Rico, 1970.* Vol. 1, Part 53, Washington, D.C.: Government Printing Office, 1973.

————. *1980 Census of Population, Puerto Rico.* Vol. 1, Part 53 A, Washington, D.C.: Government Printing Office, 1983.

————. *1977 Economic Censuses of Outlying Areas; Puerto Rico, Manufactures.* Washington, D.C.: Government Printing Office, 1980.

————. *1977 Economic Censuses of Outlying Areas; Puerto Rico, Retail Trade, Wholesale Trade, Selected Services Geographic Area Statistics.* Washington, D.C.: Government Printing Office, 1980.

————. *1982 Economic Censuses of Outlying Areas; Puerto Rico, Manufactures.* Washington, D.C.: Government Printing Office, 1985.

————. *1982 Economic Censuses of Outlying Areas; Puerto Rico, Retail Trade, Wholesale Trade, Selected Services Geographic Area Statistics.* Washington, D.C.: Government Printing Office, 1985.

United States. Department of Commerce. *Economic Study of Puerto Rico.* 2 vols. Washington, D.C.: Government Printing Office, 1979.

United States. Department of the Treasury. *The Operation and Effect of the Possessions Corporation System of Taxation; First Annual Report.* Washington D.C.: Department of the Treasury, 1978.

————. *The Operation and Effect of the Possessions Corporation System of Taxation; Second Annual Report.* Washington D.C.: Department of the Treasury, 1979.

————. *The Operation and Effect of the Possessions Corporation System of Taxation; Third Annual Report.* Washington D.C.: Department of the Treasury, 1980.

————. *The Operation and Effect of the Possessions Corporation System of Taxation; Fourth Report.* Washington D.C.: Department of the Treasury, 1983.

————. *The Operation and Effect of the Possessions Corporation System of Taxation; Fifth Report.* Washington D.C.: Department of the Treasury, 1985.

————. *The Operation and Effect of the Possessions Corporation System of Taxation; Sixth Report.* Washington D.C.: Department of the Treasury, 1989.

United States. Government Accounting Office. *Puerto Rico: Update of Selected Information Contained in a 1981 GAO Report.* Washington, D.C.: General Accounting Office, 1989.

U.S. House of Representatives. Committee on Ways and Means. *Caribbean Basin Economic Recovery Act: Hearing.* 98th Congress, 1st Session, 9 June 1983.

————. *Comprehensive Tax Reform: Hearings*, Pt. 6. 99th Congress, 1st Session, 11, 12, and 17 July 1985.

U.S. Senate. Committee on Energy and Natural Resources. *Political Status of Puerto Rico: Hearings*. 3 parts, 101st Congress, 1st Session, 1–2 June 16–17 and 19 June, and 11–14 July 1989.

————. *Puerto Rico Status Referendum Act: Report*. 101st Congress, 1st Session, 6 September 1989.

U.S. Senate. Committee on Foreign Relations. *Caribbean Basin Initiative; Hearings*. 97th Congress, 2nd Session, 22 and 31 March 1982.

Vales, Pedro A., and Hernández, David. "La modernización de la violencia: su asociación con la burocratización de la vida cotidiana contemporánea." *Revista de Ciencias Sociales* 18 (September–December 1974): 111–132.

Vasconi, Tomás A. "Cultura, ideología, dependencia y alienación." In José Matos Mar, ed. *La crisis del desarrollismo y la nueva dependencia*. Buenos Aires: Amorrortu, 1972, pp. 114–134.

Vietorisz, Thomas. *The Feasibility of Petroleum Refining Operations in Puerto Rico for Serving European Oil Markets*. San Juan: Economic Development Administration, 1957.

Villamil, José J. "Puerto Rico 1948–1979: The Limits of Dependent Growth." In Heine, *Time for Decision*, pp. 95–116.

Villar Roces, Mario. *Puerto Rico y su reforma agraria*. Río Piedras: Editorial Edil, 1968.

Velázquez, Ismaro. *Muñoz y Sánchez Vilella*. Río Piedras: Editorial Universitaria, 1974.

Wagenheim, Kal. *A Survey of Puerto Ricans in the U.S. Mainland in the 1970's*. New York: Praeger, 1975.

Wells, Henry. *The Modernization of Puerto Rico*. Cambridge, Mass.: Harvard University Press, 1969.

Wolf, Eric. "San José: Subcultures of a 'Traditional' Coffee Municipality." In Steward, Julian H., et al. *The People of Puerto Rico*. Chicago: University of Illinois Press, 1956, pp. 171–264.

Wolff, Edward N. "Capitalist Development, Surplus Value and Reproduction; an Empirical Examination of Puerto Rico." In Jesse Schwartz, ed. *The Subtle Anatomy of Capitalism*. Santa Monica, Calif.: Goodyear, 1977, pp. 140–149.

World Bank. *World Tables, 1988–89*. Baltimore: Johns Hopkins, 1989.

Index

Abbott Laboratories, 153
Acción Social Independentista, 38
Act Number 16, 151
Administrators, 123, 124
Advertising, 165
AFDA. *See* Agricultural Promotion and Development Administration
Agrarian reform, 46, 48, 68; impact, 52, 56; industrialization, 43–44; law, 41–42; proportional profit farms, 42–43. *See also* Land, redistribution of
Agricultural Adjustment Administration, 52
Agricultural Promotion and Development Administration (AFDA), 151
Agriculture, 36, 57(n6), 72, 73; national income, 46–47. *See also* Agrarian reform; Sugar industry
AID. *See* Aid to Industrial Development
Aid to Industrial Development (AID), 69
Alavi, Hamza, 17
Albizu Campos, Pedro, 33, 34, 65
Alianza Puertorriqueña, 31, 38
Alliance for Progress, 88–89
Alliances: social class, 17, 22, 27(n32)
Althusser, Louis, 10
American Federation of Labor, 33
American Metal Climax, 135
Andersen, Arthur, 165
Anti-Americanism, 37, 39, 58(n29)
Anti-Puerto Rican sentiment, 37
Argentina, 7
Assassinations, 37

Badillo Compton, 165
Badillo/Saatchi & Saatchi, 165
Banco Central, 154
Banco de Ponce, 165
Banco de San Juan, 85, 163
Banco de Santander, 154
Banco Mercantil, 163
Banco Occidental, 154
Banco Popular, 165
Banking, 57(n5), 85–86, 127, 165; commercial, 161, 163–164;

restructuring, 151, 154; taxation, 148–149; United States, 30, 118
Bank of America, 154, 163
Bank of Boston, 154, 163
Baquero, Genaro, 106
Bargain Town, 124
Baxter Travenol, 153
Bird family, 85
BOC Group, 166
Bourgeoisie, 22, 23, 27(n32), 126, 141–142(n78); developmentalism, 88, 93; finances, 85–86; industrialization and, 52–53, 54, 73; politics of, 94, 131–132. *See also* Petty bourgeoisie; Working class
Boycotts, 33
Brazil, 7
Brokerage houses, 154, 165
Byron, M. J., 179
Bush, George: on plebiscite, 178–180

Canada, 115, 163, 166
Capital, 102, 125–126, 157; foreign, 73–74, 75, 77–78, 113–121; transnational, 108–109, 110–111; United States, 90–91, 94, 110, 135–136
Capitalism, 56, 80, 122, 143, 144; imperialist, 21–22, 66; sugar corporations, 29–30
Capitalist state, 14–15; class struggle, 18–19
Cardoso, Fernando Henrique, 17, 30
Caribbean Basin Initiative (CBI), 151–152, 157, 181(n23)
Caribbean Development Program, 157
Caribbean Refining Co., 108
Carlin, 166
Carrión family, 127
Casiano, Manuel, 177
Catholic Church, 104
CBI. *See* Caribbean Basin Initiative
CGT. *See* Confederación General de Trabajadores
Chadbourne Plan, 32

197

University of Puerto Rico, 134
Urbanization, 80, 122
Urban sector, 81
Value: surplus, 21–22
Venezuela: oil from, 108, 111, 115, 135
Virgin Islands, 122

Wages, 107, 124, 125(table), 144; decline,
  145, 168; and income, 86–87;
  minimum, 101, 102–103, 137, 138(n3)
War Powers Act, 45
Water Resources Authority, 45
Welfare, 38, 50, 123

West Germany, 115, 166
Westinghouse, 115
Winship, Blanton, 34
Women, integration into the labor force,
  86; population control, 92, 167; wages,
  86, 124
Woolworth, 124
Working class, 19, 27(n32), 35, 73, 86,
  94, 147; displacement of, 122–123
World War II, 94, 99(n83)

Young, Arthur, 165
Young & Rubicam, 165

About the Book
and the Author

Since the 1950s, Operation Bootstrap has been presented to the Third World as a model for successful development; export-oriented development has become the gospel of the neo-orthodox economics espoused by the World Bank and the IMF. Exploring the political process that led to the formulation of Operation Bootstrap, Pantojas-Garcia develops the alternative view that development strategies are ideological constructs that express the political and economic interests of class coalitions, not of society as a whole. The view that development is a neutral technical process beneficial to all—i.e., developmentalism—is in fact an ideology that reflects a class position.

The Puerto Rican experience, argues Pantojas-Garcia, demonstrates that peripheral capitalism is dynamic. Shifts in patterns of capital accumulation, both internal and external, lead to changes in social and economic structure, in class coalitions, and in the ideology of development itself, as well as to intensified political conflict. Analyzing the connection between these patterns of conflict and change and accommodation among key social sectors, he finds that, even with Puerto Rico's contradiction-ridden development process and its enormous problems—the unresolved colonial status of the island, the opposition of local and foreign economic interests, the lack of jobs, to mention only a few—developmentalism provides the unifying substance that has permitted the continuity of capitalist development. As long as changes are successfully presented as "necessary for progress" and "beneficial to all," the contradictions of capitalist development can be resolved to the benefit of the dominant coalition.

Emilio Pantojas-Garcia, a political sociologist, is assistant professor in the Latin American Studies Program at the University of Illinois at Chicago.